Revisiting *Mis*
Neighbor

Revisiting *Mister Rogers' Neighborhood*

Essays on Lessons About Self and Community

Edited by KATHY MERLOCK JACKSON
and STEVEN M. EMMANUEL

McFarland & Company, Inc., Publishers
Jefferson, North Carolina

ALSO OF INTEREST

Walt Disney, from Reader to Storyteller: Essays on the Literary Inspirations, edited by Kathy Merlock Jackson and Mark I. West (McFarland, 2015)

Disneyland and Culture: Essays on the Parks and Their Influence, edited by Kathy Merlock Jackson and Mark I. West (McFarland, 2011)

Frontispiece: A portrait of Fred Rogers by John C. Tibbetts. Used with permission.

LIBRARY OF CONGRESS CATALOGUING-IN-PUBLICATION DATA

Names: Jackson, Kathy Merlock, 1955– editor. | Emmanuel, Steven M., editor.
Title: Revisiting Mister Rogers' neighborhood : essays on lessons about self and community / edited by Kathy Merlock Jackson and Steven M. Emmanuel.
Description: Jefferson, North Carolina : McFarland & Company, Inc., Publishers, 2016 | Includes bibliographical references and index.
Identifiers: LCCN 2015048985 | ISBN 9780786472963 (softcover : acid free paper) ∞
Subjects: LCSH: Rogers, Fred. | Mister Rogers' neighborhood (Television program) | Television broadcasting—Religious aspects—Christianity.
Classification: LCC PN1992.4.R56 R48 2016 | DDC 791.4502/8092—dc23
LC record available at http://lccn.loc.gov/2015048985

ISBN (print) 978-0-7864-7296-3
ISBN (ebook) 978-1-4766-2341-2

BRITISH LIBRARY CATALOGUING DATA ARE AVAILABLE

Front cover: Fred Rogers from Mister Rogers' Neighborhood (PBS/Photofest); background street scene © 2016 skeeg/iStock

Printed in the United States of America

McFarland & Company, Inc., Publishers
Box 611, Jefferson, North Carolina 28640
www.mcfarlandpub.com

To two very special people,
RAY MERLOCK
and
HENRIETTE EMMANUEL,
with appreciation for their caring presence in our lives

Acknowledgments

We would like to thank our families, Joe and Nick Jackson and Henriette, Dan, Nicholas and Marcus Emmanuel, for their love, inspiration, and support. We also appreciate the commitment and expertise of our administrative assistant, Amy Dudley, who prepared the final manuscript. Our colleagues and students at Virginia Wesleyan College have offered ideas and encouragement, and we offer our deepest gratitude.

Grateful acknowledgment is made to the McFeely-Rogers Foundation for granting permission to quote lyrics of Mister Rogers' songs.

Table of Contents

Introduction

Mister Rogers' Neighborhood, the third-longest-running television series in the history of PBS, left an indelible mark on the many pre-school children and their caregivers who made up its audience. It continues to do so. In the digital age, and more than a decade after the death of the show's founder, Fred Rogers, *Mister Rogers' Neighborhood* continues to attract an audience online, and perhaps no programming in the history of children's television has done more to develop the identity and ethics of the young child. Although educators have long espoused the value of *Mister Rogers' Neighborhood*, it has escaped the interest of scholars in other fields, whose particular lenses may provide insight into the show's lasting impact.

This book of essays reassesses Rogers' contribution to children's lives and media and to American culture. It embodies three main themes. The first is Rogers' stance on the individual, how Rogers perceived the self and presented it to his young charges. The second is Rogers' ideas about community, how various members of his neighborhood imparted important lessons on ways of contributing meaningfully to society. The third is Rogers' use of television to accomplish his goals. With television, Rogers found the perfect medium for disseminating prosocial messages to a mass audience of young children, helping them to better understand themselves and the world they live in. This volume explores how Fred Rogers' philosophy and creative choices influenced generations of children.

Finally, the essays collected here could make the case that the demands created by today's highly technological modern world have contributed to an erosion of people's willingness and capacity to listen carefully and to be present to others, and this, in turn, has profound implications for friendship and community. Rogers' ideas still resonate.

When I say it's you I like, I'm talking about that part of you that knows that life is far more than anything you can either see or hear or touch. That deep part of you that allows you to stand for those things without which humankind cannot survive. Love that conquers hate, peace that rises triumphant over war, and justice that proves more powerful than greed.
—Fred Rogers

The Performance
of the Pastoral

Chris Buczinsky

At a time when the entertainment industry lays out for our children a cornucopia of virtual reality, returning to *Mister Rogers' Neighborhood* is a journey to the center of another Earth. Re-watching Season 1, Week 1 is like going on a techno-archeological dig, past our present sensory overload and down to the foundation of our present babbling tower of communication technology, mass entertainment, and children's education. So far down, the light is dim, people and objects appear only in black and white, and the air is thick and heavy with reality. A drowsy numbness pains our senses. Absent the storm and stress we have grown accustomed to—the fast talk and quick wit; the bright flash and crazy color; the lightning pace and staccato edit— one can't help but fall asleep. But after the nap, one wakes refreshed to find Mister Rogers patiently waiting to reintroduce us to the neighborhood and to show us an ordinary but wonderful world we had forgotten.

Mister Rogers' Neighborhood is best seen as a witness to the enduring appeal of the Christian pastoral. Fred Rogers performs a naïve Self, with a New Testament morality of loving-kindness shining through every gesture. Like a nineteenth-century sprite preserving himself in a cathode ray tube, he carries into the twentieth century what is at once a vintage literary mode, a religious ethic, and a theological hermeneutic. *Mister Rogers' Neighborhood* brought the Christian pastoral—its soft colors, its wooly atmosphere, and its pacifistic morality—into the suburban home, with all its modern trappings and its still endearingly minimal, technological gadgetry. One might call his program twentieth-century America's most successful religious mission. Displaying a remarkable openness and flexibility, Fred Rogers embraced modernity in a kind of theological *jiu-jitsu*, borrowing modernity's form to better preserve and broadcast the Christian ethic. *Mister Rogers' Neighborhood* is, in short, a commercial entertainment offshoot of the revolutionary liberal theological movement that sought to reinterpret Christianity as a message of universal love with Jesus as moral teacher (Dorrien).

Since I was born in 1959, and *Mister Rogers' Neighborhood* went on the air in 1967, I missed the show. I was in school, and like all children, looking ahead—eight going on twelve. I wanted nothing to do with a little kids' program. Like many Americans, I kept seeing Mister Rogers out of the corner of my eye, this bland TV celebrity with a curiously stubborn staying power. Originally a student of religion and biblical studies, I had plans, like those of the young Fred Rogers, to be a pastor, but I ended up earning a doctorate in literature, the first cousin of religious myth. Driven by a desire to make poetry come to life, to get it off the scholar's page and into the hearts of people, I created, again like Rogers, a children's show serving suburban Chicago elementary schools. Facing down a gym full of third graders, performing poetry for them every day, I contemplated with awe the length and success of Rogers' career, and I took to studying his performance tactics online.

Fred Rogers' pastoral education, training, and mission can help us appreciate these tactics. The Mister Rogers that Fred Rogers plays is a Pastor, a new, demythologized pastor made for TV in which the kerygma, the message and moral of the pastoral, is stripped from the myth (Bultmann 12–16). Take away the pulpit, the scripture, and the overt religious symbols; leave just the man, and the viewer has Mister Rogers. In his performance on *Mister Rogers' Neighborhood*, Fred Rogers in fact pens a veritable sermon on Protestant theatricality in general and pastoral showmanship in particular. Only by walking the fine line between naiveté and cynicism, by both absorbing ourselves in sympathy with this sermon and distancing ourselves in suspicion of it, can we fully appreciate Mister Rogers' personal gift and cultural contribution. We can explicate the elements of Mister Rogers' performance through a commentary on what might be called his unstated sermon for children's performers, a homily with three main admonitions.

1. Be Yourself

In *Fred Rogers: America's Favorite Neighbor*, the narrator, Michael Keaton, sums up what is now a commonplace judgment: Fred Rogers was the "same on and off camera" (*Fred Rogers*). There is no difference between Fred Rogers and Mister Rogers; he was just "being himself." But a performer's identification with his role, however powerful and enduring, does not wipe away all difference. A performer can put so much of his heart and soul into a performance that the two become one, the role absorbing the man and the man living into the role, and this is especially the case with Fred Rogers, for whom the act of being Mister Rogers seems to have been a religious mission and a moral imperative, a case of a TV role doubling as an ego-ideal. The issue was brought home when a teenager recently asked me, with an innocence that rivals Mister Rogers' own: "Who played Mister Rogers?" The answer, "Fred Rogers," surprised her, but the question it raised was more interesting: what does it mean to "play Mister Rogers?"

Indeed it is easy to underestimate Mister Rogers' performance skills because his performance tries to deny its own status as a performance. Mister Rogers is always transparent, clear, and sincere. He therefore presents a peculiar challenge to anyone trying to analyze his style. In *Analyzing Prose,* the rhetorician Richard Lanham shows that language that holds out an ideal of sincerity, clarity, and transparency is particularly difficult to analyze because it offers so little rhetorical flourish. When a style displays little self-conscious elaboration of the powers and peculiarities of language, when it resists exploring language's metaphoric, syntactic, and rhythmic possibilities, there seems little to say about it. A style that denies it *is* a style that is, Lanham points out, a terrible candidate for stylistic analysis (Lanham 1–6).

Trying to analyze Fred Rogers' performance is a little like going up to Mister Rogers himself and pulling on his cheeks to find the real face beneath the mask. One can only imagine Fred's response. In all likelihood, he in turn would gently pull on the scholar's face, and in his unflappably kind and understanding way, turn it into another opportunity to teach. "Sometimes we do have to dress ourselves up for different occasions," he might say. "Look at how I change when I come home. But most of the time, when we're at home or in our neighborhood, we can just be ourselves." If the scholar should protest, and point to Erving Goffman's classic and definitive sociological work on *The Presentation of the Self in Everyday Life*, wherein social life is analyzed in terms of a series of dramatic performances (every social situation being a dramatic challenge demanding that each of us act an appropriate social role), Mister Rogers would probably smile and break into his disarmingly simple rendition of "You Are My Friend, You Are Special" (Goffman 253).

Many people are uncomfortable before Mister Rogers because we live in an ironic age, and in the face of sincerity the ironist is always apt to suspect he is having his chain pulled, or worse, being played (Purdy). *Barney and Friends* was such a hit in the 1990s partly because the parents of that generation, schooled in irony by the media, could only "do nice"—accept simple and sincere feelings—under the comforting guise of a pillow-like *Tyrannosaurus rex*. It is one thing for a lumbering dinosaur to sing a song about loving each other; it's another when a real man, however avuncular and unthreatening, sings, "I think you're a special person/And I like your ins and outsides." Without the distance of the screaming purple costume, the contemporary, ironic parent, always alert to "stranger danger," squirms with discomfort.

It is not that Mister Rogers is not being "real" with children, or that he isn't clearly aware of the power of roles. Anyone who has had the pleasure of entering the Neighborhood of Make-Believe, of listening to Fred Rogers through the voices of Daniel Striped Tiger, Henrietta Pussycat, or King Friday, knows how much Mister Rogers appreciates the theatrical pleasures and the educational benefits of pretending. Rather, to appreciate Fred Rogers' accomplishment, one has to carry the rhetorical analysis, one's sensitivity to theatrics, further. One must look closely at Rogers' performance at the places from which theatrics seem to be exiled—in his home, where he is just "being himself," and in the neighborhood, where he interacts with others in the "real" world. Melding the believing heart to a suspicious eye, one has to denaturalize his show, peer into the unassuming interstices of his performance, not to debunk him (the dictionary definition of a person who debunks Mister Rogers is a "jerk"), but to appreciate just how skillful Mister Rogers truly is (Culler 131–60). Everybody is indeed fancy—certainly Mister Rogers is; it's just difficult to see "fancy" under a pastel cardigan.

2. Tread Lightly, Like the Lamb

What can be more natural than Fred Rogers' primary role, as Himself in his home? Right from his entry, his role is double: the white-collar working man takes off his coat, puts on a sweater, and becomes everybody's uncle. He is a gentle, soft-tempered man—simple, direct, and kind. Out of the variegated hues that make up a human heart, Mister Rogers selects a few key colors. Just as the Impressionists eliminated bitumen from their palette, his choices all tend toward "sweetness and light." As Himself, Mister Rogers shows no sign of frustrated impatience, irritable reaction, knee-jerk dismissal, or any of the other forms of crotchetiness even the best adult shows a child. Mister Rogers is not "just being real" with children; he is modeling the moral treatment of a child.

An understanding of the pastoral as a literary genre helps unfold both the morality and the performance. The pastoral has its roots in the ancient Greek bucolic poems of Theocritus, Virgil's *Ecologues*, and Spenser's *The Shepheardes Calender*. But William Blake's *Songs of Innocence and Songs of Experience*, the most influential and *apropos* Christian-Romantic inflection of the genre, provides the best entry into Fred Rogers' showmanship. Blake's four elemental pastoral figures—the child, the piper, the shepherd, and the lamb—make up the literary composition of Mister Rogers' on-air persona. In "The Lamb," one of the work's most important poems, Blake makes a four-fold identification that is key to the Christian pastoral:

> He is meek & he is mild,
> He became a little child:
> I a child & thou a lamb,
> We are called by his name [Blake 30].

Christ, Lamb, Child, and Poet reflect one another in their salient gentle demeanor, which is also a moral imperative. In the face of worldly force, Christ displayed his power by being "meek and mild," extending his own neck to the knife (The Bible, Acts 8:32). The lamb embodies both Christ's resignation and his purity. Each of us, according to Blake, lives out this condition in the powerless stage of childhood. As the most effective way to convey the kingdom of God, the world in which the lion lies down with the lamb, the poet adopts the childlike persona (Abrams 412–18). Mister Rogers' anodyne exhortations do not come near to Blake's visionary intensity and poetic power, which is why the *Songs* are not really for children, but Blake's figures hover over Fred Rogers' ministerial performance: the Good Shepherd as the model of the Pastor; the Piper who makes music for the sheep; the Child, who meets the world with innocent curiosity; and the Lamb, whose gentle ways define the pastoral ethic.

Of course, the show faces life's difficulties (jealousy: Episode 1176; divorce: Episode 1477; competition: Episode 1481–1485), but always through a Protestant plain-speaking stripped of all energy that hints of aggression. Anyone who has watched his controversial Episodes 1521–1525 ("Mister Rogers Talks About Conflict"), in which King Friday orders his subjects to start making bombs, knows Rogers was a man of powerful convictions and courage who brought his pastoralism to bear on our most troubling social problems. Broadcasting his pastoralism in the most explicit way possible, the storyline ends when the bomb fragments are turned into record players for a dance, and Mister Rogers sings "Peace and Quiet" and delivers a benediction to his young viewers: "I wish you peace." The final episode concludes with the text of Isaiah 2:4 appearing on the screen: "And they shall beat their swords into plowshares, and their spears into pruninghooks: nation shall not lift up sword against nation, neither shall they learn war any more."

Mister Rogers approaches even these most vexing issues with a preternatural calm, an indefatigably mild care and gentle loving-kindness of the pastoral mode. Alongside the bells and whistles of a video game or the amps of a blockbuster like *Transformers*, Fred Rogers' performance appears heroically gentle and quiet. To take the measure of the pastoral influence, compare the theme song of *Mister Rogers' Neighborhood* to that of *Pee-Wee's Playhouse*. Mister Rogers' song is a friendly foyer, a conversational, melodic invitation to be his neighbor ("Would you be mine? Could you be mine?"). Pee Wee's song is a bouncing madhouse, a post-modern, frenetic invitation to anarchy. The closest thing to such energy the viewer gets in *Mister Rogers' Neighborhood* is Mr. McFeely's jittery hurry, the foil that throws into relief Mister Rogers' lamb-like gentleness.

Fred Rogers' education as a Presbyterian minister lends his show the pastoral tone that infuses his performance in all its minute details, from the trademark pastel sweaters and his almost *sotto voce* enunciation to his gentle handling of objects and his quiet sneaker glide. Take, for instance, the ubiquitous presence of what we might call Mister Rogers' *flair*. Mister Rogers is an elastic performer. Lithe and fit, his body always displays ease and lightness. But once ordinary life and "the real" become the target impression, especially as it is suffused with the morality of the pastoral, all baroque theatricality of gesture becomes verboten; extravagant movements are ruled out. In front of the camera, however, the need for showmanship cannot be squelched, so he gives his body rein only in the *margins* of his performance, in the hanging up of his coat or the putting down of a package. Watch for this attenuated energy, his flair, in the way he rides the sofa bed of make-believe back into its hideaway, or better, in the musical flourish or "ta-da" with which he ties his sneaker or tosses his shoe from one hand to another.

If there is any prop that condenses the pastoral style of Mister Rogers' performance, it is his sneakers, whose rubber soles tread always quietly, always lightly, with the soft touch of a lamb. Fred Rogers may have introduced his trademark footwear to keep the noise down on the set, but in the end the soles of his shoes perfectly embody the pastoral soul; they symbolize the imperative of gentleness he harbored in the raucous twentieth-century medium of television. Likewise, no side to his performance is more pastoral, though hidden in plain sight, than his walk. A motion that gives no cause for caution, not an inkling of any exertion that could be mistaken for violence, it is the fluid movement of a body energized in light action, supremely at ease. For an example, watch how he moves to the door to perform "It's Such a Good Feeling" (Season 11, Episode 3: "Learning to Make Pretzels"). The upbeat song demands a quick pace, and he makes his way like a brisk walker with his almost trademark glide. The up-tempo, soft-footed motion of a boy in sneakers getting ready to go outside, it is a level walk, all-horizontal, no bounce; in short, it is a walk under the regime of a minimalist, Protestant theatricality and a pastoral morality of loving-kindness.

3. Learn from People, Things and Stories

Of course, Mister Rogers carries his pastoral morality of gentleness beyond the privacy of his home and into his encounters with neighbors in the neighborhood. Throughout its 895 episodes, *Mister Rogers' Neighborhood* created a picture of an ideal community for American children. It was a model *of*, and to some extent a model *for*, community: both a framework within which children might begin to see their own neighborhood and a blueprint for the community that his audience, Mister Rogers' "television neighbor," might someday help to build (Geertz 93–94). His neighborhood moves to a clockwork but friendly step, tying together unique individuals, each with his or her own name, face, and personality, all going through their daily lives, always ready to stop (except Mr. McFeely!) and enjoy a brief but pleasant, mutually-uplifting, face-to-face encounter. Mister Rogers teaches children to observe the community with wonder as a local network of intimate, face-to-face relationships, a *gemeinschaft* in the midst of a *gesellschaft* world (Tonnes).

In Anglo religious and literary history, the prototype of the Neighbor that Fred Rogers plays is the parson naturalist of the eighteenth century. As he explores the ties that bind him to both the human and non-human members of the neighborhood, Mr. Rogers displays the enlarged sense of community of a Gilbert White in *The Natural History of Selborne* (White). Mister Rogers' neighborhood is small town or suburban, but the sensibility is rural, as the etymology of the word "neighbor" (Old English *nēahgebūr*, from *nēah* "nigh, near" + *gebūr* "inhabitant, peasant, farmer") draws out. Among his neighbors Mister Rogers demonstrates a care for others, a pastoral responsibility to the community that always transcends the specific theme of any single episode. But he melds to the pastoral role the persona of an innocent child, moving through the neighborhood as the open but inexperienced one, without knowledge and in need of teaching.

Out in the neighborhood, so many of Mister Rogers' encounters are object lessons, his performance whittling down to a handling of things in the world. One might call it a performance of curious hands. Just like a little child, once he is out among the shops and homes, he can't resist touching things, exploring them with the inquisitiveness of a child who wants to figure them out. Mister Rogers' hands become the focal point as they hold, prod, poke, lift, or turn some object in the world. In "Learning to Make Pretzels" (Season 11, Episode 3) he mixes, kneads, and pats the dough, lifting the dough break and twisting the pretzels, all the while peppering the pretzel maker with ingenuous questions. In the first week of the show he takes apart a punch clock, opening it up, looking inside, and carefully putting it back together again. In Episode 1529, titled "Work," he holds, touches, and smells an apple, and holds a price tag gun in the supermarket.

This showmanship of the everyday object has a mesmerizing power for education. But the content of these object lessons is not as important as the form. What the mode teaches, beyond the individual lesson, is an attention to individual things, an almost Buddhist mindfulness that can be traced back to his Christian-Romantic conviction of the preciousness of each individual (Hanh). Rogers makes the conviction explicit in "Everybody's Fancy" a musical lesson in the sexual differences between boys and girls. Launched from his fish tank, it begins as a lesson in environmental ethics that ties our treatment of the earth back to the way we conceive of individuals. The best way to stop polluting our environment, Mister Rogers says, is to realize that every individual is special, a creature of God's creation. "The important thing for us is to look for what's fine in everybody, and that will help us to want to take care of everybody, and," Rogers adds, "give us a really good feeling." The recognition of individuality leads to an ethic of care and the fulfillment of personal happiness.

Mister Rogers speaks as he does in deference to this respect for the individual. He looks straight at the camera, to the individual child watching at home, then down to whatever object he is talking about, then back at his television audience, which he always conceives as a single child. It is a conversational performance, eye-to-eye, mind-to-mind, all "I–Thou"; he addresses one child, the "you" that is both plural and singular (Buber). He speaks in short lines, pausing after each sentence so the child can process the idea. As a neighbor going about his business, Mister Rogers is always ready to stop to say hello, to encounter his fellow neighbor as an individual. In his invariably genial pace, he displays a model respect, greeting the person by name, often with a little handshake, saying goodbye when he must move on. Mister Rogers is a pastor without a church, or better, one whose church has become the neighborhood.

Mister Rogers carries this pastoral ethic of individual worth and its conversational imperative even into the Neighborhood of Make-Believe, where the allure of a false theatricality would tempt any performer. Though gently engaging, his puppetry is far from a rollicking performance, stepping neatly around the natural inclination of the form toward slapstick and farce. Like his encounters in his own neighborhood, the encounters in the Neighborhood of Make-Believe are talky. In the context of the Christian pastoral, the events that happen in the Neighborhood of Make-Believe are best read as parables or teaching stories. A literary genre with an impeccable Judeo-Christian religious pedigree, going back at least as far as the Good Shepherd himself, the stories of King Friday, X the Owl, Daniel, Henrietta Pussy Cat, Lady Elaine Fairchild and all the rest displace the child's questions, concerns, and issues onto imaginary characters where they can be examined in a fun way. Subsuming entertainment to substance, story to moral, the parable is a didactic form, but in the hands of Fred Rogers it is not, for all that, pedantic. Under the aegis of Rogers' ethic of Christian loving-kindness, the characters always remain on this side of amiable and pleasant, the voices—even King Friday's at his most petulant and controlling—soft and sweet.

Mister Rogers, the Arch-Presbyter of Sincerity, our television Pastor of the Anti-Ironic, brought the Christian pastoral into the twentieth century, making it palatable to an increasingly secular population. Unapologetically, Fred Rogers put the old wine of Christianity into new wine skin of television. The original nature of the Picture Picture segment—the placing of motion picture / slide screen within the traditional art frame and the magical way it conversed with him—demonstrates the friendly footing on which he wanted to place the child's relations with the new medium. If his successors were unable to keep the medium from overwhelming the message, incapable of resisting the siren song of an entertainment that rings hollow for lack of a moral center, it wasn't because Fred Rogers didn't try his hardest to show them the way.

Indeed, today, in 2016, the pastoral message of *Mister Rogers' Neighborhood*, and perhaps even more, its form, has a new and unexpected relevance. The honeymoon is over with CGI, virtual reality, and social media. We have come through the initial rush of constant information, the euphoria of video-screen magic, and the tingle of social media connectivity, and on the other side we have found its hollowness. It does not satisfy. Our children (indeed, we ourselves) need the knock on our door, the warmth of a living room, the skin-to-skin contact with our neighbors. Most contemporary children's programs assume we are in the world to be entertained. An essentially consumer model, most programming offers little sugar pills of good feeling. *Mister Rogers' Neighborhood* assumed we are in the world to learn and grow. Built on a pastoral model, it nurtured the heart and mind in the only way that is truly satisfying, by teaching children to be themselves, to tread lightly through the world, and to head out, every day, to discover their neighborhood.

Works Cited

Abrams, M. H. *Natural Supernaturalism: Tradition and Revolution in Romantic Literature*, rev., exp. ed. New York: Norton, 1971. Print.
Blake, William. *Songs of Innocence*. New York: Dover, 1971. Print.
Buber, Martin. *I and Thou*, 2d ed. New York: Scribner, 1958. Print.
Bultmann, Rudolf. *Kerygma and Myth: A Theological Debate*, rev., exp. ed. New York: Harper & Row, 1961. Print.
Culler, Jonathan. *Structuralist Poetics: Structuralism, Linguistics, and the Study of Literature*. Ithaca: Cornell University Press, 1976. Print.
Dorrien, Gary J. *The Making of American Liberal Theology: Imagining Progressive Religion*. Louisville: Westminster John Knox, 2006. Print.
Fred Rogers: America's Favorite Neighbor. Screenplay by Rick Sebak. Perf. Fred Rogers and Michael Keaton. Triumph Marketing, 2004. DVD.
Geertz, Clifford. *The Interpretation of Cultures: Selected Essays*. New York: Basic, 1973. Print.
Goffman, Erving. *The Presentation of Self in Everyday Life*. Garden City, N.Y.: Doubleday, 1959. Print.
Hanh, Thich Nhat. "The Tangerine of Mindfulness" in *Old Path White Clouds*. Berkeley: Parallax Press, 1991. Print.
Lanham, Richard A. *Analyzing Prose*, rev., exp. ed. London: Continuum, 2003. Print.
Purdy, Jedediah. *For Common Things: Irony, Trust, and Commitment in America Today*. New York: A.A. Knopf, 1999. Print.
Tönnies, Ferdinand. *Community and Civil Society*. Ed. Jose Harris. Cambridge: Cambridge University Press, 2001. Print.
White, Gilbert, and Richard Mabey. *The Natural History of Selborne*. Harmondsworth: Penguin, 1977. Print.

Social Activism for the Small Set

KATHY MERLOCK JACKSON

> The child is still in me ... and sometimes not so still.—Fred
> Rogers (*You Are Special* 171)

In 1969, when the Public Broadcasting System and the Corporation for Public Broadcasting were in danger of losing funding, Fred Rogers, whose children's show, *Mister Rogers' Neighborhood,* was threatened with budget cuts, testified before the U.S. Senate Subcommittee on Communications. In a persuasive six-minute statement, Rogers convinced lawmakers that denying funding for shows like his that were geared to the special needs of children was akin to depriving those in the next generation of their right to happy and productive lives. He even recited the lyrics to one of his songs, which gave children a peaceable strategy for dealing with anger. Rogers' persuasive testimony proved effective. Senate Subcommittee Chairman John Pastore was visibly moved, and the PBS budget was not only saved but increased to twenty million dollars. This incident solidified Fred Rogers' role as an activist for children, non-violence, tolerance, and social responsibility. Mary Elizabeth Williams, in an article in *Salon* titled "Where Have You Gone, Mister Rogers?" calls Rogers "[o]ne of the most radical figures of the contemporary history" and adds, "He was not known for fiery speeches or his daring action. Instead, he became a legend by wearing a cardigan and taking off his shoes" (Williams). A proponent of late 1960s liberalism, Fred Rogers took a stand to promote the values of social activism to an impressionable young audience of two- to five-year-olds, showing preschoolers the small things that they can do in their own neighborhoods. His goal, he said, was "to give children the notion that they can solve the problems that will come to them—that they can have a responsible attitude toward life, toward themselves, and toward others" (Rogers, *You Are Special* 37). In *Mister Rogers' Neighborhood*, Fred Rogers uses television to promote his world view of social responsibility, tolerance, and peace, establishing for children the building blocks for community involvement. Television facilitated his activist spirit and enabled him to achieve his objectives.

In the pantheon of PBS children's television, *Mister Rogers' Neighborhood* is a landmark. It debuted nationally on February 19, 1968, during a tumultuous year when activism in America peaked (Abramson 193). It remained on the air for forty years, continuing even after Rogers' death on February 27, 2003. As *TV Guide* observed, "TV is all about coveting, but Mr. Rogers is about appreciating what you already have, about caring for others and seeing the best in them.... If ever a show was equipped to thrive in the realm of reruns, it's the timeless classic ... a quiet, dependable oasis for young viewers" (qtd. in Center for Puppetry Arts). Still available online and in DVD, *Mister Rogers' Neighborhood* is second in longevity among PBS children's shows; only *Sesame Street*, which debuted in 1969 and is still aired daily in PBS markets, has been on longer. While both shows target the same preschool audience and prepare children for kindergarten, *Sesame Street* concentrates on school-readiness skills while *Mister Rogers' Neighborhood* focuses on the child's developing psyche and feelings and sense of moral and ethical reasoning. Ellen Handler Spitz notes in an article for *The Chronicle of Higher Education* that what most engaged her about Rogers' work was its "close mingling of children's emotional, cognitive, and aesthetic lives" (B16).

An ordained Presbyterian minister who obtained a degree from Pittsburgh Theological Seminary late in his life, Rogers never downplayed his role as a social advocate, and people who knew him say that he was the same person on-screen and off. He landed in children's television quite by chance. Raised in a wealthy family in southwestern Pennsylvania, he endured many childhood illnesses, including scarlet fever, and spent a lot of time indoors creating stories, playing with puppets, and developing his imagination (McGinn 61). He went on to study music in college and, in 1951, got a job with NBC. Television at the time was just a fledgling medium, and although Rogers hated it, especially its fast pace, inane pie-in-the-face skits, and commercialism, he recognized its potential to do good for the audience he wished to reach: children. By the mid 1950s, he had moved to public television station WQED in Pittsburgh, where he wrote and performed in an imaginative puppet show for children that eventually led to *Mister Rogers' Neighborhood*. Thus, the reluctant convert to television found his medium, but he fashioned it in his own style, always having, as George Gerbner commented, "something to tell rather than something to sell" (12). He spoke slowly and sincerely, as a nurturing father to his child, and unlike other rapid-fire children's shows, his averaged only two edits per minute. According to Daniel McGinn of *News-*

week, "Peacefulness isn't the first attribute you think of when you think of when you consider what makes great television. But it's the essence of the ritualized world of make-believe that Rogers crafted for children over the course of four decades in the studio" (61).

Rogers strove to help children to understand and appreciate themselves and their places in their own small worlds and, in so doing, found his message: social responsibility. He is hardly alone in this call to action. Harvard political scientist Benjamin R. Barber, who has been an advocate of education and the need to develop concerned citizens, has written a series of books echoing Mister Rogers'—and Alexis de Tocqueville's—mantra: "Are we Americans willing to be journeymen citizens? Are there institutions where we can learn liberty? Can our schools be nurseries of citizenship?" (Barber, *An Aristocracy of One* 4). Rogers understood this calling and instilled in preschoolers the awareness and tools that they need to become activists, described as

> people who see the need for change, improvement, and motivation on a large scale. They are people driven by passion, keen to share facts they want understood more widely, and led by a vision for a better future. Activism comes naturally to some, while for others it's something that's thrust upon them as a result of particular experiences or upon learning about something they passionately believe needs to change.
>
> Whatever your reasons for wanting to be an activist, you have the ability to do so no matter your age, your means, or your background. Having the belief that you can make a difference and that you have the power to do something about an issue are at the heart of creating change for the better ["How to Become an Activist"].

While the definition sounds lofty, especially for toddlers, Rogers broke down the core values of social activism into small, discrete parts that he could teach by example to young television viewers.

Although Rogers recognized the importance of television to inculcate prosocial values, he rejected the idea of a mass audience. As he said repeatedly, "I'm not that interested in 'mass' communications. I'm much more interested in what happens between this person and that person watching. The space between the television set and the person who's watching is very holy ground" (Fred Rogers Company Website, Professional Resources). Rogers also believed that television was most effective after it was turned off, when child and care-taker had uninterrupted time to talk about what they had watched. Very young children pay especially close attention when Rogers, a familiar figure who speaks slowly and soothingly, is on the screen; they follow his movements, guided by the camera and close-ups, and listen carefully to his voice. Rogers capitalized on this, being among the first to understand television as an intimate medium and regard a TV personality as an invited guest in one's home. According to Robert Thompson, director of the Center for the Study of Popular Television at Syracuse University, Rogers was a key early innovator who shaped television, especially programming for children, by realizing its potential. He says,

> Along with a very small group of people—Steve Allen from late night, Irna Phillips with soap operas, Ernie Kovacs with video art—Fred Rogers really understood what the medium of television was all about, what it could do, how it was this intimate forum that talked to you in the privacy of your own living room, and he grasped that early on.
>
> There's something about [Mister Rogers'] program, when you're in your little pajamas with feet attached to them and you're home in the comfort of your living room on the couch that was so extraordinarily comforting and quiet. It went down like a nice hot bowl of soup [qtd. in Owen A10].

As Rogers talked via television to each child one-on-one, he grasped the receptiveness of his young audience and the potential to build a better world by instilling core values in youth. In *Mister Rogers' Neighborhood*, he shows children the small things they can do to show respect for themselves and others. Roger Desmond at the University of Pennsylvania's Annenberg School of Communications notes that *Mister Rogers' Neighborhood* does what other children's shows do not: "The kid who's a preschooler is developing a sense of self.... Most television doesn't even address that. 'Who am I? Why am I here?'—that kind of stuff" (qtd. in Bianculli 47). These questions comprise Rogers' building blocks for creating social responsibility. His messages are uncomplicated. As Rogers asserts, "Deep and simple are far, far more important than shallow and complicated and fancy" (*Mister Rogers and Me*). Speaking directly to each child in plain, clear language, Rogers established the following steps of self-awareness and understanding community that build the foundational values for social responsibility and peaceful action.

Step 1: You have self-worth.

At a time when the divorce rate was rising and the number of single-parent and two-career families was increasing, children needed attention. Mister Rogers provides this by offering an uninterrupted half hour each day to talk to the child about matters of importance, take him or her places, and introduce new friends. Through songs and rituals, Rogers delivers an important message of self-validation: "I like you just the way you are." Each day he walks through the same door, changes into his casual clothes, and sings jaunty songs designed to raise a child's sense of self-esteem. In one episode of *Mister Rogers' Neighborhood*, Rogers sings one of his signature songs to Jeff, a special needs child in a wheelchair:

> It's you I like,
> It's not the things you wear,
> It's not the way you do your hair—
> But it's you I like

> The way you are right now,
> The way down deep inside you—
> Not the things that hide you,
> Not your toys—
> They're just beside you [Fred Rogers, *You Are Special* 2].

Rogers contradicts the notion in commercial television that people are defined by their possessions or appearance. He assures children of their intrinsic value. In the case of Jeff, Rogers reminds him that he knows things that others do not, such as how to operate a mechanized wheelchair, and asks him to demonstrate. Tim Menees, a cartoonist for the *Post-Gazette*, recalls a visit with his daughter to Mister Rogers' studio: "Shortly after we arrived at the station, Mister Rogers walked over and introduced himself to us. He asked our daughter Becky, then 4, how she was. Becky was dumbstruck. This was, after all, like meeting God. She blurted out, 'Mister Rogers, I have a new dress!' To which he said, as she nodded at him silently and wide-eyed, 'It's lovely, Becky. But it's what's inside you that's important'" (Menees B-6). This is the same message Rogers repeats each day in his show: everyone has inner goodness. He reminds his young charges to be mindful of their own virtues and talents rather than compare themselves to others. Rogers, incidentally, never lent his name to any product merchandising or advertising campaigns; he valued people, not products.

Step 2: Others will help you.

Just as Rogers tells each child that he or she is special, he teaches respect for the goodness of others. As Rogers recalled, "When I was a boy ... my mother would say to me, 'Look for the helpers. You will always find people who are helping.' To this day, especially in times of 'disaster,' I remember my mother's words, and I am comforted by realizing that there are still so many helpers—so many caring people in the world" (Fred Rogers, *The World According to Mister Rogers* 208). In *Mister Rogers' Neighborhood*, Rogers is quick to point out that helpers abound, that children can find people around them that they can trust. He says, for example, of Mr. McFeely, the express mail carrier and his good friend, "He's always doing something for someone" ("Making a Thank You"). When Rogers needs something, be it a sandwich, a new pair of shoes, or something repaired, he finds someone in the neighborhood to help him. When he wants to learn a new skill, such as making a pot, learning a dance, dribbling a basketball, or playing a tuba, he knows that experts who will assist are not far away, driving home the fact that each neighborhood is rich in possibilities, experiences, and support. Mister Rogers never travels very far from home—his radius is quite small—but helpers appear everywhere. This cooperative spirit contradicts what researchers George Gerbner and Larry Gross termed the "mean world" of television, apparent in the typical alarmist news and action-and-adventure-oriented entertainment sagas that characterize television. Rather than creating mistrust and eliciting fear, Rogers encourages children to regard people and new situations as friendly, not threatening.

Step 3: You are part of a community of people who are different from you.

Mister Rogers invites each child to be a part of his community and to occupy public space. With urgency in his voice, he says in his signature song,

> I've always wanted to have a neighbor
> Just like you!
> I've always wanted to live in a
> Neighborhood with you.
> So let's make the most of this beautiful day;
> Since we're together we might as well say,
> Would you be mine?
> Could you be mine?
> Won't you be my neighbor? [Fred Rogers,
> *The World According to Mister Rogers* 158].

Rogers not only invites each child viewer to be his friend, he also serves as the catalyst for new relationships with people of different genders, ages, races, and ethnicities, especially those who build and create. Through Rogers, the viewer meets many neighbors, such as Mr. McFeely the mail carrier, Chef Brockett, and Joe Negri, the music store owner, as well as others throughout the community. Yo-Yo Ma, who appeared twice on *Mister Rogers' Neighborhood*, demonstrates how to express emotion through music. Sam Weber and the Dance Theatre of Harlem introduce dance. As Mister Rogers initiates visits around the neighborhood, he meets different workers in their various jobs: pretzel maker, crayon maker, restaurant owner, bread maker, sculptor. "It is through relationships" said Rogers, "that we grow best and learn best" (Fred Rogers Company, Professional Resources). Rogers shows that each person—be it blue-collar, white-collar, or artist—is unique and functions as a contributing and valuable member of his or her community. Bob Rogers, a cartoonist for the Pittsburgh *Post Gazette*, notes of Rogers: "His messages were simple: 'You are special.' 'I like you just the way you are.' 'Please, won't you be my neighbor?' To those of us who tuned in every day, they became building blocks of self-esteem. He taught us tolerance and acceptance before we could even say the words" (Bob Rogers B4). Mister Rogers' messages of diversity and acceptance resonate when he tells children, "Some of us have one color skin, and some of us have another. That's all outside stuff. But we all have insides too, and our insides have different ways of growing. Our thoughts and our feelings grow, and there's a lot we can do about them" ("So Many Ways to Grow").

Step 4: You care about and are responsible to others in your community.

If one learns to respect those in his or her community, one realizes a commitment to them. Rogers said, "We live in a world in which we need to share responsibility. It's easy to say 'It's not my child, not my community, not my world, not my problem.' Then there are those who see the need and respond. I consider those people my heroes" (Fred Rogers Company, Professional Resources). Rogers expresses this attitude in his show. Each day he feeds his fish, which serves as a metaphor for nurturing those around him. He consoles Chef Brockett when he loses a cake decorating contest and helps him to focus on the value and enjoyment of the experience, not the disappointment. He talks to Mr. McFeely about his feelings after his divorce and helps him to remember and value the good times. Rogers said, "The best, I feel, that we can hope is to give children the notion that they can solve the problems that will come to them—that they can have a responsible attitude toward life, toward themselves, and toward others" (Fred Rogers, *You Are Special* 37). Part of that responsibility lies in learning to control emotions. In one of his songs, Rogers asks,

> What do you do with the mad you feel
> When you feel so mad you could bite?
> When the whole wide world
> Seems oh so wrong
> And nothing you do seems very right? [Fred Rogers,
> *The World According to Mister Rogers* 116].

He offers small solutions—such as punching a bag, pounding some clay, running, or stomping—and encourages children to own and express their feelings of anger but not take them out on others.

Step 5: You have valuable ideas to communicate.

Although Rogers focuses on emotions, he is also concerned with the child's intellectual life. He values learning and on a segment titled "Talking About School" makes the connection between learning and self-esteem when he says, "Sometimes learning makes you feel good about yourself" ("Talking About School"). Rogers teaches by example, encouraging children to think and talk about what they are interested in or care about. He plants the seed in children to regard expressing ideas and questioning as rights and civic responsibilities. In a segment titled "Did You Know?" Rogers says, "I'm interested in all sorts of things, and I spend a lot of time trying to learn about things. I'm curious, and I wonder about all sorts of things." He then proceeds to sing his song "I Wonder," which includes the lines "did you know it's alright to wonder?" and "did you know it's alright to marvel?" ("Did You Know?"). Rogers ends each show with a song, promising his return and further conversation: "I'll be back when the day is new and I'll have more ideas for you."

And you'll have things to talk about. I will too." Rogers never talks down to children, and in his show he addresses difficult and complex subjects: divorce, war, anger, fear, sickness, death. In an episode on divorce, he tells children he understands that they hurt but assures them that when parents split up, it is not their fault. He encourages children to think, ask questions, and express their opinions to trusted adults. In another episode on making mistakes, puppeteer Susan Linn stops by to visit Rogers on her way to see children in the hospital. In a conversation with her puppet, she allays children's fears that they go to the hospital because they are bad. You don't go to the hospital because you are bad—or even because you are good—but because you are sick, she says. Rogers proclaims, "I care deeply about communication, about words—what we say and what we hear" (Fred Rogers, *You Are Special* xiv). His shows function as conversations as he anticipates children's questions— as simple as "Is there a bathroom on the airplane?" or as complex as "Why do living things die?"—and provides thoughtful responses.

Step 6: You can think creatively and differently from others.

Rogers encouraged children to be curious and inquisitive and to express their own ideas. He nurtured the creative spirit by frequently inviting artists, musicians, and dancers to be a part of his show. In *A Place for Us*, political scientist and community advocate Benjamin R. Barber espouses the importance of the arts and humanities in developing free thinkers. "The arts," he writes, "are civil society's driving engine, the key to its creativity, its diversity, its imagination, and hence its spontaneity and liberty" (109). When Mister Rogers interprets a Picasso painting, does an umbrella dance, or asks what a window could be if it were not a window, he is helping children to think and move in new ways and develop creativity. He tells children, "There's no one quite like you." He celebrates the uniqueness of each individual, giving children license to think their own thoughts and not always follow the pack.

Step 7: You can solve conflicts peaceably.

Mister Rogers' Neighborhood reflects camaraderie and cooperation. However, it also addresses conflict, especially when the show travels via trolley to the fantasy world of make-believe. Rogers acknowledged a reality: "The world is not always a kind place. That's something all children learn for themselves, whether we want them to or not, but it's something they really need our help to understand" (Fred Rogers, *You Are Special* 36). Rogers did not underestimate the intensity of children's feelings, particularly anger, and he provided strategies for dealing with negative emotions in a constructive way. He believed that children learn by example and said, "Our children will learn a lot about expressing their feelings by watching how we express ours. And we need to let them know that the violent expressions of anger that they see around them are not the way that it has to be. Above all, we need to try to show our children that we love and value them. By doing so, we can help them learn that there is much in the world to love and value as well … and that goes for the people in it, too" (Fred Rogers, *You Are Special* 104). In a *Mister Rogers* episode titled "When Friends Fight" three friends in the Neighborhood of Make-Believe find lovely fruit and decide to make a fruit salad. However, they disagree on how and in what bowl to prepare it, and one accuses another of being bossy. They then talk things through to make up. Another episode, "Friends: Ups and Downs," takes a similar approach: using negotiation to reduce conflict. Rogers regarded all of the influences in children's lives as important in developing their ability to deal with conflict. He stated his belief: "Children who are loved and feel they are lovable are the ones who are most likely to grow into loving, rather than violent, adults. Taking the time to help our children understand their world and their place in it, as well as what they see on television, is a way of letting our children know they are unique, valuable human beings who can learn to express their own aggressive feelings in healthy non-violent ways" (Fred Rogers, *You Are Special* 107).

Step 8: You can make a difference in your community.

Fred Rogers taught by example and defended quality television shows as "'building blocks' for play" (McGinn 61). His top priority was to attend to children's emotional needs—to build their self-esteem, allay their fears, and answer their questions—but he also wanted to teach strategies for making good choices. If realized, these goals empower children to be, like Mister Rogers, a force for the good in their communities. "Peace," said Rogers, "means far more than the opposite of war!" (Fred Rogers, *The World According to Mister Rogers* 163). He provided children with the tools to be advocates for peace and social responsibility. In an episode on recycling, guests show how old wood can be made into puzzles or a bird feeder, wool clothes into woven rugs, and discarded sheets into a pillow. A recycler says, "There's a lot of things you can do with old things, but you have to take the time to make them." In the Neighborhood of Make-Believe, residents face a problem: their garbage dumps are full. The solution is for a community to work together to adopt recycling habits. Rogers says, "It's a good feeling that you don't have to solve everything yourself. You can always ask for help" ("The Environment: A Recycling"). He lets children know that problems are not so big that they are overwhelming; huge things are possible if taken in small steps and shared.

While one cannot deny that Fred Rogers functioned as an activist for social responsibility and peace, it is more difficult to determine the effect, if any, that he had. PBS never reached as large an audience as commercial children's television. Nevertheless, at its height of popularity in 1985, *Mister Rogers' Neighborhood* reached eight percent of American households daily, no small thing. As the generation dubbed "the millennials" grew up, according to Alex Bitterman, it craved "community" and "a sense of responsibility to society" (34). Demographers William Strauss and Neil Howe concur, characterizing the millennial cohort as having idealism, a greater national mission, and more values (341). Perhaps *Mister Rogers' Neighborhood* played at least some small role in planting the seed for the development of these attitudes. If Rogers was effective, it was based on two things: the example that he set for children and the trust that he engendered in them. Ellen Handler Spitz notes that although he "never preach[ed] a word about equality or diversity, Fred Rogers simply lived those principles by visiting with 'neighborhood friends' and guests from varied racial, religious, national, and occupational backgrounds, and they ranged in life stage from infancy to old age" (Spitz B16). Tom Shales, writing for the *Washington Post*, cited his authenticity as well, saying, "His philosophy comes through his actions and words. This isn't … what someone hired him to do.... At the center of it all is this trust that young viewers place in him … the sense that he is not just fooling" (qtd. in Wilcox).

Rogers was committed to creating a caring citizenry, and he realized that the place to begin was with children, empowering them to grow up feeling a part of their neighborhoods and believing that they can make a change for the better. He showed them the small things that even they could do to be happy, supportive members of the community. Rogers' activism can be summarized in one word: empathy. By anticipating and addressing children's feelings, he hoped to encourage the emotional growth that enables people to get along better and build a peaceful environment. He realized that one does not become socially responsible overnight but begins the process with tiny steps of self-awareness, connectedness, and empowerment, starting when one is very small.

Rogers' impetus for social activism lasted to the end of his life. At his final public appearance in 1997, when he accepted an Emmy Award for his Lifetime Achievement to Daytime Television, he said the following: "All of us have special ones who have loved us into being. Would you just take, along with me, ten seconds to think of the people who have helped you become who you are? Those who have cared about you and wanted what was best for you in life. Ten seconds of silence. I'll watch the time" (Fred Rogers Acceptance Speech). As he urged those in his audience to think about those who helped them, some became weepy. Rogers then said, "Whomever you've been thinking about, how proud they must be to know the difference you feel they've made. You know they're the kind of people television does well to offer our world" (Fred Rogers Acceptance Speech). By directing his audience to reflect on the kindness of others, Rogers was making a social statement, calling on his audience to be grateful rather than its emotional opposite, narcissistic and self-absorbed. Through *Mister Rogers' Neighborhood*, he did this with children as well. A force in the activism and peace movements of the 1960s, Rogers helped to create the social sensibility of a movement, contributing to a dynamic cultural moment. This, he said, was his epitaph: "to be remembered for being a compassionate human being who happened to be fortunate enough to be born at a time when there was a fabulous thing called television that could allow me to use all of the talents that I have been given" (Archives of American Television: Fred Rogers). His small steps, like those he taught in *Mister Rogers' Neighborhood*, held ramifications far beyond.

WORKS CITED

Abramson, Leslie H. "1968: Movies and the Failure of Nostalgia." In *American Cinema of the 1960s: Themes and Variations*. Ed. Barry Keith Grant. New Brunswick: Rutgers University Press, 2009.

Archives of American Television: Fred Rogers. Emmy Television Legends. Interviews, Part 4. Fred Rogers. Online video. n.d. Web. 6 June 2014.

Barber, Benjamin R. *An Aristocracy of Everyone: The Politics of Education and the Future of America*. New York: Ballantine, 1992.

_____. *A Place for Us: How to Make Society Civil and Democracy Strong*. New York: Hill and Wang, 1998.

Bianculli, David. "The Myth, the Man, the Legend." In *Mister Rogers' Neighborhood: Children, Television, and Fred Rogers*. Ed. Mark Collins and Margaret Mary Kimmel. Pittsburgh: University of Pittsburgh Press, 1996. 37–49.

Bitterman, Alex. *The College Question: Why College (As We Know It) Is Not Working for the Millennial Generation*. Buffalo: Balanne and Co., Press, 2013.

Center for Puppetry Arts. "About *Mister Rogers' Neighborhood*." n.d. Web. 6 June 2014.

"Did You Know?" *Mister Rogers' Neighborhood*. PBS Kids. Mister Rogers Songs. n.d. Web. 6 June 2014.

"The Environment: A Recycling." *Mister Rogers' Neighborhood*. PBS Kids Mister Rogers Full Episodes. n.d. Web. 6 June 2014.

Fred Rogers Acceptance Speech. Emmy's Lifetime Achievement Award. Online video clip. YouTube. YouTube 1997. Web. 6 June 2014.

Fred Rogers Company. Professional Resources. n.d. Web. 6 June 2014.

Gerbner, George. "Fred Rogers and the Significance of Story." In *Mister Rogers' Neighborhood: Children, Television, and Fred Rogers*. Ed. Mark Collins and Margaret Mary Kimmel. Pittsburgh: University of Pittsburgh Press, 1996. 3–13.

"How to Become an Activist." WikiHow to Do Anything. n.d. Web. 6 June 2014.

"Making a Thank You." *Mister Rogers' Neighborhood*. PBS Kids. Mister Rogers Moments. n.d. Web. 6 June 2014.

McGinn, Daniel. "Everybody's Next-Door Neighbor." *Newsweek*, 10 Mar. 2003, 61.

Mister Rogers and Me. Dir. Benjamin and Christofer Wagner. Wagner Brothers, 2011. DVD.

Owen, Rob, and Barbara Vancheri. "Fred Rogers Dies." *Pittsburgh Post Gazette*, 28 Feb. 2003, A1, A10.

Rogers, Fred. *The World According to Mister Rogers*. Waterville, ME: Thorndike Press, 2003.

_____. *You Are Special: Words of Wisdom for All Ages from a Beloved Neighbor*. New York: Penguin, 1994.

Rogers, Rob. "Is Your Dad Mister Rogers?" *Pittsburgh Post Gazette*, 28 Feb. 2003, B-6.

Spitz, Ellen Handler. "The Magical Neighborhood of Mr. Rogers." *The Chronicle of Higher Education* 28 Mar. 2003, B16.

Strauss, William, and Neil Howe. *Generations*. New York: William Morrow, 1991.

"Talking About School." *Mister Rogers' Neighborhood*. PBS Kids. Mister Rogers Moments. n.d. Web. 6 June 2014.

Wilcox, Leslie. "Happy Birthday, Mister Rogers." Web log posts. Leslie Wilcox Blogs. 14 Mar. 2014.

Williams, Mary Elizabeth. "Where Have You Gone, Mister Rogers?" *Salon*. 13 Mar. 2012. Web. 6 June 2014.

Good Neighbors, Moral Philosophy and the Masculine Ideal

SUE MATHESON

Gender is a powerful, complicated cultural force. As Anthony E. Rotundo points out in *American Manhood: Transformations in Masculinity from the Revolution to the Modern Era*, the set of cultural types that we have learned—the tough man and the tender, the real man and the sissy that have been accumulating cultural sanction for a century—encourage us to value certain kinds of men (291). "[S]ymbols of right and wrong manhood have become lodged in our political consciousness and in the decision-making culture of our great institution," he says, causing us "to value toughness as an end in itself" (291). Recently, North America's infatuation with toughness celebrating primitive masculinity and "male" competitive, assertive drives has been reflected in the huge demand for digital combat, online and on video. The *Call of Duty*, *Medal of Honor*, *Battlefield* and *Halo* series, solely concerned with war, feature casts of muscle-bound, testosterone-charged masculine primitives whose primitive impulses, physical strength and aggressive instincts are tested in struggles for survival. Nonetheless, however popular digital combat has become, a much older type of American manhood continues to be highly valued—represented by a 143-pound minister who displays tenderness, nurturing, and the human desire for connection and cooperation. Appearing on made-for-analog programs, Fred Rogers offers none of the excitement and adrenaline-producing action that digital combat creates. Calming, and relaxing his viewers, he is generally considered to be America's favorite surrogate father.

As Rotundo points out, manliness, the social representations of manhood are not edicts determined on high and enforced by law, and manhood itself is a learned, used, and reinforced phenomenon that is reshaped by individuals in the course of life (7). How did an ordained Presbyterian minister, a child psychologist, and an interpreter of young children's inner lives become an icon of masculinity and the ideal American man for millions of television viewers? As Mary Elizabeth Williams points out in "Where Have You Gone, Mister Rogers?" he did it "by being nice." Masculine, rather than macho, Fred Rogers never served in the military, he never smoke or drank, and he was a vegetarian. Dedicated to serving children, he improved their television programming.

A performer and composer, Fred Rogers is best known for creating and starring in *Mister Rogers' Neighborhood*. Each of *Mister Rogers' Neighborhood's* 905 episodes begins with its principle character, Mister Rogers (Fred Rogers), entering his home, singing his theme song "Won't You Be My Neighbor?" and changing into a zippered cardigan sweater (knitted by his mother) and sneakers. Typically, Mister Rogers spends his time on camera feeding his goldfish, talking to his television audience, going on a field trip to a site of interest in his Neighborhood, and visiting Neighborhood of Make-Believe with its trolley, its "tree," its "castle," and its citizens, among them, King Friday XIII. In the later seasons of *Mister Rogers' Neighborhood*, all of its episodes ended with the song "Feeling."

Born March 20, 1928, in his grandparents' house, Fred Rogers belonged to the middle class and grew up in Latrobe, Pennsylvania. Interested in music from a very young age, he graduated from Latrobe High School in 1946, studied at Dartmouth College from 1946 to 1948, and earned a B.A. in music composition at Rollins College in 1951, when he began working as a floor director at NBC in New York City for *NBC Opera Theatre*, *The Hit Parade*, and *The Kay Smith Hour*. By 1954, he had concluded that commercial television was not a suitable environment for children's television. He began working at WQED, a Pittsburgh public television station as its program manager and a puppeteer on *The Children's Corner*, a local, unscripted, live children's show with Josie Carey. On that show, some of the characters, music and puppets that would later appear in *Mister Rogers' Neighborhood*, noted for its gentleness and tranquility, were developed.

In 1963, Rogers was contracted by the Canadian Broadcasting Corporation (CBC) to develop a fifteen-minute children's program, *Misterogers*, which ran three seasons. Many of the set pieces used for *Mister Rogers' Neighborhood* (the Trolley, the Eiffel Tower, and the "tree," and the "castle") were created for *Misterogers*. While working in Canada, Rogers also co-starred with his understudy Ernie Coombs on Butternut Square on CBC TV from October 19, 1964, to February 10, 1967. When he acquired the rights to *Misterogers* from the CBC in 1966, he moved the show to WQED in Pittsburgh, where he developed the show for the Eastern Educational Network. The distribution of *Mister Rogers' Neighborhood* began on February 19, 1968. Primarily geared to children aged two to five years of age, the series is appropriate for all ages. At its viewing peak in 1985, a whopping 85 percent of the households in the United States tuned into the longest-running program on PBS. As of 2013, almost all of the 1979–2001 "second series" episodes were still in active rotation on a number of PBS stations.

In part, the incredible and on-going popularity of *Mister Rogers' Neighborhood* is attributable to Fred Rogers' promotion of pre-twentieth-century manliness in twentieth-century America. Drawing on America's foundational ethics, Rogers, in *Mister Rogers' Neighborhood*, embodies a bifurcated form of manhood that combines the characteristics of two masculine ideals that continue to underpin American culture: the Christian Gentleman—a nineteenth-century phenomenon—and *communal manhood*, the roots of which were embedded in New England before 1800.

As Rotundo points out in "Learning about Manhood: Gender Ideals and the Middle-Class Family in Nineteenth-Century America," the ideal of the Christian Gentleman was in essence an ethic of compassion that directed a man's attention to the needs and concerns of others. The ideal, he says, stressed love, kindness and compassion—"these were not only worthy attitudes for a man—they also formed the basis for right actions on his part" (38). Himself the embodiment of a Christian Gentleman, Rogers believes that "[t]he purpose of life is to listen—to yourself, to your neighbor, to your world and to God and, when the time comes, to respond in as helpful a way as you can find … from within and without" (167). Envisioning a civil society based on the assumption that it is the duty of every adult (male or female) to "help our children grow toward being caring, compassionate, and charitable adults" (Rotundo 184), *Mister Rogers' Neighborhood* rests on its creator's belief that neighbors do act as advocates for one another: "[i]n every neighborhood, all across our country, there are good people insisting on a good start for the young, and doing something about it," Rogers says (155). Expressing his confidence in human sociability and fellow feeling, he points out in *The World According to Mister Rogers* that "[t]here's a nurturing element to all human beings, whenever they themselves have been nurtured, and it's going to be expressed one way or another" (23). In order to train children to make actions that attend to the needs and concerns of others, *Mister Rogers' Neighborhood* establishes what Rogers terms a "neighborhood of care." For Rogers, participating in children's programming was an act of love and compassion—personally and professionally. He told Senator John Pastore in 1969 when he appeared before the United States Senate Subcommittee on Communications to argue for support for PBS and the Corporation of Public Broadcasting in response to proposed funding cuts by President Richard Nixon, "This is what I give, I give an expression of care every day to each child to help him realize that he is unique. I end the program by saying you've made this day a special day by just your being you. There's no person in the whole world like you, and I like you just the way you are."[1]

Rogers' appeal to the Subcommittee members' philanthropy to support programming like *Mister Rogers' Neighborhood* to improve the self-esteem and mental health of American children caused Pastore to comment, "I think it's wonderful. It looks like you just earned twenty million dollars." In 1969, America's foundational moral underpinnings clearly had not changed since the nineteenth century. Mister Rogers' address to United States Senate Sub-committee on Communications caused federal funding for PBS to jump from nine million to twenty-two million dollars. As Rogers' address and Pastore's response illustrate, the Christian Gentleman's personal conduct, unlike that of the Masculine Primitive, is committed to fostering social good not self-gratification. Because the Christian Gentleman privileges the needs of society over those of the individual, expressions for this gender ideal include phil-anthropic activities, involvement in church events, acts of self-sacrifice and a deep involvement in family life (Rotundo 38). This ideal also places a great deal of emphasis on impulse control. It is not surprising that self-mastery is an important subject addressed by Rogers in *Mister Rogers' Neighborhood* and one which Fred Rogers stressed in his Senate testimony when discussing his program's aims. Quoting from the song "What Do You Do with the Mad That You Feel?" Rogers reminded Pastore that a child needs to learn self-control (the ability to "stop when I want to") because self-mastery is the mark of being an adult: self-control "helps us become what we can … a girl can be someday a woman/And a boy can be someday a man" (Rogers 102–03).

Middle-class and morally respectable, the Christian Gentleman was con-sidered the ideal neighbor. His neighborliness belongs to the earlier concept of *communal manhood* that was developed in the social world of colonial New England, where, Rotundo notes, a man's identity (and by extension, his wife's and children's) was inseparable from the duties he owed to his com-munity. In colonial New England, men fulfilled themselves through public usefulness more than by their economic success, and the social status of the family into which a man was born gave him his place in the community more than his individual achievements did (Rotundo 2). Aptly, the individuals in *Mister Rogers' Neighborhood*, like men in colonial New England, are publically useful, being governed by a set of duties owed to others.

In *Mister Rogers' Neighborhood*, this set of duties often intersects caring with consumption. As Rotundo points out, some of our most engaging expe-riences of community in the twentieth century come from our participation in communities of consumption" (284). In the Neighborhood, consuming, be it shopping or eating is a very important activity. Rogers takes his television "neighbor" to restaurants, kitchens, factories and farms, and personally introduces the viewer to the people who work at these places, emphasizing what Rotundo calls "the importance of the sense of personal connection or support that a human community can provide" (284). Thus, in *Mister Rogers' Neighborhood*, individuals and the places which they occupy in their society are always identified by their social functions. Some characters are identified by their titles at work, like Officer Clemmons (François Clemmons), a member of the local police force, and Chef Brockett (Don Brockett), a restaurant owner and entrepreneur. Other small businessmen are identified by the nature of their work. These jobs are indicators of social functions. Mr. McFeely, for example, is the Deliveryman who connects people with one another by delivering their mail and packages. Some individuals do not even have a surname on the show. Their titles take the place of their family name as a community identifier: Emily, for example, is The Poetry Lady.

Meeting the other neighbors in the Neighborhood involves Rogers introducing the owners, managers, and workers of these places to the television viewer not only by their names but also by their functions as members of the community. The television viewer is introduced to these individuals as well, not only establishing his or her part in the program as a fellow consumer but also including him or her as a part of that community. Thus, when Mister Rogers plans to visit the cows at Taner's, the neighborhood dairy farm, he first introduces the viewer to the idea of accompanying him to meet a member of the community, Jane Henshaw, "a woman who works at the dairy farm in our neighborhood."[2] Jane, he says, "takes care of cows and all kinds of products there and I thought we'd just go over there today and see some of the cows and see where people get milk to drink." Here, the idea of community and neighborhood is emphasized by the camera's treatment of the Neighborhood. The camera cuts to a close-up of the model of Mister Rogers' house in the Neighborhood as Mister Rogers, gesturing to the viewer to join him, exits his front door. The camera pulls out to include the dairy farm located behind Mister Rogers' house in the shot and then zooms in on the farm before panning up to the backdrop of the sky that hangs behind it. This shot of the sky dissolves into a shot of the sky above the actual dairy farm, which then pans down and pulls out to reveal the barns and a farmyard filled with Holsteins and Guernsey cows. Standing outside the gate to the farmyard, Mister Rogers is included in the shot. Jane Henshaw stands in the background with the dairy herd.

In colonial New England, people thought of the world as we would now think of our neighborhood. As Rotundo points out, the New Englander regarded his or her society as being "an organic social order in which rights and responsibilities were reciprocal and in which terms like individuality or self-reliance had little place" (12–13). A colonial New Englander's identity in what was a stable and ordered social hierarchy was bound up in performance of social roles which were organized in terms of social relationships. The conjunction of these roles (father-son, husband-wife, or neighbor-neighbor, for example) was governed by a reciprocal set of duties owed to one another (Rotundo 12–13). In *Mister Rogers' Neighborhood*, each "neighbor" performs a publicly useful role—a job that involves social caring for others. The Neighborhood's dairy, for example, is publicly useful, because it produces milk for people to consume. The dairy's employees ensure that their customers' needs are cared for. Even the dairy's cows, whose job it is to produce the milk, are treated as important individuals in this community of care. When encountering the cows at the dairy in Season 14, Episode 7, Mister Rogers acknowledges their importance and awards them equal status as members of the community by greeting them with the same polite hello that he uses to greet the employees who work there.

Here it should be noted that Mister Rogers asks permission to enter the farmyard, and only enters it after Jane has given him her social trust. He introduces the viewer, his "television neighbor" to her. This introduction further establishes the existence of a personable and personal community. Significantly, Rogers emphasizes Henshaw's first name while making this introduction: "*Jane*, I'd like you to meet my television neighbor. This is *Jane* Henshaw" ("The Cows," italics mine). During the tour of Taner's dairy, the introductions are professional as well as personal, emphasizing how these "neighbors" operate in conjunction with one another. In the milking parlor, for example, Jane introduces her employee by her first name *and* her function: "I'd like you to meet Anne Bauer; she's our herdswoman" ("The Cows"). Jane's relationship to Anne is personal and professional. Just as it is the duty of the cows in the community at Taner's dairy to give milk to the Neighborhood, it is Anne's duty to milk them and send the milk on to be stored before being pasteurized.

After Rogers interviews Anne about milking and she shows him how the cows are milked, his departure from the milking parlor again demonstrates the social trust and obligations which these neighbors owe to one another. Reaffirming the intimate nature of their relationship, Rogers uses Anne's first name to thank her. He then affirms the nature of their relationship by promising to see her again and shaking her hand. Anne's response, shaking his hand, thanking him, and also saying goodbye, completes their neighborly interaction. Notably, when the entire tour of the farm and its factory concludes, the same social ritual is enacted with Jane Henshaw. Jane confirms the closeness of her relationship with Mister Rogers by saying, "It was nice seeing you, Fred" ("The Cows"). Again the exchange of thanks, handshaking, and goodbyes take place—what seem to be simple pleasantries are important rituals of social closure, affirming the obligations that one neighbor owes another and maintaining the community of care to which they belong. As

Rogers himself notes in *The World According to Mister Rogers: Important Things to Remember*, social exchanges like these direct one's attention to the needs and concerns of others and illustrate the nature of ideal neighborliness:

> Imagine what our real neighborhoods would be like if each of us offered, as a matter of course, just one kind word to another person. There have been so many stories about the lack of courtesy, the impatience of today's world, road rage, and even restaurant rage. Sometimes, all it takes is one kind word to nourish another person. Think of the ripple effect that can be created when we nourish someone. One kind empathetic word has a wonderful way of turning into many [185].

To be an effective neighbor one must recognize and understand the code of social conduct and personal virtue expected of an individual by his or her neighbors. When one considers the optimistic assessment of an orderly cosmos and the confidence in human sociability, kindness, and empathy that the viewer finds in *Mister Rogers' Neighborhood*, it becomes apparent that Mister Rogers is following in the footsteps of Anthony Ashley Cooper, the third Earl of Shaftesbury (1671–1713) on television. Enlightenment thinkers would have recognized *Mister Rogers' Neighborhood* as a "civilizing" process, one in which individuals pursue moral knowledge and moral self-transformation. Being neighborly in the Neighborhood involves refashioning and improving one's self according to a prescribed moral pattern: as Rogers points out to his viewer, "if you will look carefully, /Listen carefully, You will find a lot of things carefully / ...That's the way you learn a lot of things carefully / ...You'll begin to notice a change in you / ...That's a way to keep on growing carefully" ("The Pretzel Factory").

For the "enlightened" viewer, every episode of *Mister Rogers' Neighborhood* is an exercise in moral philosophy—that is the educational activities in the Neighborhood, in Mister Rogers' home, and in the Neighborhood of Make-Believe are not so much about discovering the truth about the Neighborhood, as they are about "discovering the truth about ourselves" (13). And like Shaftesbury, who emphasizes the "workmanship that went into being a moral agent, the improvement to which the self should aspire and the creative energy required for the self to be its own 'author'" (Klein viii), Rogers offers his television "neighbor" reflections on effectiveness of self-discipline as a method by which self-transformation and living in a morally effective way can be achieved. A humanist, Rogers not only recognizes the amount of work that is required to live a virtuous and fulfilling life, but he also regards self-knowledge and character formation as moral imperatives: "I like to swim," he says, "But there are some days I just don't feel much like doing it—but *I do it anyway!* I know it's good for me and I promised myself I'd do it *every* day, and I like to keep my promises" (105).

As Shaftesbury points out in "An Inquiry Concerning Virtue or Merit," virtuous behavior is desirable, because it "upholds communities, maintains union, friendship and correspondence amongst men" (230). In the Neighborhood, neighborly behavior is virtuous behavior. For example, Rogers' song "What Do You Do with the Mad That You Feel?" introduces anger management to children as a means towards self- improvement. In "What Do You Do with the Mad That You Feel," Rogers presents self-control as a positive, self-affirming experience: "I can stop when I want to/Can stop when I wish/ Can stop, stop, stop any time/And what a good feeling to feel like this" (103). In this song, self-control, the means by the individual reconciles self-actualization with his or her societal responsibility, enables that individual to conform to norms for social conduct and conversation.

While modeling good manners for his television "neighbor," Mister Rogers transmits a code of personal conduct which enables caring for others and encourages self-mastery via virtuous behavior. These standards for social interaction which Shaftesbury would consider to be evidence of virtuous conduct and conversation are always linked to the development of the individual's moral sensibility. Most easily charted in its tropes of "politeness" (social conventions that citizens of the eighteenth century would have considered to be signifiers of moral and cultural refinement), the *paideia* or program of ethical cultivation embedded in *Mister Rogers' Neighborhood* rests on the concept of "politeness" being the "distinctively modern form of virtue" that was developed by eighteenth-century writers like Joseph Addison and Richard Steele and was pervasive in Whig thinking through the 1870s (Klein vii).

Rogers also links the development of his viewer's moral sensibility with his or her aesthetic experience of *Mister Rogers' Neighborhood.* Bridging the ideal and real, *Mister Rogers' Neighborhood* insists that the materials for moral and cultural refinement that create an ethical society are used not only on television—they are also relevant everywhere we live. Returning to Mister Rogers' house, the camera transitions the viewer between the actual world which Mister Rogers and the viewer explore on their trips to the Neighborhood, the miniature model of Mister Rogers' Neighborhood, and the television set that serves as the exterior and the interior of Mister Rogers' house, linking the ideal with the real while reversing the process of arriving at Taner's dairy farm by cutting to a shot of a Guernsey cow standing on a hill by the Taner's tank before dissolving to a shot of a similarly-colored model of a cow on a hill by the farm in the Neighborhood. The camera then pulls back to reveal Mister Rogers' house in its setting before the shot zooms in towards its front door. There is then a dissolve to the interior of the house as Mister Rogers enters his home.

This complex transition from exterior to interior offers its viewer a sophisticated series of cinematic tropes which demonstrate that it is possible to live in a morally effective way everywhere—whether in the world of television, in Mister Rogers' Neighborhood, or in the world of the television viewer. The cinematic rhetoric of these transitions' dissolves and cuts, repeated in every episode, demonstrates that it *is* possible for the ideal to become the real, the abstract to become the concrete, and the thought to become action. As Rogers notes in *The World According to Mister Rogers*, manifesting ideas in the world requires action on the part of the television viewer: "[i]magining something may be the first step to making something happen, but it takes the real time and real efforts of real people to learn things, make things, turn thoughts into deeds or visions into inventions" (99). For example, when Mister Rogers visits the Fire Station in Season 29, Episode 9, camera dissolves are again used to link the ideal and the real.[3] As Mister Rogers exits through his front door, the camera cuts to an exterior shot of his house in the modeled Neighborhood, then pulls back and dollies while panning over the Neighborhood to rest on a shot of the Fire Station. This Fire Station, modeled after the actual Fire Station to which the camera then cuts, showcases a shiny fire engine in its driveway. When Mister Rogers walks into the shot, he approaches a fireman cleaning the fire engine. As when he visited Taner's dairy, Mister Rogers fulfills his social obligations to his neighbor by apologizing for his interruption of the man's work and politely asking for Captain Arnold. Thanking the man for the information, he proceeds into the Station. One finds that the tone of Rogers' interview with Captain Arnold is more formal than the one used during his visit to the dairy. Referring to the fireman who is interviewed as "Captain Arnold" or "Captain," Mister Rogers not only identifies his "neighbor" personally and professionally, he also transfers his respect for and his acknowledgement of the professional status of the firefighter in his community. The viewer is immediately informed that Captain Arnold is one of Mister Rogers' "friends," and learns that firefighting is "serious business" as Captain Arnold first dresses and then instructs Mister Rogers in the use of a Self-Contained Breathing Apparatus (SCBA).

Throughout this interview, a community of care that resembles the one found at Taner's dairy is evident. The same important social rituals that affirm the obligations which one neighbor owes another are foregrounded, and the esteem which Mister Rogers awards Captain Arnold is reciprocated. Mister Rogers and Captain Arnold greet one another, and, once introduced, the television "neighbor" is included in their conversation. Captain Arnold listens carefully to Mister Rogers' questions and responds to them with a respectful "Yes, sir" ("The Fire Station"). While dressing Mister Rogers in his fireproof hood and mask, the fireman demonstrates the utmost care for his friend's well-being while ensuring that Rogers is safe and comfortable in the mask. Another social obligation, one's respect for another's property, is also foregrounded throughout this interview. When shown a fire engine, for instance, Mister Rogers asks Captain Arnold for permission to inspect it and doesn't touch its steps until that permission is given.

Educating the viewer about appropriate social interaction (that is rational and therefore self-controlled), *Mister Rogers' Neighborhood* emphasizes the significance of professional relationships in the Neighborhood. While Rogers and his television "neighbor" discover how things are made, one meets one's "neighbors" and is admitted into "polite" (civil) society. Each introduction reinforces the importance of polite behavior and educates the viewer in the nature of the world. For example, when Mister Rogers tours the Graham Cracker Factory with Brigitte the Foreman in Season 31, Episode 1786, he and his viewer learn how the factory employees support and care for one another while almost 2,000 boxes of graham crackers are made from one big batch of dough.[4] As the dough is mixed, dumped into the dough dump, rolled, thinned, cut, trimmed, baked in an oven approximately the size of a football field, cut again, counted, and wrapped in their individual wax paper packages to be boxed, the employees are courteous and "polite." A microcosm of social civility in the world outside the workplace, the factory workers are governed by a set of duties owed to one another. Each place of work is in itself a small neighborhood. As Mister Rogers and the viewer tour the production line, the conjunction of roles between the line workers, such as the intersection of duties between the foreman and the dough maker and the dough maker and the dough dumper, is revealed. The import of these obligations being observed is evidenced by the successful product which is packaged at the end of the production line, and shown in the respect each worker is accorded by his or her fellow workers.

Professional relationships not only impart social knowledge—they also convey cultural wisdom to the viewer. In Season 11, Episode 1477, Mister Rogers' visit to the Pretzel Factory transmits traditional secrets to the uninitiated as Rogers learns to make pretzels.[5] Introducing Mister Rogers to the art of pretzel-making, Clyde, the owner of the factory and the pretzel maker, first reveals historical information about the pretzel before divulging the religious significance that is encoded into every snack. "Pretzels were first made in Germany, France, and Italy almost fifteen hundred years ago, and they were given to children for knowing prayers," Clyde tells Mister Rogers as they roll out pretzel dough together. He then explains the process:

> We first shape them like a great big "U." We take one [end] and cross it over the other. This is to represent children's arms praying to God. Then we take one [end] and fold it over the other. That represents your parents, Mom and Dad. We pick up the ends, and fold them on back. Be sure you have three holes and look what you've made ... the fingerprints in the pretzel [are] your trademark.... That's how yours differs from mine. That's the holy Trinity, the three holes ["The Pretzel Factory"].

Here it is important to note that however small it may be, every act in the Neighborhood, even that of making a pretzel, is an opportunity for achieving self-fulfillment and self-transformation. The pretzels created at Clyde's shop are painstakingly and thoughtfully made for his neighbors. They are all expressions of neighborly caring. Indeed, every social obligation and duty required of a good neighbor in *Mister Rogers' Neighborhood* enable the individual "to become the best of whoever you are" (185). The Neighborhood encountered in every episode of *Mister Rogers' Neighborhood* is a celebration of the talents and personalities of each individual who lives there *and* a demonstration of how that individual functions as a part of a greater whole. In short, Mister Rogers' Neighborhood is an example of humanism at work.

Welcomed and integrated into the community, the television neighbor, also a member of the Neighborhood, is never alienated from the activities at hand. In *Mister Rogers' Neighborhood*, the viewer is never merely a voyeur. Throughout each episode, Rogers converses with the viewer, including him or her in the action at hand, and his opening song, "Won't You Be My Neighbor?" immediately establishes his television neighbor as a desirable and desired member of the middle class, someone to be included: "I have always wanted to have a neighbor / Just like you!" Mister Rogers tells his viewer. "I've always wanted to live in a / Neighborhood with you" (142). More important, Rogers points out that the relationship between the viewer and his or her "neighbors" is also significant and reciprocal: "If you could only sense how important you are to the lives of those you meet," he says, "how important you can be to the people you may never even dream of. There is something of yourself that you leave at every meeting with another person" (Rogers 160).

Since end of the eighteenth century, as men have become increasingly identified with public places, particularly those concerned with the world of commerce and industry found outside the home, gender typing of space has defined places of business as being "masculine." In such places, performing one's social obligations and duties is of paramount importance, for these duties create and sustain the social trust which sustains and fosters successful social interaction. In the "masculine" world of the workplace, the Christian Gentleman expects others to be good neighbors, ethical businessmen, in order to be successful. In the twentieth century, *Mister Rogers' Neighborhood* resituates gender typing of place and space by returning the viewer to an earlier conception of gender, place, and society. When Mister Rogers goes on a tour of the Neighborhood, he introduces his viewer to the business and public spaces located outside what has come to be considered the domestic, feminine sphere of the home. In these spaces, one finds both men and women at work. Moreover, Mister Rogers' home is not a gendered place subject to feminine authority. There is no angel of hearth in charge of tending its parlor. Taking off his sport coat and dress shoes when he arrives home from work, Mister

Rogers retains his tie while donning his informal cardigan and sneakers— integrating his public, at-work persona with his private, at-home personality while retaining his authority (and credibility) in both places. Uniting what have become male and female spheres of influence, Mister Rogers lives a complete, well-rounded, and syncretic life: he goes to work and keeps house for himself, shopping, doing dishes, and feeding his fish.

In *Mister Rogers' Neighborhood*, every space is a place in which ethical, neighborly interaction occurs. The Neighborhood's public places are filled with Mister Rogers' neighbors, and Mister Rogers, himself the quintessential good neighbor, not only introduces his viewer to these people, but also welcomes the television neighbor into his own home. Rogers' orderly and self-ordered neighborly life at home returns the viewer to a time when a man's "'publick usefulness' was a crucial measure of his worth, and men who carried out their duties to family and community were men to admire" (Rotundo 13). As Rotundo points out, in New England before 1800, the family, which served as the fundamental unit of society, was the primary unit of production; farms, shops and great mercantile firms were all family enterprises. Assumed to have greater reason than woman and therefore better self-government, men in seventeenth- and eighteenth-century New England were expected to be the heads of their households. The head of a household in colonial New England was considered to be the embodiment of all of its members, and to head a household was to be publicly "useful": as heads of their households, men were expected to anchor the status system, preserve the political order, provide a model for government, sustain piety, ensure productive activity, and maintain the economic support of one's dependents (Rotundo 11–12).

Here it is necessary to remember that *Mister Rogers' Neighborhood* insists that Mister Rogers' "publick usefulness" to America outside the home lies not only in his work as a businessman (when he arrives he takes off his business jacket and formal shoes) but also in the activity of connecting people, creating neighbors, and maintaining communal relationships. As Rotundo points out, a composite of ideal traits and virtues, the ideal man in colonial England was pleasant, mild-mannered and devoted to the good of the community. He performed his duties faithfully, governed his passions rationally, submitted to his fate and to his place in society, and treated his dependents with firm, but affectionate wisdom (13–14). Modeled after the example of the ideal man in colonial England, Mister Rogers, pious, dutiful and restrained, insists that "[t]he purpose of life is to listen—to yourself, to your neighbor, to your world and to God and, when the time comes, to respond in as helpful a way as you can find … from within and without" (167).

As Rotundo points out, many social critics have recently noted that today we lack even the rudiments of a language to discuss community and connection (284–85). Such critics have overlooked the importance of Fred

Rogers and his Neighborhood to Americans living in latter part of the twentieth and the first part of the twenty-first-centuries. Important elements of the continuing tradition of the Christian Gentleman and communal manhood in America, the gender ideals that Mister Rogers and his Neighborhood transmit are not isolated phenomena in the family programming found on television in the United States. As Andrew Adam Newman points out in "Changin' in the Boys' Room," the archetypal "cardigan-wearing, all-wise father figure ... was, in fact, a media creation ... that etched itself into the collective unconscious in American culture." From 1957 to 1963, the Christian Gentleman and colonial New England manliness were embodied in the popular series, *Leave It to Beaver*, by Ward Cleaver (Hugh Beaumont). These ideals were also foregrounded in *My Three Sons* from 1960 to 1972 in the character of Steven Douglas (Fred MacMurray). Then in 1972, Fred Rogers donned the cardigan and became America's favorite surrogate father in *Mister Rogers' Neighborhood*. Other dependable and caring television husbands and fathers also wore cardigans when not in suit jackets: Darrin Stephens (Dick York) in *Bewitched* and Ricky Ricardo (Desi Arnaz) in *The Lucy Show*, for example, sported cardigans at the golf course, Wilbur Post (Alan Lane) in *Mister Ed*, Jim Anderson (Robert Young) in *Father Knows Best*, and Rob Petrie (Dick Van Dyke) in the *Dick Van Dyke Show* all dressed as household heads, wearing their cardigans after work or on the weekends. Perry Como, who invented casual, used the cardigan to create his signature look "at home" during his Christmas specials. Their representations of cardigan-wearing fathers remind us that manhood, a learned, used, and reinforced phenomenon reshaped by individuals in the course of life, is always rooted in one's experience of family and community.

Aptly, Fred Rogers valued his "publick usefulness" above his other achievements. As he told Karen Herman for the *Archive of American Television* in 1999, he wanted "to be remembered as being a compassionate human being who happened to be fortunate enough to be born at a time when there was a fabulous thing called television that could allow me to use all the talents that I had been given."[6] Since his death in 2002, Rogers has certainly been granted his wish. As Williams notes, "Fred Rogers was fearless enough to be kind. Kinder in a single day than many of us can muster up in a week. He wasn't embarrassed to be gentle; he was never too cool to be simply good." An embodiment of the Christian Gentleman *and* colonial New England's communal manhood, Rogers himself defined his life's work as "an offering of love" (Herman). When one considers the masculine types that have been culturally sanctioned throughout the twentieth century, it is tempting to include Fred Rogers in only one category, but to do so would be to mistake a tough for a tender man. Commenting on the nature of the gender ideals available today for men, Rogers himself points out that tender men are, by their very natures, extremely tough: "[c]onfronting our feelings and giving them appropriate expression always takes strength, not weakness," he says. "It takes strength to acknowledge our anger and sometimes more strength yet to curb the aggressive urges anger may bring and to channel them into nonviolent outlets. It takes strength to face our sadness and to grieve and to let our grief and our anger flower in tears when they need to. It takes strength to talk about our feelings and to reach out for help and comfort when we need it" (15). "When I was a boy I used to think that strong meant having big muscles, great physical power," he adds, "but the longer I live, the more I realize that real strength has much more to do with what is not seen. Real strength has to do with helping others" (41).

Equating social and self-worth with virtue, Shaftesbury points out how important it is "[t]o have one's affections right and entire not only in respect of oneself but of society and the public": "this," he says, "is rectitude, integrity or virtue" (192). Valuing strength of character, the manliness that Fred Rogers embodies in *Mister Rogers' Neighborhood* is ultimately an ethics of compassion and self-worth which enables boys (and girls) to become morally effective, socially useful citizens *and* powerful individuals. Ultimately, being a good neighbor is an essential expression of one's manhood, one's integrity, and one's virtue. As Shaftesbury notes,

> in the passions and affections of particular creatures, there is a constant relation to the interest of a species or common nature. This has been demonstrated in the case of natural affection, kindness, zeal for posterity, concern for the propagation and nurture of the young, love of fellowship and company, compassion, mutual succor and the rest of this kind. Nor will anyone deny that this affection of a creature towards the good of the species or common nature is as proper and natural to him [192].

Learned, used, reinforced, and reshaped throughout one's lifetime, manhood is a powerful cultural force. An American icon of fatherhood, Fred Rogers taught (and continues to teach) millions of viewers that neighborliness is an important expression of one's manhood. Being a good neighbor, of course, is not an end in itself, for it is always a means to an end. As Shaftesbury says, it is "the private interest and good of everyone to work towards the general good"; if an individual ceases to promote that social good, "he is actually so far wanting to himself and ceases to promote his own happiness and welfare" (230). More than three hundred years later, Fred Rogers' perspective on the nature of neighborliness, the conjunction of individuals that constitutes a neighborhood, accords with Shaftesbury's. In *Mister Rogers' Neighborhood*, the more things change, the more they stay the same. "Whether we're giving or receiving help, each one of us has something valuable to bring to this world," Rogers says, "that's one of the things that connects us as neighbors—in our own way, each one of us is a giver and a receiver" (136). In *Mister Rogers'*

Neighborhood, one finds that no man is an island—connected one to another, we are each part of a greater continent. In the final analysis, Fred Rogers' popularity rests on a compelling manliness deeply rooted in the American psyche. Reminding us of the complicated nature of gender as a cultural force, his depiction of manhood in *Mister Rogers' Neighborhood* counterbalances the attractiveness of the masculine primitive in the twentieth-first century by linking the members of America's digital community with their collective past and compensating our current preoccupation with violence and toughness with compassionate strength. In *Mister Rogers' Neighborhood*, the nineteenth-century America's Christian Gentleman and colonial New England's masculine ideal impart cultural and historical secrets of the middle class to young viewers, while reminding us all that friendship and the individual continue to flourish as the foundations of the American community.

NOTES

1. Rogers' address to the United States Senate Subcommittee on Communications and Pastore's response is available at http://www.youtube.com/watch?v=yXEuEUQIP3Q.

2. "Mister Rogers Visits the Cows" may be seen its entirety at http://www.youtube.com/watch?v=yMwQUZirfyg.

3. Mister Rogers' visit to the Fire Station in "Mister Rogers' Neighborhood Go Stop Go" may be viewed at http://www.youtube.com/watch?v=UUNRjF1QvOs.

4. Mister Rogers' visit to the Graham Cracker factory may be viewed at http://www.youtube.com/watch?v=NFWP0vGWA10&list=PL3ry-GpNMHO7c-3YLaDhaDxxV2Pk_A_FE/.

5. Mister Rogers' visit to Clyde's pretzel factory may be viewed at http://www.youtube.com/watch?v=W42pX8bUqkU.

6. For the interview in its entirety, see http://www.youtube.com/watch?v=NgZEb5vZTTE&list=PL02654C0264619375.

WORKS CITED

Cooper, Anthony Ashley, Third Earl of Shaftesbury. "An Inquiry Concerning Virtue or Merit." In *Characteristics of Men, Manners, Opinions, Times*. Ed. Lawrence E. Klein. Cambridge: Cambridge University Press, 1999: 163–230. Print.

Herman, Karen. "Mister Rogers on How He'd Like to be Remembered." Emmytvlegends.org, 10 Feb. 2012. Accessed 30 June 2014. http://www.youtube.com/watch?v=NgZEb5vZTTE&list=PL02654C0264619375. Internet.

Klein, Lawrence E. "Introduction." In *Characteristics of Men, Manners, Opinions, Times*. Ed. Lawrence E. Klein. Cambridge: Cambridge University Press, 1999: vii–xxxi. Print.

Mister Rogers Defending PBS to the US Senate. 29 July 2007. Accessed 20 June 2014. http://www.youtube.com/watch?v=yXEuEUQIP3Q. Internet.

"Mister Rogers Neighborhood Go Stop Go." 3 July 2014. Accessed 5 July 2014. http://www.youtube.com/watch?v=UUNRjF1QvOs. Cited parenthetically as "The Fire Station." Internet.

"Mister Rogers Visits the Cows." 12 Sept. 2010. Accessed 2 July 2014. http://www.youtube.com/watch?v=yMwQUZirfyg. Cited parenthetically as "The Cows." Internet.

"Mister Rogers Visits the Graham Cracker Factory." 29 Jan. 2013. Accessed 5 July 2014. http://www.youtube.com/watch?v= NFWP0vGW A10&list=PL3ry-GpNMHO7c-3YLaDhaDxxV2Pk_A_FE. Internet.

"Mister Rogers Visits the Pretzel Factory." 18 Jan. 2014. Accessed 5 July 2014. http://www.youtube.com/watch?v=W42pX8bUqkU. Cited parenthetically as "The Pretzel Factory." Internet.

Newman, Andrew Adam. "Changin' in the Boys' Room." *New York Times* 5 Feb. 2006. Accessed 5 July 2014. http://www.nytimes.com/2006/02/05/ fashion/sunday styles/25DIAPERS.html?pagewanted=print&_r=0. Internet.

Rogers, Fred. *The World According to Mister Rogers: Important Things to Remember.* New York: Hyperion, 2003. Print.

Rotundo, Anthony E. *American Manhood: Transformations in Masculinity from the Revolution to the Modern Era.* New York: HarperCollins, 1993. Print.

_____. "Learning about Manhood: Gender Ideals and the Middle-Class Family in Nineteenth-Century America." In *Manliness and Morality: Middle-Class Masculinity in Britain and America 1800–1940.* Ed. J.A. Mangan and James Walvin. New York: Palgrave Macmillan, 1987: 35–51. Print.

Williams, Mary Elizabeth. "Where Have You Gone, Mister Rogers?" 13 Mar. 2012. Accessed 2 July 2014. http://www.salon.com/2012/03/13/ where_have_you_gone_mister_rogers/. Internet.

Grown-Up Work and the Work of Growing Up

Valerie H. Pennanen

For most of human history, in cultures around the world, children have been expected to work. And so they have done. Generations of little hands have harvested crops, tended livestock, cooked meals, carried water in peacetime and weapons in wartime, entertained and waited on the wealthy, and labored in mines, warehouses, and factories.[1] Down through the ages as well, children from more privileged backgrounds have been allowed—or at times forced—to work with their minds: "getting lessons" from private tutors or from teachers, and encouraged to regard their studies as preparation for success in the adult world. The conviction that each and every child deserves to be schooled and sheltered from hard physical toil did not emerge in the Western world till the end of the eighteenth century. It was slow to grow and has yet to become universal. Despite numerous modern laws and international treaties designed to protect the young, as many as 245 million boys and girls in developing countries still are routinely compelled to work at demanding physical jobs; worse yet, 179 million of these children are in jobs that probably or certainly will—in the words of a 2002 report from the International Labor Organization—cause "irreversible physical or psychological damage, or ... even threaten their lives" (International Labour Organization). At the same time, ironically, adults in industrialized nations are often heard complaining that their children are lazy and underprepared for the "real world" of work.

Between the extremes of exploitation and overwork on the one hand, and lives full of self-centered leisure on the other, there can and should be a happy medium, and to find what that medium looks like, we have only to turn to *Mister Rogers' Neighborhood*. In his gentle yet forthright way, the late Fred Rogers presented work as both a key part of a person's identity and a means of bringing comfort, safety, knowledge, or enrichment to the lives of others. Mister Rogers helped young viewers to appreciate the daily lives of working adults through four types of segments on the show: meetings with familiar residents of the television neighborhood; interviews with guests; visits to the Neighborhood of Make-Believe; and, most famously, Picture Picture films about manufacturing jobs and the people who do them. But he did not stop there. With genuine respect for his audience of children aged two through five, he encouraged them daily to engage in their own, vitally important task of growing up. The relevance of Mister Rogers' ideals in regard to work—not just for middle-class Americans and their children, but for all the world and its children—and how he managed to impart those ideals to young viewers, while still entertaining them, will form the dual focus of this essay.

As millions of American children used to know (and countless adults remember), Mister Rogers begins each episode of his show with music. The gentle music-box effect of the opening notes is followed by the deeper and livelier sound of a jazz piano, and then as the tune reaches a crescendo Mister Rogers opens the door to his television house, waves cheerily, and sings, "It's a beautiful day in this neighborhood, / A beautiful day for a neighbor; would / You be mine? / Could you be mine?" He continues his song while matter-of-factly exchanging his sport jacket for a sweater, dress shoes for sneakers, until at last he sits before his audience, softly and tunefully inviting them, "Won't you please, / Won't you please, / Please won't you be my neighbor?" Designed to evoke a parent coming home from work at day's end, or perhaps at lunchtime (since Mister Rogers always switches back to business attire and leaves the "house" as the episode ends), this charming yet predictable opening sequence hints that both work and leisure are important. Moreover, by arriving always with an energetic walk, a cheerful smile, and music that suggests two different kinds of happy mood, Mister Rogers lets his young viewers see that work and leisure both can make us glad.

The fact that Mister Rogers' presence on television actually *is* his job is alluded to in various episodes, as filmed throughout the years. In a show first broadcast on April 6, 1984 (number 1528)[2] to conclude a week-long series on work, Mister Rogers gives children a tour of his studio surroundings, introduces them to musician John Costa and others involved with the show, returns to his "house" to display puppets from the Neighborhood of Make-Believe and demonstrate how he makes them talk, and displays photographs and drawings depicting the show's history. An earlier episode (Episode 1384) has Mister Rogers holding up puppets and speaking in their voices, while in a later episode (Episode 1698) Mr. McFeely and Mister Rogers watch a time-lapse video of the television house being set up. In an episode about pets (Episode 1497) Mister Rogers telephones his wife to ask if he may bring Bob Trow's dog Barney home for the night, afterward remarking to his viewers, "It's time for me to go to my real home now. You know what I mean when I talk about my *real* home. That's a place where I live with my family. *This* is my television home, where I come to visit with you each day." Likewise at the end of his visit with restaurant owner (and former Neighborhood of Make-Believe guest) Barbara Smith (Episode 1703), Mister Rogers responds to Ms. Smith's observation that she needs to get back to work by noting, "And so do I." Their cheerful, matter-of-fact parting underscores the theme of work as a basically good, rewarding thing—a theme Ms. Smith has stressed throughout the interview (see below). Granted, not every preschooler would be apt to understand or even notice Mister Rogers' references to his Neighborhood as work, but the references are certainly there; and Fred Rogers would be among the first to tell us that children, though they learn gradually, may understand a good deal more than we give them credit for.

Through encounters with familiar residents of the "television neighborhood," Mister Rogers further helped young viewers to glimpse what it means to have a job and respect oneself for doing it well, despite occasional struggles. Mr. McFeely, the "Speedy Delivery" man who comes by almost every day, is an excellent case in point. Mr. McFeely models consistently good manners (as do all the people on the show) and also, as a rule, good time management—balancing short, congenial visits to Mister Rogers' "house" with dedication to his other customers and adherence to schedule. For instance, after delivering a canvas seat for a three-legged stool, he lingers long enough to watch Mister Rogers install the seat and briefly accepts the invitation to try it out. "But," he adds, getting to his feet, "if you're a Speedy Delivery man, you can't sit for too long." With that, he bids his friend a polite farewell and exits to complete his rounds (Episode 1481). It is true Mr. McFeely at times seems in too much of a hurry, either because he is having hard time keeping things in perspective (a series first aired in 1972 shows him becoming ill from overwork and having to learn how to relax [Episode 1247 and following], or because he wants to avoid talking about a topic that makes him uncomfortable (this occurs in the opening episode of the weeklong series, "Mister Rogers Talks About Divorce" [Episode 1466]). Mr. McFeely has been known to make a mistake as a result of rushing about too fast: he delivers the wrong package to Mister Rogers' address and learns of his error only when the next customer scolds him (Episode 1591). He feels bad about the mistake for a while, in part because the customer's anger has hurt his feelings and in part because, like all of us, he hates to be wrong! Yet he is able to forgive himself with a little help from Mister Rogers' singing "You Are Special." Mr. McFeely's overall competence at his job is made abundantly clear in the numerous episodes where he appears; and his jaunty "Speedy Delivery" song (first heard in Episode 1631) reflects healthy respect for himself and his business. The fact that he charges money for his services is mentioned on at least one occasion (Episode 1528)—a reminder that what he does has genuine value.

Chef Brockett, another regular on the show, is a highly skilled baker who, like Mr. McFeely, is hurt but not devastated by occasional setbacks to his work. When Chef Brockett realizes that he has failed to chill a batch of cream sufficiently before whipping, he is disappointed, but he soon finds another use for this cream and correctly prepares a second batch (Episode 1580). In another episode, he is saddened to lose a cake-decorating contest but is also able to accept reassurance—understanding that his cakes are still fine and that his bakery holds a special place in the life of the Neighborhood (Episode 1483). An enterprising gentleman, he uses video arcade games to help promote sales of a special series of cakes, made to resemble characters from the Neighborhood of Make-Believe (Episode 1514).

Joe Negri—in real life, a professional jazz guitarist—is portrayed in the quasi-real-life segments of the show as owner of a music store. Here he sells, cares for, and repairs instruments, gives lessons, and hosts performances by other musicians, sometimes performing with them; in one memorable instance, he joins cellist Yo-Yo Ma in playing the Mister Rogers tune "Tree Tree Tree" with vocal accompaniment from Mister Rogers (Episode 1547). Mr. Negri thus emerges as a person of versatile talents, respected by himself and others for those talents (note that he and Yo-Yo Ma regard themselves as fellow musicians and music lovers, instead of rivals), and a man who draws on those talents to create a unique livelihood. In the Neighborhood of Make-Believe he appears as Handyman Negri, a change meant to reflect the importance of his repair work at the music store. (Even though in a 2010 interview for National Public Radio Negri remarked he was not *really* handy "in the least bit" [Rose], his genuine respect for professionals who work with their hands—his own father was a bricklayer—helped him play the role well [Around the Neighborhood].)

Of the several other "neighbors" who appear periodically on the show, perhaps the most interesting is Audrey Roth, who like many real-life working people has held more than one job—and performed each one well. Be it as waitress, soda-shop attendant, or owner of her own small business—Audrey Cleans Everything—Ms. Roth is a person of many talents who matter-of-factly does whatever needs doing, though we are also given to understand that she (like everyone else in the Neighborhood) is part of a larger community, whose members help each other. She employs cleaning supplies delivered by Mr. McFeely to remove a stain from Mister Rogers' shirt (Episode 1394). Her business office is in her home (Episode 1412)—another hint that work, at its best, is integral to a person's daily life and self-concept. In the Neighborhood of Make-Believe Ms. Roth goes by the name Miss Paulificate and works as a telephone operator. She also proves a capable substitute teacher for Miss Cow at the Make-Believe school (Episode 1481).

Mister Rogers' personal interviews with people from around the U.S.

(and sometimes beyond), ranging from the little-known to the internationally famous, do much to highlight the beauty, the variety, and above all the value and inherent dignity of human work. In 1983 Rogers wrote appreciatively of the numerous guests "who have generously made time in busy schedules to join us" and

> have represented a rich variety of human creativity and achievement: sports greats like Lynn Swann, virtuoso musicians such as Van Cliburn, astronaut Al Worden, great entertainers like Rita Moreno, Marcel Marceau, and Tony Bennett, and superb artisans and performers of many kinds—stonecutters, cake decorators, gymnasts, dancers. With our guests' help, I have been able to show a wide diversity of self-expression, the extraordinary range of human potential. I want children and their families to know that there are many constructive ways to express who they are and how they feel [49].

In other words, the purpose of these interviews was twofold: to help children see that every human being truly is special, and to help them begin to glimpse their own futures in a positive, even joyous way. Spanning the show's three and a half decades and numbering in scores, the interviews not only succeeded in carrying out this twofold mission; they also taught children many specific truths about what work is like and what it takes to make a success out of work. To illustrate, let us take a closer look at some sample interviews.

The visit with Jane Henshaw of Taner's Dairy Farm (Episode 1527; described in the script as "the Neighborhood Dairy Farm") highlights the importance of money management, teamwork, respect for co-workers, and also, in the case of those who work with animals, respect for animals. Upon arrival at the farm Mister Rogers takes a good look at the cows (noting their gentle faces) and explains to the children that these are two different kinds of cows: Gurnseys and Holsteins. He inquires of Jane Henshaw, "Do they like to be milked?" and receives her answer, "I don't think they mind it." Soon he meets Anne the herdswoman, who demonstrates the "milker." "Does that hurt?" he asks. "No," he learns, "It's just a gentle sucking," similar to a hand squeeze. As Rogers' young viewers continue to watch, they see how the milk travels to the holding tank; Ms. Henshaw points out the holding room, then the bottling machine, and she comments briefly on the expense of such machinery. The bottling is demonstrated, as is the packing of bottles into cartons and their transportation into the giant, walk-in cooler. Then Ms. Henshaw and Mister Rogers go outside to watch the work at the loading dock—another reminder that teamwork is essential in every good business. Ms. Henshaw explains about other products that come from her dairy and states, "When you own your own business, it's very expensive, all of those items." "I can imagine," Mister Rogers replies. "But it's very pleasing, also," Ms. Henshaw adds; then—as a polite way of saying she needs to get back to work—she bids Mister Rogers farewell: "So glad that you could come today."

Back at the "television house," Mister Rogers remarks to his viewers, "I like to go to interesting places like that. Weren't those cows beautiful? Do you know why a cow has milk?" He explains, gently underscoring the point that animals are not mere tools for human use but are living, feeling beings like ourselves. (There are of course no inhumane factory farms in Mister Rogers' Neighborhood.)

The importance of being well trained and careful in one's work, for the sake of other people's safety—perhaps even their lives—is highlighted in Mister Rogers' visit to Captain Arnold of the Neighborhood Fire Department (Episode 1744; in fact a visit to Engine Company 15, Pittsburgh Bureau of Fire). Captain Arnold begins by demonstrating his firefighting gear, putting it on while explaining it. He tells Mister Rogers that firefighters are drilled in putting on this gear so they can do it quickly. He introduces the protective hood, mask, and breathing apparatus by putting them on Mister Rogers, who quietly observes, "This is serious business." "Yes, sir, it is," replies Captain Arnold. A bit later Mister Rogers repeats the words, "Serious business" adding, "and *wonderful* business," as he and Captain Arnold go off to look at the fire truck. "Boy," Mister Rogers comments, "there's so much you need to know … to be a good firefighter." With the aid of two other firefighters, Mister Rogers allows himself to be strapped down and go for a "one-second ride" on a stretcher; after this a fourth (female) firefighter demonstrates turning on the truck's siren and emergency lights. Before saying good-bye Captain Arnold provides some clear, simple advice on fire prevention and fire safety. Back at the "television house," Mister Rogers highlights a serious yet positive thought for his young viewers: "You know, people work at fire stations so they can help other people who are having trouble with fires. Aren't you glad that there are people who want to help that way? I know I am. The people who drive those fire trucks know exactly when to go and stop and go again. Let's do that with the trolley!" Thus begins a typically smooth transition to the Neighborhood of Make-Believe, in which King Friday and Handyman Negri have just become volunteer firefighters; Lady Aberlin agrees to join them in the firefighting effort and goes to Corny's factory to tell him the news. Pleased to hear about the new organization, Corny recalls a time when fire broke out at his factory, how scared he was, and how grateful he was when help came. The sequence that follows (in which the Platypus Mound catches fire and Lady Elaine joyfully squirts her hose to put the fire out) reaffirms the dual message just sent by Captain Arnold and Mister Rogers: fires and firefighting are "serious business" indeed, but there are carefully trained, caring professionals in our midst whose work is to save people from fires—professionals who merit our respect and thanks.

The fact that work requires a strong, ongoing commitment of time and energy to make it a success—with challenges to face and problems to solve each day—is mentioned quite often in the interviews. Actress Margaret Hamilton (Episode 1453) responds to Mister Rogers' query, "Did you have—it was hard work, probably, making that movie [*The Wizard of Oz*], wasn't it?" as follows:

> MISS HAMILTON: Yes, it was. It was *lots* of hard work. Sometimes people say, wasn't it fun, it must have been fun to make it; well, it *was* fun, but it was lots and lots of hard work, just as you say—and sometimes uncomfortable. Because you had to be very careful about your costume, and you had to do various things, and when I had to eat my lunch I had to be *very* careful because my hands were all green; and when in the middle of the day the work stopped for a while and we had luncheon, I had to have a little girl who would break my bread for me, or hold a sandwich or whatever I was having and sort of give it to me in little small portions, because it was very difficult for me to wash my hands, because then all the green would come off. And then—
>
> MISTER ROGERS: 'Cause that was make-up, wasn't it?
>
> MISS HAMILTON: Yes, that was just all make-up; and then on the face too, you see, and so they didn't want to have to do that all over again. So I would be very careful about everything, because if I touched my dress, it was colored—and the green would come off on the black dress, and that wouldn't look very well. So, I had to be very careful. So there were things like that about it, for *all* of us, that were difficult. But, there were times when it was great fun and we *enjoyed* doing it. But it was *really hard* work.
>
> MISTER ROGERS: I can imagine.
>
> MISS HAMILTON: Mm-hm.

Restaurant owner Barbara Smith (Episode 1703) has a similar exchange with Mister Rogers shortly after he arrives:

> MS. SMITH: You know, Fred, this restaurant has been a dream come true.
>
> MISTER ROGERS: Ah, you've worked hard to make that dream come true.
>
> MS. SMITH: It takes hard work, doesn't it?
>
> MISTER ROGERS: It really does.

Ms. Smith proceeds to show Mister Rogers around the restaurant, emphasizing two additional points that have already been mentioned: the importance of teamwork—we learn head chef Henry is one of *many* employees, whose combined efforts make it possible to serve dinner to some 350 people daily; and the need to guard people's safety—in this case making sure that only clean, gloved hands are used to touch the customers' food, and that kitchen staff and visitors wear hats to prevent hair from falling into the food. Ms. Smith also, like Ms. Henshaw, makes it plain that while she is very happy to show Mister Rogers around and share the bliss of her "dream come true" with him, she still must watch her time. "So, Henry," she says, after Mister Rogers has departed, "I have a lot of work to do; I'm gonna clean this up, and, uh, then I'll get back to my other job." "Great," Henry replies.

Magician David Copperfield (Episode 1717) likewise states in a Mister

Rogers interview that *his* work—the creation of illusions—requires ongoing work and great care. In fact, says Copperfield, while he has loved to perform magic ever since childhood, he has also had to learn a great deal, and to this day he is still learning things "*and inventing* new things with magic!" "Human beings don't *really* fly," Mister Rogers observes, prompting the following exchange with the magician:

> MR. COPPERFIELD: No, human beings don't fly, unless [gestures toward himself] they're magicians. Unless they learn the skill of doing magic and doing illusions; and you're gonna learn there's a *secret* behind it, a skill that you have to learn. You know, it's—uh—I'm not *really* flying, I'm creating the *illusion*, making it very believable for the audience. Was it believable for you?
>
> MISTER ROGERS: I'll say! [David Copperfield chuckles.] But, uh, you had to work a long time to be able to do that.
>
> MR. COPPERFIELD: Yes, and you need to be very *careful*; it doesn't just happen. You have to really study it. That particular flight is something that we invented. You know, I invented the technology to make it look like I'm really flying.

Still another important theme about work is revealed by cellist Yo-Yo Ma in his 1985 meeting with Mister Rogers (Episode 1547): the need to grow in self-knowledge, while respecting others' right to do likewise. Mr. Ma recalls that when he first took up violin at age four, he was rather intimidated by his older sister's ability with the instrument. One day he saw a double-bass violin and wanted to play it; but his parents had him compromise on the cello, beginning with a miniature version of the instrument that nonetheless required him to sit on "about three phone books" while he played! The fact that the cello turned out to be by far the best instrument for Yo-Yo Ma is made crystal-clear throughout the visit, as is Mr. Ma's respect for his children and their right to follow their own vocations. He observes that while his son Nicholas, age four, enjoys riding around on the cello case, and while he certainly hopes the boy will grow up to care about music, it will be entirely up to Nicholas if he wants to play the cello or any other instrument. These remarks echo a point made by Mister Rogers earlier in the same episode: "Some people play an instrument," he reflects, "and other people don't. It's so important to find out what we feel good about doing, and then practice that. Lady Elaine likes to play the accordion, so she does that well. Each one of us can find something that we like, and *that's* what we'll want to practice."

It should be noted that all Mister Rogers' interviewees, including the six just named, make it clear they find deep fulfillment in their work. From Jane Henshaw's description of dairy management as "very pleasing," to Margaret Hamilton's use of the word "fun" to describe her impersonation of the Wicked Witch of the West; from Yo-Yo Ma's habit of closing his eyes to concentrate on the cello's sound, to David Copperfield's saying of his magic, "I love it. I love it. It's … kind of like being a painter. Magic is my paint," the women and men who share their vocational stories on *Mister Rogers' Neighborhood* support Rogers' point that work, provided it is freely chosen in accordance with a person's unique interests and gifts, can be one of life's truest joys. The interviewees also tend to describe their work in terms of the other people whom it touches—seeing themselves as providers of food ("I love feeding people," Barbara Smith exclaims), of other goods and / or services, of education, of beauty, or of entertainment. Incidentally the fact that human beings have both a right and a need to enjoy wholesome entertainment is subtly affirmed by the show, where entertainers get the same degree of respect as all other working persons. That professional entertainers can and do use their fame to help society in other, more tangible ways is sometimes conveyed as well. Thus Margaret Hamilton invites young listeners to practice empathy—a skill they will need in real life—by thinking in a new way about her screen character, the Wicked Witch of the West. "Mister Rogers," she says, "you know, most of us get *something* along the line, but so far as we know, that witch just never got what she wanted; and maybe she wanted those ruby slippers because they had lots of power, and she wanted more power … actually you have to think about her point of view." And David Copperfield, after teaching Mister Rogers to do a hand trick with a rubber band, explains how "Project Magic" uses tricks like this one to help hospital patients strengthen their hand muscles.

As has already been mentioned, the Neighborhood of Make-Believe provides still another context for exploring work on the show. Because Mister Rogers' Make-Believe characters and situations are often quite funny, it might come as a surprise to some adult viewers that there is (to use Mister Rogers' phrase) "serious business" beneath the play; such is the case, however, and nowhere more so than on the topic of work. It is interesting to note that the human adults who appear in the Make-Believe segments—Neighbor Aber, Lady Aberlin, Handyman Negri, Mayor Maggie, Miss Paulificate—consistently behave *as adults* (one exception being Bob Trow when dressed as Bob Dog). Some of these adult humans are understood to hold paying jobs, others are not, but they all evidently have finished the task of growing up into responsible, self-controlled, considerate, and caring people. They are content with their lives, yet open to new experiences; they enjoy literature, art, drama, and music (Lady Aberlin and Miss Paulificate love to dance); they understand the importance of work and play; and they know how to recognize, affirm, and express feelings appropriately—which means they can help the more childlike characters in Make-Believe to do likewise.

As for the puppet characters, some—Daniel Striped Tiger, Ana Platypus, Prince Tuesday—are depicted as children, with needs mirroring those of the real children in Mister Rogers' audience. These puppet children need to be sheltered, supervised, sent to school, taught good manners and respect for others, guided in making the right decisions, disciplined when necessary, reassured when they are frightened, and above all, loved unconditionally. The remaining puppets for the most part act like mature adults—the level-headed Queen Sara is a good example—but a couple behave erratically, like overgrown children. Like the puppet youngsters, Lady Elaine Fairchilde and King Friday XIII have important lessons to learn; yet because they have more power and stronger personalities than the puppet children, they can be much harder to teach! For flesh-and-blood children at home, watching the physical antics of Lady Elaine and hearing dimwitted decisions from the "mouth" of King Friday is bound to be fun, because even they know more about appropriate grown-up behavior than these imaginary "adults" seem to.

Besides basic lessons in how to act civilized—a topic to which we shall return—the childish and child puppet characters in Make-Believe also learn truths about work, including some that are not easy to face. Prince Tuesday and Ana Platypus, for instance, both have to learn that their parents' jobs are important and may sometimes intrude on family togetherness. When King Friday and Queen Sara agree to teach a course at the Royal School of Castle Management, their commitment to go out of town for several days means they must hire a caregiver for Prince Tuesday. (In a gentle irony, the subject of the royal couple's class is how parents can best balance their job responsibilities with caring for their children!) The prince feels scared and angry, briefly disappears and has to be looked for, and is only gradually reassured by both his parents and the caretaker, who in this episode is called not just Neighbor Aber but "the Associate Mayor of Care" from nearby Westwood (Episode 1516). Ana Platypus is upset when her father, Dr. Bill, fails to return home in time for a family picnic at the beach; at first her mother, Elsie Jean, tells her daughter, "He should have been here by now; perhaps he's been delayed," but a bit later Elsie Jean realizes their plans must change. She tries to help Ana understand the situation ("Ana, your father's a doctor. He *cannot* leave people when they need him"), but Ana is too angry: "But I needed him, too!" she exclaims. "I know, dear," replies Elsie Jean, "and I *am* sorry. But why don't you and I have a picnic right here, right now?" "Maybe later, Mother," Ana says sadly. "Thanks anyway." "All right, well," says her mother, "I'll be inside working when you're ready." This brief reminder that homemaking too is work, coupled with Elsie Jean's refusal to waste time placating Ana, means Ana has to do a little thinking on her own. "Everybody's always working," she muses. "I guess I have to work on my disappointment. I *did* want to go to the beach with Daddy." Help then arrives in the form of Lady Aberlin, as the following dialogue shows (Episode 1527):

> LADY ABERLIN (reading aloud from a list): X [the Owl] says yes, Corny says yes; Ana, will *you* say yes to helping us dig the hole for the swimming pool? It'll save us money!

ANA: I'm too little.

LADY ABERLIN: But everyone can help. Each in our own way. You and I—everybody.

ANA: Well, don't ask Daddy. He's too busy working all the time. He could never help.

LADY ABERLIN: Ah. [Pause.] You mean you aren't going to the beach today?

ANA: Mama says some other day, maybe. When Daddy can come. But he's always working.

LADY ABERLIN: Well—when your Dad is helping other people instead of helping you—that can feel—pretty unfair.

ANA: *I—want—him—here.*

LADY ABERLIN: If he could be here, he would be, Ana. Your father cares for you very much. That's why he works so hard. Because he cares for you. And I care for you, too.

ANA: You do?

LADY ABERLIN: Sure I do. [Pause.] Now. Let's think of something else we could do, instead of going to the beach.

ANA: Like what?

LADY ABERLIN: Like—like how's about—digging our own beach right in this neighborhood? The swimming pool, remember: we really need your help.

ANA: I *do* have a shovel. And a bucket!

LADY ABERLIN [laughs happily]: Oh! I'll report to Uncle Friday, and I'll be right back!

ANA: Okay. Bye!

Although admittedly Lady Aberlin does not explain the link between Dr. Bill's work and his care for his family, Ana hears what she needs most at this moment: her father's work entails not only helping strangers (an abstract concept) but also caring for her, because he "cares … very much." Minutes earlier in the same segment, a newcomer to the Neighborhood of Make-Believe, Ellen Paterson of Paterson's Pools, has briefly explained to X the Owl (a well-mannered, clever, slightly childlike "adult" puppet) that "money has a lot to do with work," though she acknowledges there are other types of pay too (including "a good feeling" about one's work). Children watching this particular episode of *Mister Rogers' Neighborhood* will also no doubt recall the show's opening visit to Jane Henshaw—who, as we have seen, mentions money. So the fact that Ana is not interested in hearing details about her father's work vis-à-vis money is perhaps just as well.

Puppet "adult" King Friday XIII is an intelligent, well-meaning monarch whose biggest flaw is self-importance. His pompous air, delight in long words (including the species names of his pet birds), and assumption that people will affirm him with the words, "Correct as usual, King Friday," are fun to watch and harm no one; on the other hand, his tendency to jump to conclusions (e.g., that play is bad because sometimes people fall and get hurt [Episode 1486]) and make decrees based on those conclusions (no more play!) can lead to trouble. Friday periodically has to learn that, while he is indeed king, his job title does not give him the right to push his subjects—let alone his wife!—around or minimize the importance of what they do. In an argument that needlessly scares Prince Tuesday (who has recently heard about divorce), Friday announces that he is king and will therefore do as he pleases, to which Sara sharply replies that she is *queen* and says *no* (Episode 1477). Luckily for the royal family, Friday seldom forgets to treat both his wife and her work with respect; the queen's work consists of overseeing a charity called Food for the World, assisting other charities (e.g., a fund for endangered species [Episode 1596]), and, of course, helping her husband to parent Prince Tuesday. On another occasion, King Friday asks Miss Paulificate to telephone Harriett Elizabeth Cow (Episode 1481) and ask her to come at once to the castle to discuss his idea for a Neighborhood Drawing Contest. Miss Cow responds that she cannot come over right away because she is teaching the children, and no one else is on hand to take her place. (A true professional, she would never dream of leaving her charges unattended, royal summons or no royal summons!) The problem is solved by Miss Paulificate, who agrees to cover Miss Cow's class while Miss Cow goes to the castle (and who uses this time to teach the puppet youngsters a little bit about telephone usage and manners). Even so, Miss Cow's consent to speak with the king is simply that; she does *not* promise to agree with everything he says, and as it turns out, expresses frank concern about the contest. Since everyone's artwork is unique, she observes, art can't really be judged.

Lady Elaine Fairchilde is curator of a unique place called the Museum-Go-Round. She apparently does her job well, has acquired bits and pieces of knowledge about other people's jobs, is quite adventurous—she's even traveled to outer space—and is as a rule willing to pitch in and help others with their projects. It is she who enlightens Lady Aberlin on the subject of pool construction and recruits her to help with a survey: "Listen, Toots, you don't just dig a hole and call it a pool. It takes a lotta work. You see, they're starting [to survey the ground]." "I'd better be going," says Lady Aberlin. "I'm too busy workin' to go," remarks Lady Elaine. "Report on your findings, will you?" (Episode 1527). But Lady Elaine is also a highly emotional, rather insecure "person" who at times will stop at nothing to get her own way or pay back those who have angered her. Gifted with magic powers, she has been known to use her charm "Boomerang, toomerang, soomerang" to literally turn things upside down or completely rearrange the Neighborhood of Make-Believe. She engages in vandalism at Corny's Factory—literally defacing the King Friday dolls and reworking them into Lady Elaine dolls (Episode 1493)! Yet Lady Elaine also has both a conscience and a good heart. She needs to be understood, loved, and forgiven for her bad behaviors; and as long as her friends give her another chance, she sincerely does her best to make amends. In the case of the damaged dolls, she agrees to make up for the damage by working for two days in Corny's Factory. She actually ends up improving business at the factory, convincing Corny to manufacture just one item (rocking chairs) and thereby winning him the approval of the Better Buy Business Bureau (Episode 1495).

The ideal healthy balance among work commitments, personal relationships, and self-care is exemplified in Make-Believe by Mayor Maggie of Westwood (in real life, Maggie Stewart). In the episode where Prince Tuesday disappears because he is angry about his parents' business trip (Episode 1516), Mayor Maggie—who has accompanied Neighbor Aber en route to the royal child care job—remarks that her time is short ("I must get back to my mayoring duties at Westwood"), but she nonetheless makes a point of looking for Tuesday on her way back to work; she also stops briefly to chat with Daniel Striped Tiger and sing him the song about love, "When Your Heart Has Butterflies Inside It." Afterward saying good-bye to Daniel, she tells him, "I like to sing for you…. I have such a big job that I can't always be exactly where I'd like to be," but she also promises to visit again.

No discussion of the work theme in *Mister Rogers' Neighborhood* would be complete without mention of his many short films about factory employees and the items they create. These films, which typically are delivered to the television house by Mr. McFeely and shown on Picture Picture near either the beginning or the end of the program, include some of the best-remembered moments from the show's long history. The films of course appeal to young children's curiosity about how things work and where things come from, but their deeper purpose is to honor the many thousands of men and women who work, as did Fred Rogers' grandfather,[3] in factories.

Viewers of Picture Picture have the chance to watch people making everything from common foods like bread (Episode 1749) and peanut butter (Episode 1613) to everyday conveniences like raincoats (Episode 1741) and toilets (Episode 1723); also items for children's play, such as teddy bears (Episode 1661), and objects designed to help others to create art (e.g., crayons, Episode 1481), and music (bass violins, Episode 1547). While narrating, Mister Rogers and Mr. McFeely deliberately use the words "people," "man / men," and "woman / women" as often as they can, especially in connection with close-ups of individual workers' hands and faces. The theme of these workers' skilled collaboration with their machines (as well as with each other) is suggested by sentences like "I'd like you to see how people and machines make zippers" (Episode 1516), and appreciation for the machines themselves is conveyed too, sometimes whimsically as when Mister Rogers says, "It's like a Ferris wheel, isn't it?… These crayons get lots of rides" (1481). Yet he also reminds his viewers that even the most delightful or impressive machines require human supervision. In the video about zipper manufacture, he states, "People have to be watching these machines all the time to be sure that they work just right. It takes *people* to do anything well" (1516). Mr. McFeely—who as we have seen is personally familiar with mistakes—alludes to machines' fallibility when narrating a film on how people make sneakers (1573; March 11, 1987). The job of certain workers, he explains, is to "look at each [sole] and trim off *more* rubber that the machine may have missed."

Mister Rogers comments often on the skill, knowledge, and care that people bring to their manufacturing jobs. Watching a man dribble blue dye into containers full of semi-liquid white plastic destined to become play balls, he says to Mr. McFeely, "He knows just how much of each color to add, doesn't he?" (Episode 1727). Likewise, watching a woman sewing together the canvas top of a sneaker, he observes, "Look how fast she works. Oh, it must take a lot of practice to do that job right" (Episode 1573). He also points out the beauty of certain sights in the factories, exclaiming "Beautiful!" of a newly made batch of crayons (Episode 1481) and noting, as a machine folds vanilla extract and food coloring into fortune cookie dough, "That's very pretty to watch! It looks like a painting … a moving painting" (Episode 1721). Last but not least, the factory workers' humanity is affirmed via remarks on what they might be *thinking* as they work. For instance, as Mister Rogers watches a woman apply the first layer of rubber trim to a sneaker, he muses, "I wonder if she ever thinks about all the people who might be wearing a pair of the shoes she's helped to make" (Episode 1573).

As regards children's work, Mister Rogers uses an enjoyable array of show-and-tell methods, Make-Believe segments, and songs to convey that theirs is a threefold task: they need to learn about the world around them, they need to grow (physically and emotionally), and they need to play—both because play is intrinsically healthy, and because play gives children a chance to try out adult roles and start dreaming about their own futures. "Some of the things that children do for their work," he explains in one episode, "look like play. Well, playing and understanding things is a big part of children's work! And some children grow up to use some of their play in their grown-up work. I did that with puppets. You see, when I was a little boy I used to play with puppets. I would make them talk, and I'd think up all sorts of stories about them. Well, I think that helped me when I decided to use puppets on television" (Episode 1528). The stories told by many of Mister Rogers' interviewees about their own childhoods, for instance how young Margaret Hamilton loved to dress up as a witch, or how little Barbara Smith used to beg her mother and grandmother to let her help in the kitchen, make the same point. A video screened at the television house by Maggie Stewart (Episode 1744) depicts children at a day care center busy with dress-up and role-playing. The youngsters are shown caring for dolls, preparing and serving imaginary meals, and pretending to be angels, fairies, doctors, and firefighters, while in the background John Costa's piano softly plays the tune "It's You I Like." After watching the video Mister Rogers declares, "That is *very* important play!" to which Ms. Stewart replies, "Yes, indeed, it is." "And very *serious* play," adds Mister Rogers. "They are some of my good friends," Ms. Stewart observes—her tone and words very much in keeping with show's respectful stance toward children.

A number of Mister Rogers' trademark songs concern growing, whether physically ("Everything Grows Together, Because You're All One Piece") or emotionally ("What Do You Do with the Mad That You Feel When You Feel So Mad You Could Bite?"), or both ("You're Growing, You're Growing, You're Growing In and Out"). There is a Mister Rogers song about perseverance ("You've Got to Do It") and the aforementioned song about love, which includes these lines about empathy:

> When your heart can sing another's gladness,
> Then your heart is full of love.
> When your heart can cry another's sadness,
> Then your heart is full of love.

The song echoes the Biblical concept of love both here (compare Romans 12:15) and in the closing lines:

> When your heart has room for everybody,
> Then your heart is full of love.

Loving other people in the fullest sense means respecting them, and as we have seen, the show repeatedly stresses the truth that each and every human being is special.

Finally, in the song "Did You Know?" Mister Rogers presents growing up as a process richly rewarding and filled with joy—just as adult work can and should be. The song makes the point so eloquently that it deserves to be quoted in full:

> Did you know, did you know,
> Did you know that it's all right to wonder?
> Did you know that it's all right to wonder?
> There are all kinds of wonderful things!
> Did you know, did you know,
> Did you know that it's all right to marvel?
> Did you know that it's all right to marvel?
> There are all kinds of marvelous things!
> You can ask a lot of questions
> About the world and your place in it,
> You can learn about people's feelings,
> You can learn the sky's the limit!
> Did you know, did you know,
> Did you know when you wonder you're learning?
> Did you know when you marvel you're learning

> About all kinds of wonderful,
> All kinds of marvelous,
> Marvelously wonderful things?

In the years when Mister Rogers paid "visits" five times weekly to millions of American homes, day care centers, and schools, a thought that surely occurred to many adults was "What happens when kids find out the real world *isn't* like Mister Rogers' Neighborhood?" Granted, the show covers many serious real-life issues including divorce, death, and war, but it is nonetheless set in an idyllic world of peaceful skies, safe homes, and friendly businesses, and the people who "live" there are on the whole remarkably happy—happy with their lives, and happy with their work. In Mister Rogers' Neighborhood, no one ever comes home from work angry, exhausted, frightened, or despondent; there are no George Baileys grieving over their broken dreams, no Dagwood Bumsteads sleeping at their desks out of sheer boredom, and no one remotely like Garfield the Cat as seen in a current poster, where, clad in a tie, slumped over and holding a briefcase, he glumly remarks, "I might as well work, I am in a bad mood anyway." The "real" world as most Americans know it is full of people like George Bailey, Dagwood, and Garfield, not to mention thousands of workers who quietly endure their jobs for the sake of their families but feel little or no personal connection with their work. Real-life America is a place where all too often, businesses exploit people (as well as animals and the environment) instead of helping them. And it is home also to great numbers of poorly paid, underemployed, and unemployed men and women.

Yet it has been often and truly said that even the poorest person in the U.S.A. is rich compared to the majority of human beings on the planet. Outside America, particularly in the developing world, millions live in unspeakable poverty. Hunger for many is a fact of life, sanitation for many more is poor or nonexistent, schools are ill equipped and neglected, and in many places adults and children both are obliged to work at difficult, even dangerous jobs that are all about survival and not at all about self-actualization.[4] With such glaring contrasts between the culture of Mister Rogers' Neighborhood and the world outside, and with Fred Rogers himself now part of the "real" world's past, what can his teachings about work—and life—mean for us today?

To begin by stating the obvious, Mister Rogers' Neighborhood is a place that *deserves* to be real and deserves to be duplicated (with cultural variations) all around the globe. Imagine what it would mean if every boy and girl on earth, regardless of culture or country, had a chance to grow up the "Mister Rogers" way: experiencing love; learning to appreciate beauty; developing self-respect, in conjunction with respect for others; learning to handle feelings constructively; identifying interests and talents; dreaming dreams, and playing and working hard to make them come true. Of course the dreams wouldn't all come true, and everyday life would still be filled with challenges. But it would be a dramatically better life than most people know today.

Suggesting that the world could actually *become* more like Mister Rogers' Neighborhood may seem naïve. Yet it is worth keeping in mind that the happiness we see in the Neighborhood is based on genuine human happiness—and happiness is contagious! Moreover history has shown that change for the better is always possible, and it may come about more quickly than anyone expects. Consider the fact that less than two centuries ago nearly four million men, women, and children in the United States were legally enslaved (Constitutional Rights Foundation website) and thousands more who were technically free toiled six days a week, ten to fourteen hours a day, for wages so low that they shock us today (Dublin). Putting an end to slave, quasi-slave, and child labor worldwide is a daunting task, but progress is nonetheless being made in places as diverse as India (Marwaha) and Cameroon (UN Women website), Latin America (Child Rights International website), and the Philippines (World of Work article republished on ILO website). Children are being rescued—or, in some cases, are rescuing themselves—from inappropriate work and embarking on the childhoods that they yearn for and need. Adults meanwhile are claiming their right to earn decent livelihoods and to make better choices for themselves, their sons, and their daughters.

If parents wishing to honor Fred Rogers' legacy would resolve both to love their children unconditionally ("You Are Special") *and* to instill in them a belief that work can and should be good for everyone, the long-term results could be amazing. The process might start with parents' reflecting on the work they themselves do, and which aspects they find most rewarding. They could then make a point of conveying a genuine "good feeling" about work to the children—perhaps by saying things like "I was really glad to help so-and-so today" or "Today was a hard day, but there was one really good thing about it" bearing in mind that (as Mister Rogers knew) paid employment, volunteer work, and home-making are all equally real and important ways of working. The parent who is struggling to find paid (or better-paid) employment, or who longs to escape from a dull or stressful job, admittedly may find it hard to send a positive message about work to his or her child. Even so, the adult should try to minimize the negatives, lest the child conclude that work is mainly something to worry about and / or avoid. If a parent decides to leave a workplace for moral reasons, then a matter-of-fact, age-appropriate explanation could be used to teach the child that work and values belong together. Parents also should help their sons and daughters learn about other adults' work, why it matters, and why people themselves matter. Children should be given regular and varied opportunities to help others, both at home and in the community, and they should also have opportunities to watch adults work, so they can better understand the joy of collaboration and the intrinsic rewards of doing tasks well. And they should have abundant time to play and explore their own gifts and talents.

Finally, as boys and girls turn into young men and women, they should be helped to see that while the world around them is far from perfect, *they* are far from helpless. They may not love every minute of the work which they will one day do as adults, but they will still be able to find ways to make work useful and satisfying. And as they gradually realize how lucky they are—and learn how unfair life still is for adults and children in many other parts of the world—they can be encouraged to get involved in humanitarian efforts to ensure better working conditions for people around the globe. If future generations can be taught to view work as a good and important part of life and to settle for nothing less, on their own behalf and that of others, then the world may one day surprise us by looking a lot more like Mister Rogers' Neighborhood.

And what a beautiful day that will be.

NOTES

1. The history of child labor is an immense topic that has been the subject of many excellent scholarly works. See for example the 999-page 2009 volume edited by Hugh D. Hindman, *The World of Child Labor: An Historical and Regional Survey.* For valuable insight into the life of child workers in classical antiquity, see Christian Laes's *Children in the Roman Empire: Outsiders Within* and Robert Knapp's *Ordinary Romans*, both published in 2011.

2. Most of the episodes cited in this essay are episodes that I have personally watched and re-watched on television and / or online (the PBS website and YouTube contain full episodes and excerpts from many classic Mister Rogers shows). Information on episodes from 1972 (Mr. McFeely falls ill and learns to relax) and early 1975 (Audrey Roth treats a stain on Mister Rogers' shirt; a tour of Audrey Roth's home office) appears in the electronic catalogue of the library at St. Vincent's College in Latrobe, Pennsylvania (Fred Rogers' hometown); the home page for this catalogue is http://biblio.stvincent.edu:2082/search~S1. I would like to express my warmest thanks to Ms. Brittany Smith, Communications Coordinator for The Fred Rogers Company, who very kindly took time to read a penultimate draft of this essay, directed me to the library web site, and provided me with access to an informative 1974 *Family Communications* article about Joe Negri, professional musician and "handyman" of Mister Rogers' Neighborhood.

3. Rogers wrote of his deep affection for his grandfather in 1983, 231 and 240.

4. Janine Maxwell's heartbreaking, challenging book, *It's Not Okay with Me* (2006)—about her personal experiences with orphaned children in Swaziland—is perhaps the best-known current work to describe conditions that are almost unthinkable to the average middle-class Westerner.

WORKS CITED

Around the Neighborhood: A Family Communication. "Joe Negri: A Handyman in Make-Believe." Vol. 2, no. 5 (Oct. 1974).

Child Rights International Network. "Latin America: Children Demand Workers' Rights." 21 Nov. 2011. http://www.crin.org/resources/infodetail.asp?id=26687.

Constitutional Rights Foundation Home Page. 22 May 2013. http://www.crf-usa.org.

Dublin, Thomas. "Women, Work, and Protest in the Early Lowell Mills: 'The Oppressing Hand of Avarice would Enslave Us.'" *Labor History* 16 (1975) 99–116; republished at http://invention.smithsonian.org/centerpieces/whole_cloth.

Hindman, Hugh D. *The World of Child Labor: An Historical and Regional Survey.* Armonk, NY: M.E. Sharpe, 2009.

International Labour Organization. A Future without Child Labour. Global report under the Follow-up to the ILO Declaration on Fundamental Principles and Rights at Work, International Labour Conference 90th Session 2002, Report I(B). Geneva: International Labour Office, 2002. Available online at http://www.ilo.org/declaration.

Knapp, Robert. *Ordinary Romans.* Cambridge: Harvard University Press, 2011.

Laes, Christian. *Children in the Roman Empire: Outsiders Within.* Cambridge: Cambridge University Press, 2011.

Marhawa, Puja. "Child Labourers' Plight: Underpaid and Overworked." *DNA India* 3 May 2011 http://www.dnaindia.com/print710.php?cid=1538786 .

Maxwell, Janine. *It's Not Okay with Me.* Enumclaw, WA: Wine Press Publishing, 2006.

Rogers, Fred, and Barry Head. *Mister Rogers Talks with Parents.* New York: Berkley Books, 1983.

Rose, Joel. "Joe Negri: from Handyman to Jazz Guitarist." National Public Radio interview, 9 Aug. 2010 http://www.npr.org/templates/story/story.php?storyId=128821517.

Saint Vincent College electronic catalogue. 22 May 2013. http://biblio.stvincent.edu:2082/search~S1 (home page).

UN Women (United Nations Entity for Gender Equality and the Empowerment of Women). "Exploited Domestic Workers in Cameroon Organize Themselves to Defend Their Rights." 13 Nov. 2012 http://www.unwomen.org/2012/11/exploited-domestic-workers-in-cameroon-organize-themselves-to-defend-their-rights.

World of Work Magazine 51, June 2004, republished as "World Day against Child Labour: New Report Highlights Plight of Children Working as Domestic Labourers" at http://www.ilo.org/global/publications/magazines-and-journals/world-of-work-magazine. .

Dis-Alienating the Neighborhood: The Representation of Work and Community[1]

Tim Libretti

In the opening scene of the first chapter in Henry Roth's 1934 classic novel of childhood *Call It Sleep,* the pre-adolescent protagonist David Schearl finds himself in his family's kitchen experiencing a sense of powerlessness before the mystery of the kitchen sink and the larger public utility system of plumbing, which human labor and ingenuity have created to meet our most basic needs. Roth writes,

> Standing before the kitchen sink and regarding the bright brass faucets that gleamed so far away, each with a bead of water at its nose, slowly swelling, falling, David again became aware that this world had been created without thought of him. He was thirsty, but the iron hip of the sink rested on legs tall almost as his own body, and by no stretch of arm, no leap, could he ever reach the distant tap. Where did the water come from that lurked so secretly in the curve of brass? Where did it go, gurgling in the drain? What a strange world must be hidden behind the walls of a house! But he was thirsty [17].

The scene registers David's consciousness of the world, particularly our social infrastructure, as created by people, and yet it also allegorizes the concept of the alienation or estrangement of labor which describes the condition in which the world human labor has created confronts one "as something alien, as a power independent of the producer"(Tucker 71). The rest of the novel plots David's growing comprehension and discovery of his estrangement ("[w]hat a strange world") from this alien, hidden world and his conquest of the terror he so often experiences to enjoy a sense of empowerment over this world Roth often represents as monstrous.

I open this essay invoking this representation of the terror and power-lessness of the childhood experience because it seems to me Roth captures a dominant sensibility of childhood that *Mister Rogers' Neighborhood* emphatically and repeatedly addresses—and relieves!—episode after episode as Mister Rogers unravels for us, particularly through the show's representation of work and labor, the mysteries of the made world, as well as the reality of our own abilities to take part in making our world, with which we engage constantly in our everyday lives. Indeed, when I read this opening scene from Roth's novel, what always comes to mind for me, as a kind of antidote to young David Schearl's sense of powerlessness, is the beginning of the episode of *Mister Rogers' Neighborhood* (Episode 1528) in which Mister Rogers is trying to fix the faucet on his kitchen sink so he can have the water he needs. Unable to do so because he doesn't seem to have the proper washer, Mister Rogers remains as calm and patient as usual and takes us on a visit to the workshop of his handyman neighbor Bob Trow, whom we encounter as he is in the middle of fixing a shovel that has come apart. Mr. Trow stops what he is doing to fix the faucet; and when Mister Rogers comments that this help will save him some money, Mr. Trow comments, "We're saving on money, but we're not saving on work. Somebody's got to do it. Work takes time, you know." This scene dramatizes many central themes of the show overall. First, in contrast to David Schearl's orientation toward the kitchen sink, the scene highlights Mister Rogers' lack of fear toward engaging the complexities of his world as he calmly takes apart his faucet to see if he can fix it. Secondly, when he can't fix the faucet, he does not give in to frustration or quit, but rather relies on the collective knowledge of the people in his Neighborhood to help him out, underscoring how our inevitable dependence on one another is also mutually empowering. Third, Mr. Trow's comments remind us to appreciate and honor the work and expertise that others possess and that helps make our lives possible. Finally, the scene shows us a world in process, in a stage of repair, highlighting for us and for children especially that the world is always in a state of being made and re-made and that we can participate through our work and through obtaining knowledge of our world in the way Mr. Trow and Mister Rogers have.

The vision and understanding Mister Rogers presents of work and labor really center the show's principal ideals of community and neighborhood in cultivating in children a consciousness of the world as process, not as finished product, and an understanding that their relationship with objects really constitutes relationships with the people around them, both near and far. Mister Rogers repeatedly highlights how the crayons we use, the marbles we play with, the sweaters we wear, the food we eat, the electricity we call on to light our homes, the mail that shows up on our door posts, have origins in human labor; and his show traces these origins by revealing to us the processes of production in the crayon or marble factory or the work the utility operator does on the power lines, while also introducing us to the actual people who perform this work and make our lives possible, such as the mainstay characters of the mail carrier Mr. McFeely or the handyman Mr. Trow. While we often live in a complex system in which our actual relationships with people are distant and even invisible, through the Neighborhood Mister Rogers seeks to make those connections visible and intimate. In orienting the child's consciousness to comprehend the world as always in the process of production and not as a static finished objective entity, Mister Rogers simultaneously cultivates in children a sense of empowerment—one that counters and relieves the kind of terror and powerlessness David Schearl experiences—in their ability to take part in producing and shaping our world through their creative actions, whether we call them work or play—a distinction Mister Rogers insistently challenges. In their form and content, the episodes of *Mister Rogers' Neighborhood* ask us to undertake, indeed themselves orchestrate, a renegotiation of our relationship with objects[2] such that we become intensely aware of (1) the way our interactions with objects actually situate us in a complex web of relationships with people, (2) the way the work people do for us is essential for making our lives possible, and (3) the way we impact or can potentially impact the world through our work, especially that work we do not even typically recognize as such. With great sophistication that has the appearance of simplicity, Mister Rogers demystifies the abstractions of our complex political economy and comprehends them for us in the kernel of human relationships that they constitute, cultivating an appreciation and gratitude for the work people do, a re-thinking and re-valuing of work itself, and an affective comprehension of the work people do to meet each other's collective needs as expressions and behaviors of love in a larger social sense. As he asks us to think about the collective work we do as the most profound way we relate to one another, Mister Rogers presents a cultural vision and set of values starkly at odds with our dominant national values today, particularly the way U.S. culture tends to valorize an individualist ideology.

In Episode 1472, in which Mister Rogers takes us to a sweater factory, we see a great example of the complex and layered way his show theorizes work as a central activity that forges—and also acts as the nexus of—human relationships, indeed loving relationships, motivating a re-assessment of the way we value both people and the work they do. The episode begins (after his standard entrance and song, of course) with Mister Rogers showing us a picture of his mother and explaining that she is the one who knits the trademark sweaters he wears and for which he trades his sport coats at the opening of each episode. The camera zooms in on the particular cardigan he wears this day to capture the detail and intricacy of each individual stitch, highlighting the craft and care his mother puts into her knitting, as he informs us that she uses "needles, yarn, and her hands" to make these sweaters, which, he elaborates, "is one of the ways she has of saying she loves somebody." Beginning with this effectively artisanal type of production or work performed within the intimate familial context of a parent working lovingly to clothe her son, Mister Rogers presents a scenario that enables most viewers to comprehend the act of production in the service of meeting human need as an act of love and as an act that puts people in relationship with one another. At the end of the episode, Mister Rogers reflects on what he sees as one of the appealing aspects of things: "They remind you of people," he says. This statement, asserting the affective dimension of objects for us, underscores also the fact that objects, as the concretization of human labor, represent quite literally, indeed constitute, relationships between people, although often the reality of these relationships contained in objects such as a sweater are not immediately visible to us. Our vision or our consciousness is not trained for the most part within our culture to apprehend an object in terms of its history as a made object that people produced so that we can satisfy a need or desire, as we see in the opening scene of *Call It Sleep,* above, in which David Schearl most simply knows that he is thirsty and wants a drink but cannot comprehend at all where the water will come from or what human labor went in to making possible his ability to draw a glass of water from the faucet. Mister Rogers quite intentionally intervenes in the development of children's consciousness, training it to understand the object world historically so that we understand the work people do to make our world possible, asking us to renegotiate our relationship with objects such that we recognize that our relationships with objects are actually relationships with people. Certainly, in representing for us the small and local circuit of his mother making a sweater for him, Mister Rogers makes it easy for the viewer to grasp the sweater as an embodiment of a loving relationship. Mister Rogers shows us his mother's picture so we can easily link the sweater to its maker, understanding its history; and his focus on each stitch emphasizes again the sweater as an object of labor, putting us in a position to appreciate the sweater not simply as a static finished product but as a dynamic process. He asks us, too, in ways he models, to appreciate not just the sweater but its maker and also to adopt an attitude of gratitude for the maker by recognizing not just the work but the love and affection that others put into making sure our needs are met.

As profound as this episode is in what I've described already, it continues even further, methodically and meticulously, to re-orient our consciousness to grasp the world historically and trace back processually the origins of our object world to the scenes of labor where we find the people who make our world and with whom we are engaged in an incredibly meaningful relationships which, typically within our culture, we fail to recognize, as labor remains largely invisible and on the margins of our consciousness. For Mister Rogers, just as his mother is a loving caregiver, so are those who work to provide for us in the world at large, though they often get lost in the complexity and abstraction of our very large economy. The logic of this episode, then, as Mister Rogers takes us on a visit to a sweater factory, is to enlarge our consciousness to comprehend the aggregate sets of relationships in which we are engaged in our socio-economic world so that we can appreciate both affectively and intellectually people and the work they do for us on a larger social scale. He begins in the smaller household or family context as a microcosm of the larger social world of production, a local world which children—and all of us, frankly—can wrap their heads around more easily, and then moves from the home to the larger industrial factory where we produce goods and services to meet human needs on a much larger scale. Indeed, as we witness the process of how a sweater is made on the video tape Mr. McFeely brings to play in Picture Picture, the first scene we see features workers unloading enormous spools of yarn from trucks and bringing them into the factory, as Mister Rogers exclaims, in his modulated way as the factory floor is revealed, "Look at all those people and all those machines." We then move methodically through the larger automated looms operated by people, through the steaming of the material, to people tracing patterns on the cloth, to others cutting the cloth, to people sewing different parts of the sweater and so forth. As we see a woman at a sewing machine attaching a collar, Mister Rogers comments, "That must take a lot of practice, Mr. McFeely." This focus on the craft and skill of the worker and the care the worker must put into her task echoes his focus on the care and craft of his mother's stitch, and he implicitly asks us to make this connection and to value each similarly.

While it might be hard to say that the individual workers have any kind of specific love or affection for any specific individual who will later wear the sweaters they collectively make, Mister Rogers wants us to recognize that *the very behavior is loving and caretaking*, that we are engaged in broad and expansive sets of relationships in which people we don't even know are taking care of us and working to meet our needs, to provide for us. This behavior, rooted in the reality of our radical interdependence as a society, is a kind of love, and by bringing us to the scene of labor Mister Rogers moves us to understand the meaningful nature of the relationships in which we are engaged in our world—*for our own good and benefit*—which we can't always see. In this sense, Mister Rogers is giving us a new vision, cultivating a perceptual form that can potentially transform how we feel, think, relate to others, and comprehend the world. Just as we recognize the intricacy of his mother's knitting, we can recognize and appreciate the intricacy of the enormous processes of production in which we take part reciprocally, in mutually dependent but also mutually empowering ways, to take care of each other.

Moreover, Mister Rogers, through this episode, identifies the work we do as a kind of love, even if a social love with a different kind or degree of intimacy and affection than we experience in a family relationship. Indeed, this idea is reinforced more than once throughout his many episodes, as we see in Episode 1530 when Mister Rogers takes us on a tour of his studio to reveal to us once again the processes of production, in this case of his show. He introduces us to the various people who are necessary to make his show possible: "It takes a lot of people to make television programs.... And all those people care about you. They want to make the best programs they can for people like you." Understanding the intricacy and care of the production processes that make our lives possible—that is, to understand our world historically—puts us in the frame of mind to appreciate others because we understand the human relationships in which our lives are embedded and the care and love others are giving us through their work.

The thrust of *Mister Rogers' Neighborhood* to humanize—or deeply grasp the human dimension—of our larger socio-economic system works on many levels and has many consequences. First, as I've suggested, one mission *Mister Rogers' Neighborhood* repeatedly fulfills is that of making labor, which is typically invisible to us, visible in all its intricacies. By making work and the worker visible and intelligible, the show places us in a position to understand and appreciate the work that makes our lives possible. How can one appreciate what one cannot see or understand? This appreciation, which functions for Mister Rogers as a kind of stance on life that impacts how we treat others and how we (re)imagine social relationships, becomes a basis for challenging the incredibly deleterious cultural development in our political economic system which Harry Braverman has termed "the degradation of labor." By this term, Braverman is referring to two phenomena. First, the term describes the way an intensified division of labor has eroded craft and artisanal expertise by taking work and breaking it into smaller and smaller tasks, thus deskilling the worker. Where before, for example, one chef might have produced a delicious hamburger, at McDonald's the production of the hamburger is broken down into a series of simplified and repetitive operations performed by an assembly line of people. The effects of this division of labor from the business perspective are that the worker can easily be replaced as the skill required is easily learned and that the work "merits" a lower wage. Second, the term refers to the way this process then supposedly enables us to devalue the necessary work people do; we come to refer to such types of work as "unskilled," justifying the low wage at which the work is remunerated and, hence, in social terms, valued and appreciated. *Mister Rogers' Neighborhood*, though, insistently counters this type of valuation that results from the degradation of labor. As we watch production at the sweater factory, for example, both Mister Rogers and Mr. McFeely continually highlight the work people are doing, which we typically might take for granted or not notice, and its importance, the vital role it plays in our collective lives. At one point Mr. McFeely narrates the production process, saying, "Then the collar goes on. But not by itself. A person has to do it." Mister Rogers then responds, "It takes a person." When at one point the segment focuses on the woman who is packaging the sweater in plastic so it can be shipped, a task I would venture to say many of us don't think about, Mister Rogers notes, "Each person has his or her own job there." Mister McFeely responds, "That's right. They all work together to make sweaters." Thus, we are being asked, or instructed, to recognize not just the necessity of each task but also the collective and social nature of work which entails the interdependence of each task. Implicitly, this dialogue suggests we cannot value any one task over another—or devalue any task beneath another—because they all depend on each other and are equally necessary to making and bringing to us the goods and services we need to live. Indeed, within this conversation, it is even pointed out that "it takes a lot of people to run the Speedy Delivery Service." While we might see only Mr. McFeely as the representative of the Speedy Delivery Service, we are being taught to understand and consider that we might not see all the work going on and to be aware of our potential blindness, one Mister Rogers works hard to cure while he also seems to understand that maybe he can't make every task visible, so he nods to invisibility. Mister Rogers, in making the work people do visible and in asking us always to consider and imagine those who might not be visible to us, fosters a stance of appreciation for the works of others, which he roots in an understanding and recognition of our interdependence and the collective or social nature of work.

What is the importance, or what are the possible consequences, of Mister Rogers' cultivation of the sensibility or act of appreciation and historical vision for our material lives? Let me offer one explanation. As I write this essay for this volume, a debate is taking place in the United States regarding income inequality and whether or not federal and state governments should raise the minimum wage. It strikes me that the way of looking at the world Mister Rogers presents suggests a position in this conversation. We tend in our culture to think about a job as something an individual does to earn a wage or salary to support himself or herself and perhaps a family; we tend not think about the ways the work others do serves us and makes our lives possible. Think, for example, about what you ask people or what you wonder when you learn what someone does for a living. Do you wonder how that person's work benefits your life and our collective social life? Or, do you wonder how much money that person earns doing that job? Let me risk asserting that, regardless of how you individually answered these questions, as a culture we tend to be concerned about the latter. The attitude or stance Mister Rogers encourages us to take toward the world, however, is one in which we appreciate the way we are served, the way our needs are met both individually and socially, by the necessary work others do for us because we can't realistically do everything for ourselves in this complex world (hold down a job, grow our food, build our own house, make our own clothes, teach our children, etc). His vision militates against valuing work in terms of its relative importance to other kinds of work and instead promotes recognizing the use value and necessity of the work people do for us all to live. He asks us to understand the work we do as a society collectively ("That's right. They all work together to make sweaters"). His vision moves beyond the measure of wage as he underlines our mutual dependence on one another and as he asserts the work we do *for each other* as acts of love, of mutual caretaking. His vision of understanding work collectively is not consistent with a meritocratic value system that makes value distinctions between the kinds of work people do and the contributions they make to the world. Mister Rogers sees all work that serves a social purpose and meets a human need as equally vital.

While Mister Rogers is not engaging in making public policy or leading a revolutionary movement, he is nonetheless cultivating a sensibility and way of comprehending socio-economic relations as in some sense deeply human and intimate relationships, which, if such a sensibility were adopted, would necessarily, it would seem, lead to a material transformation of the form and content of our current socio-economic relationships. Mister Rogers, for example, does not make an economic or monetary value distinction between the acts of making an opera and making a sweater (each of which he features in different episodes), even if our current market-based political economy would likely decide an opera singer "deserves" more to perform his or her job than the worker in the sweater factory. Rather, Mister Rogers tends actually to equate these different kinds of social production in terms of their vitality and necessity to meeting the collective needs of our society and creating a humane and vibrant world which cultivates human creativity with the objective of realizing the most productive world to meet human need so we can create beyond need.

The political economic ethos of his show, particularly as it represents work, moves us beyond market measures or rationalities that determine worth and allocate wealth, asking us to appreciate and value equally all the types of work that make our lives possible. Indeed, Mister Rogers often tries to help us see beyond the abstract conceptual mechanisms that organize and order our political economy to the more basic and fundamental purposes of an economy, which are to produce and to distribute goods and services to meet human need. We see some of these expressions of political economic thought in Episode 1528 in which the people in the Neighborhood of Make-Believe, in order to save money, are repairing their own plumbing system after a pipe burst. X the Owl has been tasked with renting the appropriate tools, and he finds himself engaged in tedious negotiations and calculations with the rental agent Corny to procure the necessary equipment on his limited budget. At one point, they each complain about their respective tasks, as X the Owl declares, "Buying is a lot harder than selling." He finally concludes, "All the same, I wonder if it wouldn't be easier if people just gave each other all the things they needed instead of buying all the time and selling all the time." The wish X the Owl exasperatedly expresses here is really for an economic system that does not chiefly produce profit through buying and selling, such that the meeting of need is subsidiary to profit-generation, but rather meets human need directly, first and foremost. How this episode thinks about work bears directly on X the Owl's utopian economic vision and also on how Mister Rogers himself often conceptualizes value in ways different from our current economic system. As King Friday XIII says in this episode, "All work should change things for the better." And as Mister Rogers says later in the episode, "Work changes things. Children can change things by cleaning a room, by picking up toys…. Good work can make good change." My point here is that Mister Rogers values work not through any abstract monetary measure that allows it to be exchanged in a market setting but rather for the material impact it has on the world. He values work that directly shapes us and contributes to bettering us and meeting our needs, such as making something, healing us, teaching us, serving us, repairing our things, laundering our clothes, cleaning our streets, etc. The acts of buying and selling are primarily market-driven behaviors symptomatic of an economy which is designed to meet profit first and need in a subsidiary way and which assigns relative value to work in monetary ways based on what the market bears, not necessarily on the work's intrinsic value in terms of its necessity in making our lives possible. Mister Rogers asks us to think or see through abstract economic forms such as money to understand the value of the work each does in terms of the need it fulfills in our world. His sense of appreciation (a complex word) moves beyond the simple notion of price to a more profound sense of value.

Indeed, in his attempts to cultivate this faculty of appreciation, we see once again that scale is an important issue for Mister Rogers, as he works to extend our perceptual and emotional modes, our sensibilities, which we exercise quite regularly in the intimate, local, and personal realms of our lives to the larger and perhaps more complex world we might typically experience as abstract. Throughout the show, he works to demystify the abstractions of our complex political economy so that children can understand socio-economic relationships in terms of the human relationships and consequences they actually and concretely entail. In Episode 1529 in which Mister Rogers visits a grocery store, for example, he meets Wayne, who now with his brother owns the store which was his father's, as Wayne is putting price tags on some canned goods. He asks Wayne how he determines the prices of the goods he sells; and Wayne then proceeds to explain and to make the abstraction of price concrete and human for the viewer, presenting the human relationships underlying price with a clarity which I would venture most adults do not possess or think consciously about when shopping. He explains that his store buys the goods from a warehouse for a particular cost and then adds on an amount to cover labor, electricity, rent for his building, and so on. Thus, Wayne reminds us, among other things, that when we purchase groceries we are also engaged implicitly in acknowledging the work someone did to produce and bring us that food and also in remunerating that person for his or her service in making our lives possible. This moment echoes an earlier one in Episode 1526 when Mister Rogers visits a post office, and he reminds us, "It costs money to send a letter because the people who work for the post office have to get paid somehow." It strikes me that in part we might understand the wonder and brilliance of Mister Rogers and Wayne here by considering how they challenge the Walmart phenomenon, or the mania in consumer culture to buy goods and services at the lowest possible price. Wayne invites us to comprehend that the quest for lower prices almost necessarily entails depreciating (rather than appreciating!) the work that—and the worker who—produced the goods we are buying. Lowering the wage of this unknown and invisible worker makes it more difficult for that worker to take part in enjoying and availing himself or herself of the collective work we do as a society to take care of each other. As Mister Rogers and Wayne make clear, the purchase of a good or service in a place such as a grocery store is not an isolated act but rather engages us in a wide range of human relationships. It is not that Mister Rogers asks us not to understand ourselves as individuals; rather he asks us to understand our individual identities in richer and fuller ways by understanding that we realize ourselves most fully in a social and collective context—and necessarily so, because we need the fruits of other people's labors to meet our basic needs and to make it possible for us to develop our special talents. If we had to spend our time doing the work to satisfy our basic needs, we would be exhausted and unable to develop our creative abilities fully. Throughout the many episodes of *Mister Rogers' Neighborhood,* we see promoted an ethos that encourages us to recognize our interdependence with others so that we can recognize not just that others we may never see are taking part in caring for us but also that we have a self-interest in making sure those on whom we depend are taken care of and appreciated as well. If we genuinely recognize and value those whose work enables our lives, would we seek goods and services as cheaply as possible knowing that in impacting the wages of workers negatively we potentially undermine the health and well-being of those on whom we depend, threatening our own well-being? Thus, the faculty or skill of appreciation Mister Rogers fosters in his viewers involves as well a perceptual, and frankly sensual, approach to grasping the complex yet fundamentally human interrelationships that comprise our political economic system and that inform the conceptual mechanisms, such as price, at work within it.

What Mister Rogers enables and encourages us to see, finally, is that the work we do is not at bottom about earning a wage, regardless of how we might organize our socio-economic system counterproductively, but about meeting each other's needs in our collective social lives. In another scene in the grocery store, for example, Mister Rogers stops near the cooler housing gallons of milk and tells us, referring to an earlier episode, "That reminds me of the time we were at the dairy." And then he comments, "Think about all the people who will be drinking this milk, taking it home to their families." He asks us at once in this moment to return through our memory to the scene of labor and production, the dairy which we visited in a previous episode, and also to conceive of the milk in terms of its use value, contemplating the need the milk will meet in nourishing the families who drink it and rely upon it. He effectively, insofar as it can be done in the realms of language and cognition, disalienates the producer and the consumer, underscoring the human and social relationship that is involved in the acts of both production and consumption, a relationship often masked or abstracted in the modes of distribution and exchange in our current political economy in which producer and consumer often never meet. What is important to underline here is that a key piece of work *Mister Rogers' Neighborhood* performs is the cultivation of a particular habit of thought, or mode of consciousness—which is alternative to the norm in our culture—that orients children to apprehend and perceive the world in historical terms: that they understand the world not in static or abstract terms but in the dynamic and concrete ones of human and social relationships. Even the simple act of memory—of remembering the origin of an object in human labor, such as a gallon of milk—moves us to apprehend not just objects but the relationships with others in which we are, in some sense, intimately even if seemingly distantly engaged. Indeed, even as Mister Rogers discusses taxes, he attempts to countervail the effects of alienation by encouraging us to see that taxes are not monies taken from us but investments we make in ourselves and each other for our individual and collective good; that is, he frames the paying of taxes as a collective and cooperative activity that puts us in relation with one another to realize our common interests most effectively. As he explains taxes in Episode 1526, "People put money together to have roads, schools, fresh water, which everybody needs." Again, he effectively trains children to see through or analytically comprehend abstract economic forms in terms of how they work in our system to address human need and how they concretely encompass and enable human relationships.

In asking us, effectively, to see through economic forms such as that of wage or tax through which we organize or express—as well as abstract and mask—socio-economic relationships, Mister Rogers in many ways throughout his show challenges a condition arguably quite prevalent in our society, the condition Karl Marx designated with the concept of alienation.

As Marx explains the concept, there are four main ways in which people experience this condition. They can be alienated from themselves, from others, from their labor, and from nature. For Marx, human nature is defined by its desire to create and produce, and particularly by its desire to create in consonance with a larger social purpose. Marx uses the term *species being* to designate this informing impulse or drive in human nature to engage in creative activity, our life activity, that is connected to or aligned with a social purpose or mission. What happens under the alienating conditions of capitalism, for Marx[3] is that our work, instead of being our driving life activity that connects us with others and links us to a broader social purpose, becomes simply a means to our individual existence. We work to collect a wage so we can pay rent, buy bread, clothe ourselves, and so on. We even come to conceive of our work as simply a means to existence, such that the construction worker doesn't wake up in the morning with the thought that he is going out this day to build a home so he can serve a vital social need by providing a place for a neighbor to live in, but rather with the stultifying thought that he is working another day for another dollar to pay rent and support only himself and perhaps a family when in reality his work is supporting many. In this scenario, we can see that the worker is, in Marx's terms, alienated from himself in that he is no longer connected to his nature, to his *species being*, in that he is disconnected, through the wage form, from a sense of his larger social purpose; and he is alienated from others because his work is not in a conscious sense putting him in relation with others, even if in some sense it actually does. It is also often the case that the worker experiences the world she has helped make as now alien to herself and as having power over her. The worker may participate in building a home, for example, which then she cannot afford to live in; or one might work in food production but find oneself at the end of the week unable to feed one's family.

One of the central ways Mister Rogers addresses or redresses this condition of alienation on his show is through the repeated though perhaps implicit challenging of the dominance of the commodity form in our contemporary socio-economic system. Here I invoke the analysis of the Hungarian literary critic and philosopher Georg Lukács who in his landmark work *History and Class Consciousness* traces the commodity as the root form that structures cognition and consciousness within the culture of capitalism. It is the commodity form that structures how we think and how our consciousness apprehends reality, leading us to take for granted the categories of reality of our contemporary socio-economic system. For Lukács, problems in the capitalist stage of historical development all lead back to the question of the commodity structure, which he identifies as the central structural problem of capitalism. Chief among the problems emanating from the root form of the commodity is the phenomenon Lukács identifies as reification, the process by which the world, persons, and experience are transformed into things as they are organized and reconstituted by the system of market exchange and commodity production. What happens, in Lukács' analysis, when the commodity structure organizes our social life "is that a relation between people takes on the character of a thing and acquires a 'phantom objectivity,' an autonomy that seems so strictly rational and all-embracing as to conceal every trace of its fundamental nature: the relation between people" (84). The phenomenon of reification refers particularly to how the commodity form structures our consciousness such that we apprehend the world not as sets of relationships between people but as a fixed, static thing already made. Thus, for example, when we go to the supermarket to buy a loaf of bread, we tend not to think about the bread in terms of the workers who made the bread or the long line of the labor process required to bring it to our table, from the people planting seeds to grow the grain all the way to people packaging the bread and transporting it to market where workers unpack it and place it on shelves. Instead, our consciousness tends to apprehend the loaf of bread as a finished product as opposed to grasping it processually in terms of the history of its production. When we grasp it as a finished or ahistorical product, a thing, our consciousness fails to apprehend the real sets of human relationships in which we are engaged when we purchase and consume the product. In structuring our blindness to the history and human relationships involved in the goods and services we use and consume, the commodity form fosters our condition of alienation. The constant, careful, and patient focus on precisely the processes of production that make our world possible and bring to us the goods and services we all need to live is how *Mister Rogers' Neighborhood* effectively performs a de-reification of consciousness in the way it asks us to understand that when we buy, use, or consume "things," we are actually engaged in relationships with people. In this sense, *Mister Rogers' Neighborhood*, in challenging the commodity form's drive to transform relationships between people into things, also works to ameliorate conditions of alienation both by putting the viewer back in relation with those who make our world and by encouraging us to see the world as always unfinished and in a state of process. The message is that we can participate through our own work in shaping and directing this world—we need not view it as an alien entity over which we have no control and before which we are powerless, for "good work can make good changes."

From the elements of *Mister Rogers' Neighborhood* highlighted thus far, I have clarified how the processes of de-reification and disalienation are central to the show, particularly in terms of the way the show represents work and the objects we produce. The Frankfurt School critic Theodor Adorno once wrote in a letter to fellow cultural critic Walter Benjamin that "every reification is a forgetting: objects become thinglike at the moment when they are seized without all their elements being contemporaneous, where something of them is forgotten" (Jay 229). Indeed, what we forget is the origin of objects in human labor and the sets of human and social relationships these objects embody. Mister Rogers never lets us forget. Whether he is reminding us as we gaze upon a gallon of milk in the grocery store about the dairy where we witnessed the process of milk production or connecting the sweater he wears with his mother who knitted it as he shows us her picture, he always places in the forefront of our apprehending consciousness people and the work we all do to make each other's lives possible by meeting our collective needs. Indeed, perhaps nowhere do we see more clearly, if in some way only metaphorically, the conflation of or identity between people and objects than in Episode 1477 in which Mister Rogers shows us how pretzels are made. We learn in this episode that the pretzel form represents children's arms folded in prayer and the three spaces represent the Christian holy trinity. We see quite clearly here the way we project or inform human, indeed sacred, meanings into our object world. Our object world has a human personality. The process of de-reification in the show always asks us to remember, indeed it highlights, the human dimension of the object world.

Mister Rogers' focus on process—the way his shows detail how products in our world are made—also highlights the de-reifying dimension of *Mister Rogers' Neighborhood*, as this focus countervails what critic Fredric Jameson sees as the dominant middle-class mode of consciousness, which is characterized by a contemplative stance toward the world. Instead, the show privileges what Jameson identifies as a working-class mode of consciousness. Jameson describes and distinguishes both as follows:

> For the bourgeois, the commodity is a solid material thing whose cause is relatively unimportant, relatively secondary: his relationship to such an object is one of pure consumption. The worker, on the other hand, knows the finished product as little more than a moment in the process of production itself: his attitude toward the outside world will thereby be significantly altered.
>
> For he will see the objects around him in terms of change, rather than the timeless "natural" present…. Moreover, inasmuch as he knows the interrelationship of tools and equipment to each other, he will come to see the outside world not as a collection of separate, unrelated things, but as a totality in which everything depends on everything else. Thus, in both ways he will come to apprehend reality as process, and the reification into which the outside world had frozen for the middle classes will be dissolved [Jameson 187–88].

Indeed, when Mister Rogers attempts to fix his faucet and visits Bob Trow, we see them both working with tools as they repair and even make their world, such that we see the world in a constant state of rebuilding, of making, and we see how Mister Rogers shows us "the interrelationship of tools and equipment." This mode of consciousness, I believe, is meant to empower children, to help them overcome a sense of powerlessness and befuddlement toward the world, such as David Schearl experiences in the opening passage. Mister Rogers teaches children to feel comfortable and unafraid about taking part in building their world, using tools to impact or repair their surroundings, or taking risks in taking on something as large as a plumbing system. Overcoming what Jameson characterizes as a "contemplative stance" toward the world constitutes a chief achievement of *Mister Rogers' Neighborhood.*

Mister Rogers also fosters an understanding that as one participates in making the world, one is necessarily working within a network of relationships. Thus, another effect of the project of *Mister Rogers' Neighborhood* to grasp the fundamental human dimension of our socio-economic relations is the show's implicit challenge and re-thinking of American culture's defining ideology of individualism. As one sees the world in process and sees the history of objects, linking them to the people who produced them, one comes to understand the vast network of social relationships in which one lives and upon which one depends. We see that we rely on the work others do for us to make our lives possible, rather than insisting that our achievements are ours alone. In our current culture, we tend to honor the "self-made" person who has made her own fortune and achieved success through her own hard work. Yet this successful person, Mister Rogers might say, likely doesn't do everything herself but is likely quite dependent on others to have personal needs met. We tend as a culture to mistake "an ability to buy" for the reality of "having done." That is, one might amass a fortune and be able to buy anything to meet one's needs and desires, but that doesn't mean one isn't depending on others to produce food, clothes, roads, stamps, and so on. Money often masks our social relationships, as Mister Rogers constantly reminds his viewers. Indeed, our dominant ideology of individualism, in part enabled by the money form, is also a kind of reification, as this ideology fosters a forgetfulness of the real relationships of interdependence in which we live. In reminding us of this interdependence, Mister Rogers actually brings us to a more complex and profound understanding of individualism, bringing us to recognize that in order to develop to our fullest and do all the good work of which we are capable, we must depend on others to help us meet our needs. The show reminds us that individuals rely on society for the full development of their individuality.

Another act of memory *Mister Rogers' Neighborhood* enacts over and over again, which is almost implicit or inevitable given that it is a children's show, is that the show reconnects us with the childlike dimensions of work as play which the alienating conditions of many workplaces can strip from adults.

Episode 1530, for example, features a beautiful, even lyrical, extended montage of the work that children do, including snapshots of children playing the piano, feeding a guinea pig, painting pictures, taking in groceries from the car, building with blocks at play, setting the table, and so forth. Mister Rogers tells us, "Some of the work children do looks like play, and some of the things children do at play they'll use in their work when they grow up." Indeed, Mister Rogers' puppets are probably one example of this point. What we get in this moment is an expansive notion of work that reconnects us with our species, breaking down the distinction between work and play that develops when work becomes alienating, when it is organized under exploitive and oppressive conditions. Indeed, Mister Rogers' show exemplifies this point. Is he at home or at work? Does he come home to work, as he takes off his hard shoes and slips on his more comfortable sneakers? He challenges the forgetting of reification by asking us to remember a different way of thinking about and experiencing work, which might help us imagine a different way of being, a way of organizing our society that encourages people's creativity in the service of the collective good.

Additionally, in offering this more expansive understanding of what constitutes work, Mister Rogers is again training us to appreciate what others do for us, how the work of others makes our lives possible. And this moment, again, offers a way of valuing contributions that exceeds or exists outside of a market rationality. Indeed, the work featured, such as taking in groceries, isn't paid labor, just as historically a lot of typically "women's work" in the home wasn't paid and wasn't even recognized as labor. Mister Rogers insistently redefines work or labor and in doing so challenges market-based economic value systems, putting forth a more egalitarian and expansive sense of value.

As Mister Rogers represents work, he effectively re-imagines, or helps his audience of children perhaps imagine for the first time, a world of possibility they can effect or take part in effecting through their creative activity in the world, call it work or play. He teaches us to see work as perhaps one of the most profound ways we interact with, care for, and love each other.

NOTES

1. I want to acknowledge Elijah and Caleb Libretti for their brilliant insights, thoughts, and wonderings; their incisive, joyful, and rigorous analyses and observations; and the many hours they devoted to watching and re-watching episodes of *Mister Rogers' Neighborhood* with me with a shared sense of scholarly adventure and of the importance of giving expression to the meaningfulness of Mister Rogers' work. They are really co-authors of this essay. We worked together with love for each other, love for Mister Rogers, and the kind of love Mister Rogers had for people and the world. Whatever success and meaning this essay achieves owes much to their contributions and care. The faults, of course, are mine.

2. I take this phrase "renegotiate our relationship with objects" from Colson Whitehead's fabulous novel *The Intuitionist.*

3. I want to stress that Marx does not see alienation as a condition exclusive to capitalism. Pre-capitalist modes of production, such as feudalism, were also certainly class societies that fostered the condition of alienation. I am merely here focusing on capitalism.

WORKS CITED

Braverman, Harry. *Labor and Monopoly Capital: The Degradation of Work in the Twentieth Century.* New York: Monthly Review Press, 1974.
Jameson, Fredric. *Marxism and Form.* Princeton: Princeton University Press, 1971.
Jay, Martin. *Marxism and Totality: The Adventures of a Concept from Lukács to Habermas.* Berkeley: University of California Press, 1984.
Lukács, Georg. *History and Class Consciousness.* London: Merlin Press, 1971.
Roth, Henry. 1964. *Call It Sleep.* New York: Avon Books.
Tucker, Robert C., ed. 1972. *The Marx-Engels Reader.* New York: Norton.
Whitehead, Colson. *The Intuitionist.* New York: Anchor Books, 2000.

Fantasy as Free Space: Mister Rogers' Neighborhoods

Susan Larkin

Like many children growing up in the 1980s, I watched *Mister Rogers' Neighborhood* on a regular basis. My favorite part of the show was when trolley would come beeping through to take us to the Neighborhood of Make-Believe. I doubt that, as a child, I could have articulated why I liked Daniel Striped Tiger, King Friday, Henrietta Pussycat, or X the Owl. The puppets weren't flashy or particularly clever, and they didn't participate in epic adventures. It is only in looking back that I realize the appeal of that world of make-believe: it wasn't really fantasy at all, at least not fantasy as it is most commonly thought of today. Rather than a place of splashy special effects or dystopian angst, *Mister Rogers' Neighborhood* carved out a space that managed to combine elements of utopia, imagination, reality, and fantasy. Fred Rogers wove together his television Neighborhood and the Neighborhood of Make-Believe to create a nurturing fantasy space that allowed viewers the freedom to be "just the way you are." Additionally, and even more importantly, the interconnected nature of the Mister Rogers' television Neighborhood and the Neighborhood of Make-Believe provided space for viewers to contemplate the issues and expectations of the larger world.

Like much of the best children's literature and programming, *Mister Rogers' Neighborhood* is deceptively complex. The Neighborhood of Make-Believe segments within the show, in concert with the "real" framework surrounding it, are a unique and masterful manifestation of fantasy. They offered a space where it was acceptable to be "just the way you are," even if that way was angry, sad, or socially unacceptable. The puppets in Make-Believe were often all of those things. The puppets not only served as models showing that it was okay to feel and express emotion, but also modeled how to work through and cope with those emotions. The contrast between these two segments of the show—the Neighborhood of Make-Believe and Mister Rogers' television Neighborhood—is important. The Neighborhood of Make-Believe, clearly identified as fantasy by its sets, puppets, and costumed adults, is more realistic in feeling and emotion than Mister Rogers' television Neighborhood. There is never any strife in the television Neighborhood, which is occupied largely by benevolent adults. The puppets in the Neighborhood of Make-Believe seem to span a range of ages and behave far less ideally. When working in concert, the two neighborhoods create a space that is neither utopia nor quite real, but that uses fantasy to foster in its audience a fairly sophisticated reflection of a variety of issues, ideas, and emotions.

This encouragement to think independently and in ways that may challenge ideology is one of the most important aspects of fantasy. Jack Zipes, in "Why Fantasy Matters Too Much," ponders the questions of whether the world is moving too quickly, and in too many directions, for fantasy to retain its relevance. He asks, "When the normal is so fantastically abnormal, what role can fantastic artworks play in our lives?... Is there hope for the fantastic much less hope for us to alter our social relations of exploitation and delusion?" (78). Zipes concludes that fantasy does, in fact, matter greatly, and that it can have great influence. He lauds works by authors such as David Macaulay and Peter Sís as examples of how "the fantastic can foster alternative thinking and viewing and negate spectacle and delusion" (83). The Neighborhood of Make-Believe that Rogers creates can appear to be a simplistic and sometimes even a condescending fantasy world on the surface. However, despite the simple puppets, sets, and stories, the Neighborhood of Make-Believe is able to accomplish exactly what Zipes applauds fantasy for doing as it challenges viewers to think carefully, thoughtfully, and often outside of established patterns within a protected space.

Mark Shelton asserts that *Mister Rogers' Neighborhood*, in creating this protected space, is not the simplistic, overly positive program that it is often categorized as. Rather, it is actually a subversive show in that Rogers is allying with children against adults and that, in essence, he is building a community to stand against the larger world (185–86). Explaining that "the world outside the individual is a place we seek refuge *from*," Shelton continues on to note that "many children (and some adults) find exactly that refuge in *Mister Rogers' Neighborhood,* a place with an ally who escorts children on expeditions to places (geographical and otherwise) that are by definition dangerous places, because they are outside the place where children spend their lives: inside themselves" (186). All of the journeys that occur in Mister Rogers' television Neighborhood are guided, explained, and scaffolded. Rogers then uses the Neighborhood of Make-Believe as a place where the puppets can take the risks and model independent behavior for the community of viewers. Or, to put it into Shelton's context, to act against the larger outside world. The television Neighborhood is the refuge; the Neighborhood of Make-Believe is the practice area for the outside world. This practice area is as safe as the television Neighborhood because it has been clearly established as fantasy and as being in the control of Rogers and the viewers. As Shelton notes, "it works because all the things that children quite early on recognize as false are represented as false by *Mister Rogers' Neighborhood*, something that we adults tend to forget to do in constructing worlds for children. ... Rogers gives children a clearly false world, and uses it to teach them how to deal with the real one" (191).

Rogers actually offers two false, or fantastic, worlds for viewers. The Neighborhood of Make-Believe lacks physical realism, but portrays very authentic feelings and situations. Mister Rogers' television Neighborhood is occupied by real people who exist in an idyllic setting free of most discord or difficulty. Neither setting is perfect, but both demonstrate a basic respect and compassion for individuals and experiences of all types. Excursions as mundane as trips to the grocery store are experienced with the same wonder and interest as a visit with Yo-Yo Ma.

Ma, in an interview after appearing on *Mister Rogers' Neighborhood*, comments on what may be the key element to creating that idyllic world: "Kids of a certain age really have no barriers and are not socialized to have certain ... they don't have to be 'cool,' they don't have to be 'with it,' or whatever. I think Fred Rogers deliberately opens himself to such an extent that to a socialized person it seems somewhat ridiculous to act that way" (qtd. in Zukerman 79). In other words, Rogers is so authentic and open that he is acting outside of ideological expectation. There is a freedom that comes with that. Mister Rogers' Neighborhood is not perfect; Rogers and his viewers deal with difficult events—death, divorce, and disability, among others—but these challenges are approached honestly and openly. The emotions that are the result of these events are respected and encouraged, as is the contemplation of the events themselves. Rogers deals both with issues that may seem trivial to adults—a squabble with a friend, jealousy, shyness—but also issues perceived as more weighty. In a 1970 episode titled "Death of the Goldfish," Rogers works through death and the emotions that can come with loss and grief.

Early in the episode, Mister Rogers notices that one of the fish in his aquarium has died. Mister Rogers asks viewers if they see the lifeless fish, talks about how you know if a fish is ill or dead, scoops it out of the aquarium, holds it up for examination by the viewer, and prepares it for burial. The death of the fish is approached with the same equanimity as any other event in the neighborhood. As he buries the fish, Mister Rogers talks about a beloved pet dog whom he lost as a child and how sad that was. At the end of the episode, he sums up:

> If you ever have a pet who dies, or if you're sad about something that you've lost or something like that, it helps to say that you're sad. Often it even helps to cry. Let people know how you feel. And sometime, if you feel like jumping around like Bob Dog in Make-Believe, do that too. Everyone has different things that he does when he's sad. That's why everybody is special, because everybody is different. That's why I like you so much ["Death"].

The death of the fish is treated respectfully, but not melodramatically. The message communicated in the television Neighborhood is then given more context by the events that play out in the Neighborhood of Make-Believe. There, loss manifests a bit differently. Trolley stops working and Bob Dog fears that it has died. He reacts with far more emotion than Mister Rogers did when his fish died. His upset manifests loudly as he hops around and howls. He calms somewhat when Queen Sara reassures him, "Trolleys are machines, they aren't alive, so they can't die" ("Death"). Unlike the goldfish, the trolley survives as Dr. Bill Platypus is able to find and fix the cause of the problem, a wheel off its track.

This segment in the Neighborhood of Make-Believe shows Bob Dog working through his grief at possibly losing the trolley. No one tells him to calm down or be quiet when he is jumping around and making noise while he is worried. He gets facts from Queen Sara, support from Lady Aberlin, and is allowed to freely and energetically articulate his emotions. Bob Dog enacts Mister Rogers' advice and expresses his sadness. As when the fish died earlier in the program, there were no false platitudes and no sense that death is something that children must be protected from.

Segments such as this seem to be forgotten as *Mister Rogers' Neighborhood* continuously gets categorized as overly sweet and positive. Bob Garfield, in his foreword to *Mister Rogers' Neighborhood: Children, Television and Fred Rogers*, describes his initial perception of the program as one of "saccharine sincerity, of maddening beatificity, of low wattage" (ix). Garfield's opinion changes dramatically after watching another children's program, *The Ren and Stimpy Show*, which causes him to reassess *Mister Rogers' Neighborhood*. However, whether loved or loathed, *Mister Rogers' Neighborhood* is rarely recognized for its depth of subject matter. The fact that the program never shied away from difficult topics is perhaps best illustrated by the first episodes distributed nationally in 1968. The theme of the show that week was change. The Neighborhood of Make-Believe was in an uproar because Lady Elaine had moved some of the neighborhood buildings. King Friday was appalled at the moves and set up border guards and barbed wire to keep out other possible agents of change. He and other puppets wear army helmets and require anyone approaching the castle to give their name, rank, and serial number.

On the second episode of the week, Mister Rogers and Betty Aberlin discuss King Friday's actions in the Neighborhood of Make-Believe:

> MISTER ROGERS: He [King Friday] has established border guards.
> BETTY ABERLIN: In the Neighborhood of Make-Believe?
> MISTER ROGERS: Edgar, poor thing. He has to walk back and forth and be sure that no one will come in.
> BETTY ABERLIN: That sounds like a war.
> MISTER ROGERS: It certainly does. But at least there isn't any shooting yet.
> BETTY ABERLIN: Well, do you think I should take a make-believe gun or something?
> MISTER ROGERS: I don't know that you'll need that, course you could always use your finger if you need that ["King Friday"].

Instead of a gun, Aberlin heads off with a cape that Mister Rogers gives her for protection as he tells her that he "hope[s] that you will be brave and strong as you head off to the Neighborhood of Make-Believe" ("King Friday"). Arriving there, Lady Aberlin is asked for her name, rank, and serial number and quickly learns King Friday's battle cry and reasoning behind the border guard:

> KING FRIDAY: Remember our battle cry, Edgar? Down with the changers!
> EDGAR: Down with the changers. Down with the changers, we don't want anything to change.
> KING FRIDAY: Cause we're on top!
> EDGAR: That's right, cause we're, at least you're, on top.
> KING FRIDAY: Very good ["King Friday"].

Edgar, singing all of his words, is far less sure of these ideas about change than King Friday is, but follows instructions. Over the course of the week, Lady Aberlin, Chef Brockett, Handyman Negri, and the puppets become increasingly unhappy about the militant state of the Neighborhood of Make-Believe. Lady Aberlin, Daniel Tiger, and the puppets launch a fleet of balloons with messages of peace to convince the King that they do not want to live amongst all of the strife. King Friday eventually backs down and has a conversation with Lady Elaine, who created the change that started all of the trouble. He then accepts the change in the Neighborhood and allows the border guards to stand down ("The End").

The exchange between Edgar and King Friday also articulates a most basic, but often unspoken power dynamic: those in power dislike any change that threatens their control. While the program doesn't spend a lot of time considering Edgar's comment, King Friday, the authority figure, is the one who eventually capitulates and is seen as having erred. The adults, or those in power, are not always automatically assumed to be correct. Right and wrong are not presented as simple. The show may not have a deep examination of power constructions, but neither does it dumb things down for a child audience. There are no easy answers to the armed standoff that develops—the characters have to work the problems through, and often stumble as they do so. Unlike the sitcom format where everything is solved before the last commercial break that we have come to expect on television, few of the issues that arise in the Neighborhood of Make-Believe are solved in a single episode.

These episodes focusing on change demonstrate how the program handles issues. Mister Rogers offers support from the protected "reality" of his television Neighborhood and then the puppets and other characters work through the issues in the Neighborhood of Make-Believe. The issues are handled directly and without any attempt to protect viewers from reality. Rather than sheltering viewers, Mister Rogers and the puppets put the issues into a context that best positions viewers to contemplate their meaning.

This space protected for contemplation is often mistaken for a utopian space. Shelton argues that "Fred Rogers makes his Neighborhood a place where nothing bad happens to the children who spend time with him there, and good things do" (183). Shelton's assertion is true from one point of view. By most adult standards, nothing bad does happen in Mister Rogers' Neighborhood; there are no real threats. The guns and guards are clearly labeled as pretend. However, from a child's perspective, bad things do happen, particularly in the Neighborhood of Make-Believe, a place where there is far more conflict and many more obstacles than in Mister Rogers' television Neighborhood. These bad things are often revealed to be not as formidable as initially perceived, or even to be positives, but the puppets actually experience a lot of adversity. From the border guards of the 1968 episodes to the death of the goldfish to a large number of skirmishes and disagreements among the puppets, the residents of the Neighborhood of Make-Believe face a number of challenges.

Psychologist and puppeteer Susan Linn, who actually appeared on *Mister Rogers' Neighborhood*, feels that, by encountering the challenges, the puppets "draw forth the underside of childhood.... They tap into the vein of fear, anger, awkwardness, and unadulterated self-centeredness that lies beneath the sunny surface of childhood" (93). The Neighborhood of Make-Believe is an honest and truthful place where people try to learn how to do the right thing, but do not always succeed. The puppets are not static characters, but have good moments and bad ones and grow and regress. They are supported by the adults—Lady Aberlin, Handyman Negri, Mayor Maggie, etc.—who pass through, but the adults do not solve their problems or make the bad things stop. They offer the puppets the means through which to confront their own demons. For example, in a 1973 episode, Daniel Striped Tiger is afraid to sleep over at Grandpere's. He discusses his discomfort with Lady Aberlin, but while she listens attentively, she offers no advice, instead asking him what he is going to do ("Mister Rogers"). And while Rogers and the other adult presences do not solve the problems, they also do not minimize these occurrences. While having to meet new people or sleep away from home may not be judged to be "bad things" by adults, to many children these are difficult and traumatic things. When Daniel does finally sleep at Grandpere's, he is very proud of himself and Lady Aberlin and Mister Rogers reinforce this feeling: "Daniel was very proud of himself. He didn't need anybody to paste a star on his forehead or anyplace else. No, he was proud inside.... It's good to talk about proud things, isn't it?" ("Daniel Sleeps"). Daniel's achievement is recognized and celebrated. Rogers uses the Neighborhood of Make-Believe as a safe place where traumas of all kinds can be explored and the successful navigation of them is recognized and celebrated.

The Neighborhood of Make-Believe is a safe place because it never attempts verisimilitude. While the scenery is elaborate, the puppets are clearly simply cloth and plastic. As Roderick Townley comments, "all the inhabitants of the Neighborhood of Make-Believe have immobile, impassive faces. Lady Elaine's face seems actually crude. There's not a soft, expressive, high-tech, Muppetlike creature in the lot" (73). This lack of detail and information puts the children in partial control of creating the story. Townley sees the puppets as "projective devices onto which the child casts his own meaning. It is the child's power of visualization that helps the puppets make the transition to 'reality'" (73). The children do create the meaning; the entire *Mister Rogers' Neighborhood* program is working to empower children to define and interact with the world in positive and productive ways. The program never tried to suggest that the puppets or the space they inhabit is real. Each entry into the Neighborhood of Make-Believe is preceded by a discussion framing the adventure that is about to occur. Mister Rogers and his viewing friends control the make-believe. Rogers often ends his introduction of the segment by saying, "Let's make-believe." Make-believe, then, is something that is consciously conjured up, owned, and controlled. Rogers even has a couple of episodes where he spends time showing his viewers how the Neighborhood of Make-Believe is created and how he works and voices the puppets.

This willingness to show how the Neighborhood of Make-Believe is created and how the puppets work makes clear what role Rogers feels that fantasy should occupy. To Rogers, fantasy is not about mysticism; fantasy is a free space to try things out. The space is freeing because it is safe and because it is unhampered by many societal constraints or expectations. George Gerbner, in his study of how story works on the Mister Rogers program, feels that the stories created "offer ways to control the chaotic life of the streets and neighborhoods in which many children live. Children are starving for story, the kind that builds on hope, the kind that echoes for a lifetime" (13). The stories that Rogers tells within the Neighborhood of Make-Believe are child-centered and driven. Even his television Neighborhood is adult-centered, but make-believe is the domain of the child. The adult characters in the Neighborhood of Make-Believe support the puppets, but the puppets drive the action. When the neighborhood is at war in that first week of episodes, Lady Aberlin, Chef Brockett, and Handyman Negri participate in and voice some of the conflict and concerns, but the problems and solutions come from the puppets.

This domain is a safe space, but is always presented as a temporary haven. As Ellen Handler Spitz notes in "The Magical Neighborhood of Mister Rogers," "there is always a return" (B16). The Neighborhood of Make-Believe is not presented as anything other than a place to visit. It is always there to visit, but remaining there is never a question. Trolley always comes along to take the viewers back to Mister Rogers. Make-Believe is the free space, where, through the puppets, the viewers can operate outside of adult and societal constraint. But they are encouraged to return and, like the puppets, to address the issues that may present themselves.

This return echoes the path of the hero in Joseph Campbell's archetype. After separation and initiation, the hero must return. This is often the most difficult part of the journey, for after the hero has found himself or herself, he or she must re-integrate into society after having undergone the transformation into hero. In Mister Rogers' Neighborhood, however, the return is scaffolded. Trolley is one part of this. One of the memorable landmarks of the show, the trolley works to mark the shift from real to make-believe and back. Townley, in considering the transitions within the program, notes that Rogers himself felt that "the matter of transitions is one of the most important aspects of the whole thing" (68). While the trolley transitions to make-believe and back, the shoes and sweater rituals at the beginning of the program transition the reader into Mister Rogers' Neighborhood and then out again (Townley 70). Every episode begins and ends with the same songs and changing from work shoes to sneakers and back and outer coat to sweater and back. These transitions mark the shift between the world that the child occupies, Mister Rogers' own idyllic television Neighborhood, and the Neighborhood of Make-Believe. Viewers do not have to handle the ambiguity of being unsure of their setting and thus the corresponding expected behavior.

This strategy, as Townley notes, is in stark contrast to that of most children's programs, which are more likely to follow the *Sesame Street* model of short segments and rapid shifts between them (68–69). Townley argues that "such recurrent modules, popping out of the visual maelstrom at unpredictable moments, hardly add up to a sense of continuity. Such an approach encourages children to accept disorder as a representation of the way the world really is" (69). Thus, *Mister Rogers' Neighborhood* is presenting a vastly different worldview from programs such as *Sesame Street*, even if some of the basic content is similar. The ways that viewers are able to interact and process the content are drastically different. Rogers builds in time and space to move from idea to idea and works to connect them. Every episode, as it is moving from setting to setting within the show, is building on what has come before. Take, for example, the April 5, 1984, episode entitled "A Visit to a Grocery Store." This episode, part of a week of shows constructed around the theme of work, is built around the idea that we can't all have everything we want. Mister Rogers starts with a trip to the neighborhood grocery store to pick up a few things. While there, the viewer learns how the grocery store works and what the people who work there do. As he wanders the aisles, Mister Rogers also discusses wanting everything that you see, but not being able to get it all: "When I was a little boy and came to the grocery store with my parents, I'd say I want one of this and one of this and one of this and one of … I'd want one of everything in the store. But of course I couldn't have it. Nobody can have everything" ("A Visit").

The episode then shifts to the Neighborhood of Make-Believe, where the community is struggling with some broken pipes that have left them without water. They learn that it will cost three thousand to fix the pipes, and they have to find a way to afford the repair. King Friday and Lady Aberlin are distraught by the cost and lament that they cannot afford the repairs. Queen Sara quickly cuts off the unproductive laments and tells the King and Lady Aberlin to act, to talk to people and ask for ideas, rather than to bemoan the situation. Each decides to talk to a certain group and ask for ideas. King Friday then remarks that he feels a bit better now that they have developed a plan to address the problem and Queen Sara tells him that that is because "We're doing something about our problem, not just sighing about it" ("A Visit"). When Lady Aberlin talks to Daniel Tiger, Ana Platypus, and Prince Tuesday, the "child" puppets, at the school, they suggest using the money earmarked for the swimming pool to fix the pipes. This solution is adopted, but King Friday is disappointed at having to forgo the swimming pool. Lady Aberlin comments, "I guess that not even kings can have everything they want," and King Friday replies, "Nobody can have everything, niece Aberlin. I learned that a long, long time ago" ("A Visit"). Mister Rogers reinforces this message once again upon the return to his house in the television Neighborhood. This episode also demonstrates the regard that children are held in, for they are ones to correctly assess priorities and come up with a solution. The fact that it was the child puppets who solved the water problem is another example of how the Neighborhood of Make-Believe is a child-centered space.

The water issues in the Neighborhood of Make-Believe and the grocery store visit in the television Neighborhood come together to offer multiple perspectives into wants and needs. In this way, all of the different components of the program are interconnected. Rogers' emphasis on transitions offers a means of moving from one space to another and values that movement. Rogers noted that we "hurry through transitions and try to hurry our children through them as well. We may feel that these transitions are 'nowhere at all' compared to what's gone before or what we anticipate is next to come'" (qtd. in Townley 68). Rogers changing his shoes is not an insignificant act that is delaying the beginning of the program, it *is* the beginning. While society pays a lot of attention to a few particular transitions—high school to college, moving from house to house, adding or losing a member of the family—many other transitions are not seen as needing support or contemplation. Rogers' focus on the oft-neglected space of transitions offers children a space and time to consider the ideas that his television Neighborhood and the Neighborhood of Make-Believe present. The emphasis on transitions supports transfer of the emotions, thoughts, and strategies that have been addressed and developed during the program and provides time and space to put ideas together. What may seem to be a slowly paced show is actually a space for thought and reflection. This contemplation is encouraged by Rogers, who frequently asks his viewers what they think, or to consider an idea or question.

This questioning is key. It reveals the importance of the role that the viewers play. Rogers is constantly breaking the fourth wall to interact with them. Watching *Mister Rogers' Neighborhood* is not a passive experience. Viewers have as important a role to play in the neighborhood as Mister Rogers does and are key members of the community. In their 2003 article focusing on *Harry Potter*, John Kornfeld and Laurie Prothro examine concepts of home and family and how community works to define and create these. They focus on what they call the "transformational journey—which all young people must take to discover who they are and where they fit in the world, to create their own version of home out of the strangeness they encounter when they are 'away'" (121). This journey, as they note, is a fixture of young adult literature, but is also of value for younger children, and, I think, is a key fixture in *Mister Rogers' Neighborhood*. The journey to the Neighborhood of Make-Believe that Mister Rogers and his viewing friends take in each episode works to scaffold Kornfeld and Prothro's transformational journey to find self and home. They argue that "the concept of home is inextricably entangled with that of family—individuals who together 'created worlds of their own, with particular kinds of boundaries separating them from the larger world'" (121). Mister Rogers and his viewers, his television friends, are a family and do, for the twenty-eight or so minutes of each episode, create a family and their own world and space. The Neighborhood of Make-Believe, with the trolley as its boundary marker, is an even more protected space. With a couple of rare early exceptions, not even Mister Rogers intrudes on the Neighborhood of Make-Believe.

The puppets, and the Neighborhood of Make-Believe, function as models, not the role model adult figures like Mister Rogers and the other adult neighbors who offer wisdom, but as more realistic models illustrating what it looks like to stumble a bit. Linn notes that "the program also relies on modeling to encourage self-expression and mastery. With affect ranging from eagerness to reluctance, the puppets consistently share their feelings with each other, and are rewarded for doing so. They are encouraged to overcome their fears and to move from passivity to action" (92). The puppets and viewers are all part of the community that Rogers builds.

Rogers is at the center of the community, but he doesn't function as its commander. Unlike King Friday, who barks orders at and expects deference from his subjects in the Neighborhood of Make-Believe, Rogers positions himself as a guide and as a friend. He clearly respects his television friends. As Spitz observes, "Fred Rogers never forgot that his work was being seen within his audience's actual living, playing, and sleeping spaces and that, being invited inside, so to speak, required respect for the sanctity of those spaces as private and protected realms" (B16). He enters his viewers' space gently. His opening song asks the viewer to please be his neighbor. It is an invitation, not a command.

The invitation is to enter the fantasy space that Rogers has created, to step into the free space that is his television Neighborhood and the Neighborhood of Make-Believe. This space that *Mister Rogers' Neighborhood* invites viewers to occupy is a masterful manifestation of fantasy, one that, through the combination of the television and make-believe neighborhoods, is both wildly imaginative and starkly real. Fantasy today incorporates imagination and reality, but is more commonly associated with resplendent effects and technological marvels. The fantasy that Mister Rogers created was less spectacular, but far more thoughtful and encouraged contemplation in addition to action and adventure. Fred Rogers, using a few puppets and some imagination, created one of the more welcoming, nurturing, and valuable fantasy worlds that children have had a chance to occupy.

Works Cited

Campbell, Joseph. *The Hero with a Thousand Faces*. 1949. Princeton: Princeton University Press, 1972. Print.

"Daniel Sleeps Away from Home." *Mister Rogers' Neighborhood*. PBS. *Amazon Instant Video*. 17 May 1973. Web. 30 Aug. 2014.

"Death of the Goldfish." *Mister Rogers' Neighborhood*. PBS. *Amazon Instant Video*. 23 Apr. 1970. Web. 2 July 2014.

"The End of the First Week." *Mister Rogers' Neighborhood*. EEN. *Amazon Instant Video*. 23 Feb. 1968. Web. 18 July 2014.

Garfield, Bob. Foreword. *Mister Rogers' Neighborhood: Children, Television, and Fred Rogers*. Ed. Mark Collins and Margaret Mary Kimmel. Pittsburgh: University of Pittsburgh Press, 1996. ix-xv. Print.

Gerbner, George. "Fred Rogers and the Significance of Story." *Mister Rogers' Neighborhood: Children, Television, and Fred Rogers*. Ed. Mark Collins and Margaret Mary Kimmel. Pittsburgh: University of Pittsburgh Press, 1996. 3–14. Print.

Linn, Susan. "With an Open Hand: Puppetry on *Mister Rogers' Neighborhood*." *Mister Rogers' Neighborhood: Children, Television, and Fred Rogers*. Ed. Mark Collins and Margaret Mary Kimmel. Pittsburgh: University of Pittsburgh Press, 1996. 89–100. Print.

"King Friday Challenges Change." *Mister Rogers' Neighborhood*. EEN. *Amazon Instant Video*. 20 Feb. 1968. Web. 18 July 2014.

Kornfeld, John, and Laurie Prothro. "Comedy, Quest, and Community: Home and Family in Harry Potter." *Critical Perspectives on Harry Potter*, 2d ed. Ed. Elizabeth Heilman. New York: Routledge, 2009. 121–38. Print.

"Mister Rogers as a Boy." *Mister Rogers' Neighborhood*. PBS. *Amazon Instant Video*. 5 Mar. 1973. Web. 30 Aug. 2014.

Shelton, Mark. "A Neighborhood with Forest *and* Trees: Allies, Coalitions, Kids, and Mister Rogers." *Mister Rogers' Neighborhood: Children, Television, and Fred Rogers*. Ed. Mark Collins and Margaret Mary Kimmel. Pittsburgh: University of Pittsburgh Press, 1996. 183–194. Print.

Spitz, Ellen Handler. "The Magical Neighborhood of Mister Rogers." *The Chronicle of Higher Education* 49.29 (2003): B16. *Education Research Complete*. Web. 9 Aug. 2014.

Townley, Roderick. "Fred's Shoes: The Meaning of Transitions in *Mister Rogers' Neighborhood*." *Mister Rogers' Neighborhood: Children, Television, and Fred Rogers*. Ed. Mark Collins and Margaret Mary Kimmel. Pittsburgh: University of Pittsburgh Press, 1996. 67–78. Print.

"A Visit to the Grocery Store." *Mister Rogers' Neighborhood*. PBS. *Amazon Instant Video*. 5 Apr. 1984. Web. 3 Aug. 2014.

Zipes, Jack. "Why Fantasy Matters Too Much." *Journal of Aesthetic Education* 43.2 (2009): 77–91. Print.

Zukerman, Eugenia. "Musical Notes: An Interview with Yo-Yo Ma." *Mister Rogers' Neighborhood: Children, Television, and Fred Rogers*. Ed. Mark Collins and Margaret Mary Kimmel. Pittsburgh: University of Pittsburgh Press, 1996. 79–87. Print.

The Presence
of Mister Rogers

Steven M. Emmanuel

Each episode of *Mister Rogers' Neighborhood* begins with the affable Fred Rogers walking through the door of his television house—and into the living rooms of young viewers eagerly awaiting his visit. He greets them with a cheerful smile and a heartfelt invitation, delivered in the show's theme song "Won't You Be My Neighbor?"[1] The piano accompaniment, performed live with the improvisational stylings of John Costa, imparts a sense of spontaneity to the scene. In both style and message, the music underscores the vitality and uniqueness of this moment in the lives of neighbors.

To be a neighbor, in the moral and spiritual sense of the word, entails a kind of presence that goes beyond mere physical proximity; it is a way of being that expresses care, compassion, and unconditional acceptance of the other. Fred Rogers embodied this ideal of neighborliness in his personal and public life. Indeed, it was his extraordinary capacity to be fully present to others that made him such an endearing figure for millions of children (and grown-ups) who watched his show.[2]

An ordained Presbyterian minister with a special calling to work with children, Rogers considered the space between the television screen and his viewers as nothing less than "holy ground" (*Fred Rogers: America's Favorite Neighbor*). He believed that the task of filling that space for an audience of preschoolers required an accurate understanding of how children process their experience of the world. Applying the insights gleaned from his study of child psychology,[3] Rogers developed a relational approach to pedagogy based on the premise that each child is a unique individual "with great potential for constructive living" ("Statement by Fred M. Rogers" 9), and that the most important thing a child needs in order to grow into a healthy, responsible, loving adult is the experience of acceptance and care.[4] As Rogers explained, "Life holds few easy answers, but one thing is sure—it's through relationships that children grow best and learn best…. No matter how old or young we are, we learn best from people who care about us" (qtd. in Bafile).

Whereas other educational programs such as *Sesame Street* focused mainly on literacy and numeracy skills, Rogers was chiefly interested in facilitating the affective development of children. Working within a broadly eudaimonistic framework, he helped his young viewers navigate the world of feelings, encouraging the development of personal and social skills necessary for building self-esteem and healthy relationships. To this end, much of his attention was focused on helping children discover what he called "'the good feeling of control' which each well person has" ("Statement by Fred M. Rogers" 7). In dealing with the topic of anger, for example, he explained that this emotion is a natural part of human experience, and that a healthy approach to dealing with angry feelings when they arise is not to suppress them but to acknowledge their presence and find creative ways to channel them into nonviolent outlets. Rogers treated other feelings such as fear, jealousy, frustration, and disappointment in a similar manner, encouraging children to take ownership of their emotional lives, while at the same time promoting the virtues of patience, kindness, acceptance, and compassion—qualities necessary for living a happy, productive life in community with others.

The television neighborhood Rogers created was a place where children could regularly experience the feeling of acceptance and care. To create the sense of a caring relationship with his viewers, Rogers drew deeply from his own spiritual practice. His capacity to be present to others had been cultivated through years of contemplation and self-reflection. As author Amy Hollingsworth reveals in her book *The Simple Faith of Mister Rogers*, Fred Rogers' personal life was defined by the themes of slowing down, taking time, prayer, and silence (Hollingsworth 1–32). By embodying a caring presence for his viewers, Rogers taught children the importance of slowing down and taking the time to become aware of what is happening, both inside and outside themselves. He encouraged them to develop the capacity to be present to themselves and others.

Although "caring relationships" and "presence" figure prominently in contemporary discussions about teaching, they might seem out of place in the context of television. After all, as author Nel Noddings points out, the building of caring relationships in teaching depends on a kind of presence that involves attentiveness and responsiveness to the expressed needs of students (*Caring* 16–19, 180).[5] This requires "a feedback loop, where teachers can take action, can watch how students respond and can be moved and changed by these responses, thereby shaping their next caring act" (74). The importance of this interpersonal level of engagement is widely affirmed in the theoretical literature on presence in teaching. Carol R. Rodgers and Miriam B.

Raider-Roth, for instance, define presence generally as "a state of alert awareness, receptivity, and connectedness to the mental, emotional, and physical workings of both the individual and the group in the context of their learning environments, and the ability to respond with a considered and compassionate best next step" (265).

As a mediated personality, Rogers obviously lacked the physical presence that classroom teachers normally rely upon to establish a sense of connectedness with their students. Moreover, even though viewers could see and hear Mister Rogers, his inability to see or hear them precluded the kind of reciprocity that mutually caring relationships require. Although one might point out, as Rogers did, that he had something akin to a feedback loop in the form of correspondence from viewers, this could hardly compare to the spontaneous give-and-take of a classroom teacher's face-to-face interaction with students.

Rogers had given some thought to this problem long before he became a television personality. While working as an NBC floor manager on the *Gabby Hayes Show*, Rogers asked the host what he thought about when he looked at the television camera, knowing that thousands of children were out there in the viewing audience. Hayes explained that he tried to think of just one child ("one little buckaroo"). Reflecting on that "superb advice" in an interview many years later, Rogers said, "I think of the children that I know and many of the aspects of life that they are dealing with" (*Fred Rogers: America's Favorite Neighbor*). In this way, his expressions of care, compassion, and acceptance could be seen as authentic, in so far as they were connected to real children and real concerns. Even though the problems experienced by the children he knew were in some respects unique to their individual situations, Rogers viewed these differences as variations on "the general themes of childhood" ("Statement by Fred M. Rogers" 7), making it possible for his messages to resonate with any child that might be watching the show.

Perhaps the most salient point to consider, however, is that Rogers conceived of television as a very personal medium. Indeed, he seemed to be aware, if only intuitively, of the phenomenon of "parasocial bonding." As he remarked in a draft to his 1969 Senate statement,

> It has taken public television much too long to recognize the highly personal nature of the medium. People look to other people for relationships; even through television. I'm sure that you know people who feel very personally involved with those whom they see regularly on their television sets.[6]

More than a decade earlier, Donald Horton and Richard Wohl had coined the term "para-social interaction" to describe the "seeming face-to-face relationship" that viewers can experience with certain television personalities (Horton and Wohl 215). This sense of "interaction" was much more likely to occur, they suggested, when television hosts appeared as themselves and spoke directly to the viewing audience. Mister Rogers was a good example of the sort of personality Horton and Wohl had in mind. First of all, he was a real person, and the sense of his realness was enhanced by the sharp distinction maintained between the fantasy segment of the show (the Neighborhood of Make-Believe) and the reality segments featuring Mister Rogers. Next, he spoke directly to his viewers, often sharing stories about his own childhood experiences. Finally, unlike other children's programs of the day, *Mister Rogers' Neighborhood* did not have a regular cast of children or a studio audience that interacted with the host. Apart from brief conversations with visitors to his television house, the majority of Rogers' attention during these segments flowed in the direction of the viewer, whom he referred to as "you," "my television friend" and "my television neighbor."

Recent research confirms that very young viewers are not only able to experience a sense of meaningful interaction with mediated personalities, but that certain para-social relationships can serve their emotional needs as effectively as social relationships involving face-to-face interactions (Hoffner 313–14, 326). It is therefore quite plausible to suppose that children watching Mister Rogers might have a strong sense of his being present to them, as well as being seen and accepted by him. Noddings seems to acknowledge this possibility when she observes that acts at a distance can "bear the signs of presence: engrossment in the other, regard, desire for the other's well-being" (*Caring* 19). It should be noted, however, that Rogers did not set out merely to create the illusion of presence. His intention from the beginning was to *be present* to his viewers. Although he treated the camera in a sense as proxy for the viewing child, he was always consciously directing himself to the child he could not see.

Rogers' innovative use of presence in the television medium contributes something new and important to our understanding of the concept. At a time when more and more educational content is being shifted over to "distance learning" platforms, it would be useful to take a closer look at how Rogers brought his caring presence to the screen. There are four main ways in which he did this: (1) his loving gaze, (2) his use of loving speech, (3) his situational awareness, and (4) the integrity of his teaching self.

Rogers' Loving Gaze

From the moment he enters the scene, Rogers establishes and maintains a strong visual connection with the camera as proxy for the viewing child. Even in wide shots, as he moves through the familiar routine of changing into his trademark cardigan and sneakers while singing his invitation to "be my neighbor," Rogers repeatedly glances back toward the camera, signaling his active awareness of the viewing child. This visual connection is strongest, however, in more settled moments when he lets his gaze come to rest on the camera. In these medium close-up and close-up shots, Rogers' slightly widened eyes and natural smile project warmth, openness, acceptance, and care. With this *loving* gaze he acknowledges and embraces the viewer as neighbor. "The whole idea," as Rogers once explained in an interview, is "to look at the television camera and present as much love as you possibly could to a person who might feel that he or she needs it" (qtd. in Madigan 155). Rogers' way of looking into the camera was an offering of love in its simplest form.

The moral and spiritual significance of how we regard others was well noted by the French philosopher and mystic Simone Weil. Because the proper relation to our neighbor is always essentially one of profound care and concern, she wrote, it is "indispensable ... to know how to look at him in a certain way." In her words: "This way of looking is first of all attentive. The soul empties itself of all its own contents in order to receive into itself the being it is looking at, just as he is, in all his truth" (Weil 115).[7]

As an expression of love, the salient feature of this gaze is the displacement of the ego, which gives way to an absorbing concern for the well-being of the other. Noddings, who cites Weil in her description of the caring teacher (*The Challenge to Care in Teaching* 15–16), uses the term "engrossment" to capture the quality of consciousness associated with caring attentiveness. "Engrossment" signifies a complete openness and receptivity that goes beyond empathy in the weaker sense in which one merely imagines what it would be like to be in the other person's situation ("The Caring Relation in Teaching" 773). As Noddings explains,

> I do not "put myself in the other's shoes," so to speak, by analyzing his reality as objective data and then asking, "How would I feel in such a situation?" On the contrary, I set aside my temptation to analyze and to plan. I do not project; I receive the other into myself, and I see and feel with the other [*Caring* 30].

Following Weil, Noddings affirms that "caring is always characterized by a move away from self" (*Caring* 16).

The displacement of the ego is also a central feature of what moral philosopher Iris Murdoch called "a just and loving gaze" (Murdoch 34). This way of looking, which is "the characteristic and proper mark of the active moral agent," requires setting one's own ideas and interests aside—letting go of one's self-serving notions and preconceptions about the other in order to be fully present to the reality of the person who is there (Murdoch 34).

Fred Rogers' loving gaze exemplifies the egoless quality noted in the discussions of Weil, Noddings, and Murdoch. His countenance shows no hint of an agenda or ulterior motive; it is a look that says "I am here for you," "I accept you exactly as you are." The openness and acceptance expressed in this gaze is further reinforced by Rogers' calm, reassuring demeanor, which encourages in his viewer a feeling of safety and trust.

At the same time, one can also clearly sense in Rogers' gaze a very focused energy that reflects not only his awareness of the viewer, but also his awareness of being present to the viewer as one who cares. This reflexive aspect of the gaze is what imparts to it the compelling quality of an invitation, quietly drawing the viewer in, thereby creating an atmosphere of intimate rapport.

Rogers' Use of Loving Speech

"One of the most important tasks of growing up," Rogers wrote, is "the discovery of 'who I am' in each of us" ("Statement by Fred M. Rogers" 1).[8] With gentle questions he encourages his viewers to be curious, to wonder, and to reflect. He speaks slowly, frequently pausing to allow his words to be received and considered, giving the viewer the space to attend to whatever he or she might be feeling or thinking about at that moment. In this way, Rogers encourages each child to experience himself or herself as a unique center of value in the world.

To facilitate this process of self-discovery, Rogers attempts to create an atmosphere of trust and respect based on the unconditional acceptance of the viewing child "exactly as he or she might be feeling" (6). He expresses this with loving words of affirmation. These messages are sometimes spoken, sometimes sung directly to the camera in familiar musical numbers such as "It's You I like," "I'm Proud of You," and "Everybody's Fancy." Episode 1718 features a version of "You Are Special," in which Rogers combines his loving gaze with a heartfelt rendition of the song.

Knowing that children need honesty from the adults in their lives,[9] Rogers always chooses words that are simple and true. His straightforward and honest way of speaking respects the intuitiveness of children—their keen ability to sense whether an adult really cares and can be trusted with their confidences. When broaching delicate subjects, Rogers uses language that reflects an understanding of how children process their experience of the world.

Rogers' use of speech is "loving" in that it reflects an empathic understanding of children. Attuned to the "inner dramas of early childhood," he devotes a lot of time to exploring the fears that children experience in daily life (for example, going to the doctor or getting a haircut), as well as the complicated feelings associated with loss, disappointment, and change. He guides his viewers through weighty topics such as divorce and death, and helps them to cope with unsettling events in the world by offering comforting words of reassurance and hope.

A good example of Rogers' use of loving speech is in the episode where he addresses the death of a goldfish (Episode 1101). The scene begins with Rogers gently drawing attention to a fish lying at the bottom of the tank. "Do you see a dead fish?" he asks with a note of concern. "A dead fish would be one that isn't swimming or breathing or anything at all." As he carefully scoops up the fish and presents it to the viewers in a close-up shot, he says he has heard that by putting "a very sick fish in some water with salt, it might revive it, bring it back." So he tries this. Noticing little effect, he looks up at the camera, eyes wide, as if to ask the viewers whether they have noticed any change. The motion of the water seems to be making the fish "go back and forth," he observes, "but it's not moving itself." Rogers taps lightly on the side of the container, but the close-up shot indicates there is no sign of life. He looks up at the camera again, this time with an expression of acknowledgement. "I guess the salt isn't going to help it," he says in a solemn voice. "I guess we better bury it."

Later, after burying the goldfish in the backyard, Rogers relates a personal story about the death of his childhood dog Mitzi. Here again, his language is plain and honest: "When I was very young I had a dog that I loved very much. Her name was Mitzi. She got to be old … and she died. I was very sad when she died, because she and I were good pals. And when she died, I cried." He tells of how his grandmother comforted him: "she just put her arm around me, because she knew I was sad. She knew how much I loved that dog."

Talking about his own feelings of sadness at the loss of his good pal, Rogers concludes the scene with these words: "My dad said we'd have to bury Mitzi, and … I didn't want to. I didn't want to bury her because I thought I'd just *pretend* that she was still alive. But my dad said that her body was dead, and we'd have to bury her. So we did." There is something very comforting about this simple, straightforward statement about the reality of death and the need to accept it, as well as the importance of talking about the natural feelings of sadness that go along with that. He offers this message in an even tone, without any drama. In fact, one of the things that stands out about this story is the way he smiles throughout his telling of it. Though the event was clearly a painful one, recalling the memory of it is not, because it brings to mind the deep affection he felt for his dog and the loving expressions of care and comfort that he received from family members.

Back in the house, Rogers mentions that his aunt and uncle had given him a toy dog, which he shows the viewers before pulling out a framed picture of the real Mitzi. With the toy dog he demonstrates the way he played with it, placing it alternately in a prone position (dead) and then an upright position (alive): "I used to make it go like this … then make it pop up again like that … pretending." But the picture elicits real feelings associated with his memories of Mitzi: "I really missed her when she died." Here Rogers reinforces the distinction he mentioned earlier between pretending and what is real. In terms a child can understand, he explains that the reality of death and our feelings of loss are manageable when we are able to put them in their proper context. Rogers then sings a song (a variation on "Sometimes People Are Good"):

> Sometimes people get sad.
> And they really do feel bad.
> But the very same people who are sad sometimes
> Are the very same people who are glad sometimes.
> It's funny, but it's true.
> It's the same, isn't it for me?
> Isn't it the same for you?

The message of this simple song is empowering. On the one hand, it calls attention to the transient nature of feelings, and to the fact that feelings do not define the people who have them. On the other hand, it affirms that all people experience the same feelings (e.g., sadness, anger, fear, and their opposites) at one time or another. Thus, as children are learning that their feelings are manageable (the sad can become glad again, and the angry can find peace), they are also discovering the basis of compassion for themselves and others.

At the conclusion of the episode, Rogers sings "Some Things I Don't Understand" and reminds the viewer one last time that it is healthy to talk about feelings with others: "If you ever have a pet that dies or you're sad about something that you've lost…, it helps to say that you're sad. Often it even helps to cry. Let people know how you feel."

In one of a series of episodes dealing with divorce (Episode 1476), Mr. McFeely becomes agitated when Rogers mentions the topic and he makes an abrupt exit. After noting McFeely's reaction—one that many of his viewers are probably experiencing at that very moment—Rogers calmly takes a seat and asks, "Did you ever know any grown-ups that got married and later they got a divorce?" Still looking directly into the camera he pauses for a moment before continuing: "Well, it is something that people can talk about—and it's something important." He then mentions a certain boy and girl who "cried and cried" when their parents got divorced. "Do you know why? Well, one reason was that they thought it was all their fault. But of course it wasn't their fault. Things like weddings and having babies, and buying houses and cars, and getting divorces, are all grown-up things," he explains. He pauses one more time, letting his message sink in, before transitioning to the Neighborhood of Make-Believe sequence dealing with the same topic. But the main point—that children are not responsible for their parents getting divorced—has been delivered directly from Rogers in a calm and reassuring way. Later in the show, he will explore other aspects of divorce, for instance, that parents still love their children even if they don't live together, and he will reiterate the importance of being able to talk about the feelings associated with divorce. But he comes to the main point early and delivers it in simple, straightforward terms that a child can understand and accept.

Rogers' loving use of speech reveals that he is present in his words. Ronald L. Hall refers to this ethical quality of speech as "reflexive integrity" (Hall 75). Having a reflexively integral relation to one's words is a necessary condition for being able to speak authentically, that is, in a way that reveals who one is. As Hall explains, "the mark and test of the realization of a self is the extent to which a speaker *owns his words, owns up to them, is present in them,* and *present in them before some other*" (Hall 74). In speaking from the heart, as Rogers does when candidly describing his own sadness and tears at the loss of his childhood pet, he not only reveals himself to viewers, but at the same time he models an important quality of character: the courage to "be yourself" with others. In the 1978 PBS Series *Old Friends ... New Friends* (Episode 213), Rogers remarks to psychologist Tom Cottle, "There's real courage in risking to be yourself and allowing the people you're with to be themselves, too.... A good conversation, like a good friendship, is an encounter between two people who have a true interest in each other. It sounds simple, but it's not." By speaking from the heart, we create the conditions that allow others to speak from the heart as well—we create the conditions for people to be present to each other as neighbors.

Loving speech depends on having the capacity to listen. "Listening," Rogers says, "is where love begins: listening to ourselves and then to our neighbors" (*World According to Rogers* 93). Listening to ourselves means paying close attention to the feelings, thoughts, and emotions that shape the way we respond to others. But loving speech also depends on our ability to listen to others with an open heart—without judgment or expectation—so that we can really hear them and know how to respond in a way that demonstrates our understanding and compassion. For Rogers, receptive listening is one of the most important ways that we can be present to others. This kind of listening is, in his words, "a very active awareness of the coming together of at least two lives.... One of the most essential ways of saying 'I love you' is being a receptive listener" (92).

As a mediated personality, Rogers is of course unable to listen to his viewers. However, he does model the practice of receptive listening, particularly in the way he will ask viewers a question and then pause, as though waiting for the answer. He does this while making solid visual contact with the camera. But Rogers models the behavior of receptive listening in a more complete way in his interactions with others on the program. One particularly compelling example of this is the well-known episode featuring Jeff Erlanger, a ten-year-old quadriplegic boy who visits with Rogers to talk about what it is like to be in a wheelchair (Episode 1478). In this scene, which takes place just outside the television house (there is no wheelchair access), Rogers immediately sits down on the porch step, bringing himself right down to Jeff's eye level. After briefly turning back to the camera to introduce Jeff to the television audience and explain the reason for his visit, Rogers turns back to his guest, giving him his patient, undivided attention.

Rogers is relaxed and focused, his loving gaze on full display. His body language reflects that he is following every word Jeff says. His questions demonstrate that he is listening carefully and empathically to the inner experience his guest is describing. He is alive to the challenges of being disabled and the special problems posed by Jeff's particular condition. But even as Jeff courageously shares the heartbreaking details of his own personal sufferings—the spinal tumor, the surgeries, the chronic pain—Rogers receives his story with a remarkable equanimity of spirit that is devoid of shallow pity or emotionalism. He looks completely past the disability to the *person* who is there before him. Near the end of the conversation, Rogers invites Jeff to join him in singing "It's You I Like," adding "I'd like to sing that *to* you and *with* you." By singing both *to* and *with* his friend, Rogers brings together the acts of loving speech and listening. The result is one of the most moving and memorable moments in the history of the show.

Rogers' Situational Awareness

"Situational awareness" refers to the very deliberate and mindful way that Rogers moves around the studio space and interacts with others. It captures the presence of mind that Rodgers and Raider-Roth describe as "bringing one's whole self to full attention so as to perceive what is happening in the moment" (267). Rogers brings this quality to whatever he is doing: whether it is feeding the fish, showing something he has brought to share with his television friends, demonstrating how something works, or attending to his guests. This mindful awareness is "situational" because it extends to what is going on around him. Even as Rogers is giving his careful attention to the task at hand, he is always aware of the larger context in which that activity is taking place.

In the goldfish episode, every aspect of the scene demonstrates extreme care—in the way he discovers and retrieves the fish, the way he attempts to revive it, the meticulous way he wraps it for burial, the thoughtful way he selects the appropriate spot for the grave, and the respectful way he performs the ritual. Later in the show, Rogers enlists the help of his friend Bob Trow, who carefully assists him with making a wooden marker for the goldfish grave. Bob has artistic ability, and knowing instantly from Rogers' description which of his fish has died, he draws a picture of it on the board with the word "fish" written underneath it. Then they walk solemnly together into the backyard where Rogers carefully places the marker.

It is Rogers' mindful awareness of what is happening in the moment that underlies his practice of inclusion. Even in the midst of a conversation with a guest, he will make a point of glancing back at the camera periodically, reminding the viewers that they are included in what is happening. A typical example of this occurs in Episode 1718, which features a visit with the Uptown String Quartet. Rogers begins by introducing the musicians to the television audience. Gesturing toward the camera, he says, "I'd like you to know my television neighbor." After being introduced they all wave to the camera. To get things rolling, Rogers says, "I'd like my friends to hear how the instruments sound." While the musicians perform, Rogers looks up at the camera occasionally, reminding the viewers that he and they are enjoying this music together. Rogers' presence is reinforced by this sense of sharing a common experience with his viewers. After the musicians perform an original jazz composition ("Vibes") that demonstrates the unique qualities of each individual instrument, Rogers asks them about their childhood experiences with music. In this way, he makes the conversation directly relevant to his audience. The musicians take turns sharing some childhood memories. Afterwards, they play Rogers' own "You Are Special" in a pizzicato arrangement. This number draws attention to the underlying message that every person (like every musical instrument) is a unique individual with a unique voice. This performance also serves as a musical prelude to Rogers' singing of the same song when he returns to his neighborhood house.

Encouraging the capacity to be aware of what is happening, both inside and around oneself, is a key feature of Rogers' pedagogy of presence. At the very beginning of this episode, which is devoted to the theme of "being yourself," Rogers sings the song "Look and Listen":

> If you will look carefully,
> Listen carefully,
> You will find a lot of things carefully.
> Look … and listen.
> It's good to
> Look carefully.
> Listen carefully.
> That's the way you learn a lot of things carefully.
> Look … look and listen.
> Some things you see are confusing.
> Some things you hear are strange.
> But if you ask someone to explain one or two,
> You'll begin to notice a change in you.

If you will
Look carefully.
Listen carefully.
That's a way to keep on growing carefully.
Look, look, look, and listen.

The concluding lines remind the viewer that the process of learning and growing depends on one's being able to slow down and take the time to pay attention. The growth mentioned here does not refer only to cognitive development. Looking and listening are activities that facilitate a child's affective and moral development as well.[10]

The Integrity of Rogers' Teaching Self

As author Don Hufford points out, presence is essentially "a revelation—a revealing of who I am" (Hufford 12). Yet, as Rodgers and Raider-Roth explain, teachers in the traditional classroom setting often experience a conflict between the socially (institutionally) constructed image of themselves as "teachers" and who they are as "persons":

> When a teacher acts solely from an artificially constructed notion of who she should be, she becomes remote from herself and presence becomes difficult. There is a disconnection, a disintegration of self, that precludes bringing focused attention to bear. With this disintegration, there is a subsequent lack of what Parker Palmer (1998) called integrity.... Integration, wholeness, reliability and groundedness in a person all speak to what is required for a teacher to be able to trust herself and the actions which are an extension of that self [272].

Hufford agrees, noting that the expression of one's individual identity is "necessary to a sense of *presence*" (12).

The integrity of Rogers' teaching self is revealed in the continuity of his personal character over time. There are no surprises lurking beneath that gentle, unassuming exterior. He is the same loving, caring, accepting person every day. He is reliable, grounded, self-aware. By showing his viewers this integrated self, Rogers naturally inspires their trust, as well as a deeper sense of connectedness.

Fred Rogers' identity as a teacher is connected with larger social issues that he feels compelled to address as a citizen and a person of conscience. Committed to teaching about peace and social justice, he attempts to empower children to create a better world—a more peaceful, just, and compassionate world based on the recognition that we are all neighbors. He does this by modeling the virtues of neighborliness—by looking, speaking, and acting in ways that demonstrate care and unconditional acceptance, and by directing the viewer's attention to the essential goodness that resides within every person: "When I say, 'It's you I like,' I'm talking about … that deep part of you that allows you to stand for those things without which humankind cannot survive: *love* that conquers hate, *peace* that rises triumphant over war, and *justice* that proves more powerful than greed" (*The World According to Mister Rogers* 189).

Conflict and anger were among the most important issues addressed on the show. Episodes 1521–1525[11] and 1691–1695 were devoted entirely to these topics. However, Rogers touched on the topic of anger many times, performing the song "What Do You Do with the Mad That You Feel?" in no fewer than thirty-three episodes (*The Neighborhood Archive*). The message conveyed in this song was so important to Rogers that he recited the lyrics in his 1969 testimony before the Senate Subcommittee on Communications as evidence of the social value of publicly funded educational television.

At the conclusion of Episode 1523, after Rogers sings "I'm Proud of You," he adds, "I'm very glad that you're a part of the world. Because you can help to make it a better and better place for people to live so that people won't have to be so scared of other people." Episode 1524 ends with a message that situates the issue of conflict in a global context: "Rules are very, very important. Not just for games but for all things. Even big things like countries. Countries have to have rules to protect people, too. And someday you'll be helping to make the rules for your country. I trust that you'll make the best kind you know how." In the final episode of this weeklong series (1525), Rogers closes the show in an utterly unique way. After he sings the usual closing theme "It's Such a Good Feeling," the camera moves in for a close-up shot, and Rogers begins to talk about the importance of what he and the viewers are doing together:

> We prove to each other and to other people that we *can* talk about all kinds of things. And that's because we care about one another. I hope you'll talk with the grown-ups you love about how they feel about things like war and peace, being angry and loving. That way you'll be able to find out what the history of your family is, and all the many ways they've celebrated peace in their lives.

Then he steps out onto the porch, where he sings "Peace and Quiet." This is a song he performed on several shows in 1968–1969, at the height of the Vietnam War (Episodes 8, 80, and 1016). He mentions that he had written it for his father, adding, "I'd like to sing it for you before I go. Maybe you could learn it, too. It's a very simple song." The first part is repeated three times:

Peace and quiet.
Peace, peace, peace.

We all want peace.
We all want peace.

Rogers then wishes his viewers peace, and as he leaves the frame the text of Isaiah 2:4 appears on the screen for approximately ten seconds (exactly as it appears below):

> "And they shall beat their swords
> into plowshares,
> And their spears into pruning forks[12];
> Nation shall not lift up sword
> against nation,
> Neither shall they learn war
> any more."

The deep connection between peacemaking and neighborliness is expressed in many ways on the show. It is especially noteworthy that Rogers' treatment of the concept of peace always has both an inward and an outward focus. *Mister Rogers' Neighborhood* teaches children that the important work of peace begins inside, as they begin to develop emotional self-control and cultivate the prosocial qualities of patience, kindness, and compassion that are necessary in order to be able to care for themselves and others.

In the many episodes that deal with animals and the environment, Rogers always stresses the point that the scope of care is broad: it includes self-care, as well as caring for others, for animals, and for the health of the planet. In Episode 1498, one in a weeklong series devoted to pets, Rogers says, "Everyone needs some kind of care. Caring for people helps them know that you love them. Caring for animals helps them know that you love them, too." Similarly, Episode 1617, one in a weeklong series on the environment, closes with Rogers singing "I Like to Take Care of You." Connecting this concept to the process of moral growth, he says, "It's really good to take care of yourself, and it's good to take care of other people too, *and things*. When you're able to take care of yourself, you can feel that you are growing."

Episodes 1616–1620 discuss the concept of recycling. Rogers places this activity in a social context, emphasizing that taking care of the environment is something we can do in our own small ways, but that it also involves the cooperative efforts of everyone in the community. At the beginning of Episode 1618, Rogers shows his viewers a handcrafted puzzle made from recycled wood. While he takes it apart and admires the beauty of is construction, he recalls an earlier visit with Mrs. McFeely, who showed him a few things she had created from recycled materials, including a milk carton that she had turned into a bird feeder. Afterwards, Rogers tells his viewers that good memories are things that can be recycled, too. At the conclusion of the episode, Rogers returns to the wooden puzzle, which has yet to be reassembled. This sets up the final message, which reinforces the theme of social cooperation: "This puzzle is too difficult for me to put back together by myself," he concedes. "So I'm going to ask a friend to help me do it. Sure, it's a good feeling that you don't have to solve everything by yourself."

Although Rogers' own efforts were directed at the preschool set, it was his hope that public television stations around the country would begin to develop their own local "personalities" capable of communicating in a very personal way with audiences of all ages ("Statement by Fred M. Rogers" 4). He envisioned the possibility of public television creating a network of "interpersonal relationships" in which viewers would be treated with genuine care and respect. "In whatever we produce," he wrote, "we *must* communicate the feeling that we really *care* about our audience. No matter whether we present a soap opera or an automobile repair show, whether we develop pre-school instruction or teach flower arranging, our aim must be the building of self-esteem and greater self-understanding in our viewers" ("Statement by Fred M. Rogers" 4).

With *Mister Rogers' Neighborhood*, Rogers demonstrated that television can be a powerful vehicle for positive social change. He was able to do this because, as Rodgers and Raider-Roth point out, "presence offers us a moral imperative, a psychological stance and an intellectual trajectory that can root the world of teaching and learning in its essential purpose, the creation of a just and democratic society" (284). Fred Rogers might have preferred to say "a just and *loving* society." Either way, one would be hard pressed to find a more compelling model for presence in teaching—whether in a conventional classroom or a distance-learning setting—than Mister Rogers.

Notes

1. The lyrics to this and other songs mentioned in this essay can be found on the website *The Neighborhood Archive—All Things Mister Rogers*.

2. In his memoir entitled *I'm Proud of You: My Friendship with Fred Rogers*, author Tim Madigan speaks of Rogers' "sacred presence and compassion" (168).

3. This was done under the supervision of Margaret B. McFarland, an associate professor in the Department of Psychiatry at the University of Pittsburgh. A theology student at the time, Rogers was assigned to work with McFarland to gain experience in counseling children.

4. Rogers would have agreed with Max van Manen's view that pedagogy requires a knowledge of how young people experience things, what they think about, how they look at the world, what they do, and, most importantly, how each child is a unique person. A teacher who does not understand the inner life of a child does not know who it is that he or she is teaching (van Manen 139).

5. See also Noddings' "An Ethic of Caring and Its Implications for Instructional Arrangements" 219–20; "The Caring Relation of Teaching" 772; and *The Challenge to Care in Schools* 15ff.

6. This statement was included in a draft copy of Rogers' 1969 Senate statement.

7. From the essay entitled "Reflections on the Right Use of School Studies with a View to the Love of God," in *Waiting for God* (1951). Qtd. by Noddings (*The Challenge to Care in Schools* 15).

8. "Statement by Fred M. Rogers, Senate Hearings on Public Broadcasting," dated May 1, 1969. Archived at the Fred Rogers Center, St. Vincent College, Latrobe, PA. This text was the basis of Rogers' testimony before the Senate Subcommittee on Communications, in which he argued against proposed funding cuts for public television.

9. The song "I Like to Be Told" explains this point for parents watching the show.

10. Another song with a similar theme is "I Like to Take My Time."

11. Aired in November 1983, one month after the U.S. invasion of Grenada.

12. It is curious that the word "forks" appears here in place of the conventional "hooks." As there is no precedence for this translation, one wonders whether it is an unintentional—or perhaps, given Rogers' love of music, intentional—conflation of "pruning hooks" and "tuning forks."

WORKS CITED

Bafile, Cara. Interview with Fred Rogers. *Education World.* 2002. Last accessed: May 15, 2015.

Dewey, John. *Democracy and Education.* Carbondale: Southern Illinois University Press, 1916.

Farber, Jerry. "Teaching and Presence." *Pedagogy: Critical Approaches to Teaching Literature, Language, Composition, and Culture* 8.2 (2008): 215–25.

Fred Rogers: America's Favorite Neighbor. Prod. Margaret Whitmer, Joseph J. Kennedy, IV. Hosted by Michael Keaton. DVD. Family Communications and WQED. 2004.

Hall, Ronald, L. *Word and Spirit.* Bloomington: Indiana University Press, 1993.

Hansen, David T. *Exploring the Moral Heart of Teaching.* New York: Teachers College Press, 2001.

Hoffner, C. "Parasocial and Online Social Relationships." In S. L. Calvert and B. J. Wilson, eds., *The Handbook of Children, Media, and Development.* Malden: Blackwell, 2008, pp. 309–33.

Hollingsworth, Amy. *The Simple Faith of Mister Rogers: Spiritual Insights from the World's Most Beloved Neighbor.* Brentwood: Integrity Publishers, 2005.

Horton, Donald, and Richard Wohl. "Mass Communication and Para-Social Interaction: Observations on Intimacy at a Distance." *Psychiatry* 19.3 (1956): 215–29.

Hufford, Don. "Presence in the Classroom." In Thomas, Cornell (ed.), *Inclusive Teaching: Presence in the Classroom: New Directions for Teaching and Learning,* Number 140. San Francisco: Jossey-Bass, 2014.

Madigan, Tim. *I'm Proud of You: My Friendship with Fred Rogers.* Los Angeles: Ubuntu Press, 2012.

Murdoch, Iris. *The Sovereignty of Good.* London: Routledge and Kegan Paul, 1970 [2001].

The Neighborhood Archive—All Things Mister Rogers. Last accessed: May 15, 2015.

Noddings, Nel. *Caring: A Relational Approach to Ethics and Moral Education.* Berkeley: University of California Press, 2013.

_____. "The Caring Relation in Teaching." *Oxford Review of Education* 38.6 (2012): 771–81.

_____. *The Challenge to Care in Schools: An Alternative Approach to Education.* New York: Teachers College Press, 1992 [2005].

_____. "An Ethic of Caring and Its Implications for Instructional Arrangements." *American Journal of Education* 96.2 (1988): 215–31.

Palmer, Parker J. *The Courage to Teach.* San Francisco: John Wiley & Sons, 1998.

Rodgers, Carol R., and Miriam B. Raider-Roth. "Presence in Teaching." *Teachers and Teaching: Theory and Practice* 12.3 (2006): 265–87.

Rogers, Fred. "Statement by Fred M. Rogers, Senate Hearings on Public Broadcasting" (dated 1969). Archived at the Fred Rogers Center, St. Vincent College, Latrobe, PA.

_____ . *The World According to Mister Rogers.* New York: Hyperion Books, 2003.

Weil, Simone. *Waiting for God.* New York: G.P. Putnam's Sons, 1951.

A Different Voice: Mister Rogers and the Ethic of Care

RICHARD BILSKER

> When you combine your own intuition with a sensitivity to other people's feelings and moods, you may be close to the origins of valuable human attributes such as generosity, altruism, compassion, sympathy, and empathy.—Fred Rogers (*World* 147)

I grew up on *Mister Rogers*. I watched it every day until, as my mother says, my older brother made fun of me for watching it. I had a vague recollection that I met Mister Rogers when I was very young at an event at my local PBS station, WVPT in the early 1970s. The people at the archive at fredrogers.org could not confirm that there was an appearance, but their records do show that there was a giveaway through the station of the LP, *A Place of Our Own*. I still have that LP.

As an adult, I appreciate him even more and enjoyed watching with my son when he was at the right age for it. Rogers was aware of this rather nostalgic phenomenon: "adults tell us that when they 'tune in' to our program, they come away with a renewed sense of self-worth" ("Family Communication" 72). At the same time, the "Mister Rogers is not cool" idea has a long history. NPR personality Bob Garfield discusses it in his foreword to *Mister Rogers' Neighborhood: Children, Television, and Fred Rogers*:

> Over the course of twenty-five years, I'd come to detest Fred Rogers, along with everything and everyone around him…. Twenty-five years of saccharine sincerity, of maddening beatificity, of low wattage … of Mr. McFeely … of folks just dropping in at eight o'clock in the morning and receiving a cheerful hello [Garfield ix–x].

So he decided to expose his kids to *The Ren and Stimpy Show* instead. As he points out, *Ren and Stimpy* can be described as "thirty minutes of sadistic interplay between an oafish and guileless cat and a skittish paranoiac Chihuahua" (xii). While watching Ren and Stimpy he realizes that he has got it backwards. Kids do not need an antidote to Mister Rogers, but rather they need Mister Rogers as "the antidote to everything else" (xii).[1] Why the change?

> Mister Rogers may have a very serious wardrobe disorder, but he has never once neglected my children in favor of housework, tax preparation, or the Redskins-Eagles game. He has never reneged on a promise; when he says they're going to the sneaker factory, by God they're going, and right now. He has never exploded like flash powder before their eyes, causing them to shudder at the suddenness and excessiveness of the fulmination. He has never made Mommy cry—and if he had, he wouldn't have subtly shifted the blame to her [xiii].

In other words, Mister Rogers *cares*. There is evidence of this in many of the aphorisms in his book *The World According to Mister Rogers: Important Things to Remember*. These are illustrative of his outlook:

> There's a nurturing element to all human beings, whenever they themselves have been nurtured, and it's going to be expressed one way or another [23].
> Love isn't a state of perfect caring. It is an active noun like *struggle*. To love someone is to strive to accept that person exactly the way he or she is, right here and right now [53].
> As different as we are from one another, as unique as each one of us is, we are much more the same than we are different. That may be the most essential message of all, as we help our children grow toward being caring, compassionate, and charitable adults [184].
> When I was a boy and I would see scary things in the news, my mother would say to me, "Look for the helpers. You will always find people who are helping." To this day, especially in times of "disaster," I remember my mother's words, and I am always comforted by realizing that there are still so many helpers—so many caring people in this world [187].
> When I was ordained, it was for a special ministry, that of serving children and families through television. I consider that what I do through Mister Rogers' Neighborhood is my ministry. A ministry doesn't have to be only through church, or even through an ordination. And I think we all can minister to others in this world by being compassionate and caring. I hope you will feel good enough about yourselves that you will want to minister to others, and that you will find your own unique ways to do that [188].

By all accounts, there is very little difference between his private and public personas.[2] The ideas quoted above are instantiated in the television show.

Carol Gilligan and the Ethic of Care

The ethic of care, as described by Carol Gilligan, provides an interpretive lens through which to revisit *Mister Rogers' Neighborhood*. In 1982, Carol Gilligan published her groundbreaking work in developmental psychology, *In *a Different Voice*. The book is, in part, a criticism of the view of moral development put forth by Lawrence Kohlberg, who was a colleague of Gilligan's at Harvard, though Gilligan is now at New York University. Kohlberg's model was influenced by the work of Swiss psychologist Jean Piaget, who studied how children acquired concepts like space, time, number, geometry, and causality. Kohlberg determined in his 1958 doctoral dissertation there are six stages of moral development. Gilligan's book noted that in numerous tests which asked young people to give their responses to moral dilemmas, girls scored lower on Kohlberg's scale than boys did. Gilligan argues that Kohlberg based his model primarily on studying boys. Girls, she says, seem to be speaking in a different voice (hence the title of her book).[3] She argues that it is not a lower developmental stage, but rather a different approach to the problem. In the years after her book, the two voices have come to be called justice and care. Philosophers and psychologists have been addressing these ideas with great interest for the last thirty years (Bilsker 569).

The rational rule-following ethic of justice has been the dominant one in moral philosophy since at least the eighteenth century. There have been some notable exceptions that can be seen as precursors to an ethic of care. David Hume, Jean-Jacques Rousseau, and Arthur Schopenhauer are examples that show that an ethic of care is not only advocated by women historically.

David Hume was one of the first philosophers to argue that the importance of reason in ethical decision-making was less important than passion (emotion). Hume argued that reason can direct the impulse to act, but is not the source of the impulse. He famously said that reason "is, and ought only to be the slave of the passions" (Hume 415). Moral impulses and distinctions are not derived from reason, but rather sentiment. The origin of sentiment is sympathy (454–470).

For Rousseau, too, reason is not paramount. Pity is the foundation of ethics, according to Rousseau. Pity is a

> natural sentiment moderating the action of self-love in each individual and so contributing to the mutual preservation of the whole species. It is pity that sends us unreflecting to the aid of those we see suffering... the human race would long ago ceased to exist if its preservation had depended strictly on the reasoning power of the individuals that make it up [43–48].[4]

So the natural human reaction is to help and it is only pushed to the background if brought to the level of conscious rational deliberation.

Schopenhauer's ideas revolve around his understanding of will. For Schopenhauer, Will is what drives everything, a blind striving power. It is opposed by intellect, which is the ability to reason. Will is in nature and non-human animals, as well as humans. Humans have to realize, according to Schopenhauer, that if will-to-live in humans is the individual manifestation of this blind striving, that aside from the phenomenal, perceptible selves, humans are all the same. If that is the case, then ethics should be informed by that idea. Harming another is wrong, then, because it is actually harming the self. He even uses a phrase from Hinduism, *tat tvam asi* (this art thou) to illustrate the idea (*World as Will* 367–378). Thus, the only truly ethical acts arise out of a motive of compassion (*Basis of Morality* 140–147).

Michael Slote in his article "Autonomy and Empathy" argues that it is possible to define caring in a way that is compatible with the thoughts of even earlier philosophers like Aristotle and Francis Hutcheson, when caring is understood as empathy (Slote 294–295, 298–299). So, the work in philosophy that comes out of Gilligan's developmental psychology revives some old ideas that have been less popular in the history of philosophy, especially the last two hundred years.

Gilligan highlights differences between the two ethics by pointing out that "the logic underlying an ethic of care is a psychological logic of relationships, which contrasts with the formal logic of fairness that informs the justice approach" (Gilligan, *Different Voice* 73). She also describes them in terms of perspectives on morality and self, as the ethic of care supports attachment and the ethic of rights / justice supports separation (164–65). There is a conflict between the two:

> To understand how the tension between responsibilities and rights sustains the dialectic of human development is to see the integrity of two disparate modes of experience that are in the end connected. While an ethic of justice proceeds from the premise of equality—that everyone should be treated the same—an ethic of care rests on the principle of nonviolence—that no one should be hurt [174].

In a later article, Gilligan and Jane Attanucci note that though there is a "contrast between the justice and the care perspectives … most people who participated in this research used considerations of both justice and care in discussing a moral conflict they faced" (Gilligan and Attanucci 76). It is difficult to reconcile these two perspectives, so there will have to be a dialogue. Gilligan's results are corroborated also by D. Kay Johnston with regard to adolescents examining dilemmas in Aesop's fables. She observed that "both genders employ both systems of reasoning, although they employ these systems differently. This differential use seems to be related to the context of the fables and the view of relationships held by the problem solver" (Johnston 69). Also, as noted by Nona Lyons, research shows that the ethic of care "appears to be a systematic, life-long concern of individuals. It does not appear to be a temporary, stage- or level-specific concern, or subsumed within a morality of justice" (Lyons 42).

Nel Noddings was one of the first philosophers to further the conversation and move the discussion from the psychology of moral development to moral philosophy. In her work *Caring*, she makes a distinction between "caring for" and "caring about." Caring *for* is like taking care of your family, actively engaging your time and emotions. Caring *about* is more like how you feel bad for storm victims in a distant land or those that are in other ways worse off than you are. You care about what happens to them, but you are not going to fly around the world and save everyone. You can care about lots of people, but you cannot care for more than a small-ish circle around you. Further, you cannot care for so many that you do not care for self.[5] Mister Rogers states something similar:

> Mutually caring relationships require kindness and patience, tolerance, optimism, joy in the other's achievements, confidence in oneself, and the ability to give without undue thought of gain. We need to accept the fact that it's not in the power of any human being to provide all these things all the time. For any of us, mutually caring relationships will always include some measure of unkindness and impatience, intolerance, pessimism, envy, self-doubt and disappointment [Rogers, *World* 78].

Noddings and Mister Rogers are in agreement that caring is a foundation of human relationships.

Mister Rogers in His Neighborhood

A 1993 week-long series of episodes deals with love ("Mister Rogers Talks About Love," Episodes 1661–1665, February 22–26). Over the course of the week, Mister Rogers imparts maxims in an ethic of care consistent with the features of the ethic of care described above.

In the neighborhood, Mister Rogers interacts with many people who demonstrate different aspects of love. At the same time, two plot lines run through the make-believe portions of the shows. First, King Friday seems out of sorts, always telling everyone in his kingdom that they need to be working more and not playing. The second theme is that Lady Elaine Fairchilde wants to put on a play—a soap opera called "As the Museum Turns."

In Episode 1661, Mister Rogers shows the audience a stuffed bear in a suitcase and Mr. McFeely comes by with a video of a factory that makes stuffed bears. After discussing how many people love stuffed bears and a bear costume Mister Rogers has, Mr. McFeely notes that "people can't love unless somebody loves them first." This maxim clearly lines up with the ethic outlined above. The first hint that something is bothering King Friday occurs when he is seen irritated that Queen Sara wants to enjoy her day. Lady Aberlin wears a bear costume in the Neighborhood of Make-Believe, and the viewer learns that there is more than meets the eye, until Daniel Striped Tiger recognizes her at the end, from her kind way of talking. What is outside is less important.

The next day (Episode 1662), Mister Rogers visits a friend, David Ford, an ornithologist. Love of birds—and learning in general—is another expression of love. This is tied in at the end, as well, when Mister Rogers feeds his fish. In the Neighborhood of Make-Believe, King Friday is seen trying to train his birds on sticks (*Troglodytes aedon* and *Mimus polyglottos*) and getting frustrated that they, too, are not working hard enough for him. Since King Friday seems irritated in the previous episode, it might not be that this is the cause of his attitude. To complicate his mood, one of the birds accompanies Mayor Maggie to visit the museum-go-round, where the idea is suggested to Lady Elaine that she put on a play. When the show returns to the neighborhood, Mister Rogers invites his viewers to write their own plays based on what they love, since everyone has good ideas. Showing love is another form of care.

The opening of Episode 1663 is significant as Officer Clemmons shares a wading pool with Mister Rogers as the two rest their feet. Officer Clemmons sings a song:

> There are many ways to say I love you
> There are many ways to say I care about you.
> Many ways, many ways, many ways to say
> I love you.
> There's the singing way to say I love you
> There's the singing something someone really likes to hear,
> The singing way, the singing way, the singing way to say
> I love you.
> Cleaning up a room can say I love you.
> Hanging up a coat before you're asked to
> Drawing special pictures for the holidays and
> Making plays.
> You'll find many ways to say I love you.
> You'll find many ways to understand what love is.
> Many ways, many ways, many ways to say
> I love you.
> Singing, cleaning,
> Drawing, being
> Understanding,
> Love you.

The audience is also shown a video with people doing all of these things, in addition to taking care of pets, playing sports, and other activities. In the Neighborhood of Make-Believe, King Friday is again insistent that everyone be working. Prince Tuesday wants to take a walk and goes with Mr. McFeely to make a delivery to the museum-go-round. Out of sight of the royal family, but visible to the viewer, Lady Aberlin overhears King Friday chastising Queen Sara and Prince Tuesday about not working and appears distraught. Mr. McFeely explains to Prince Tuesday that doing a good job is a sign of love. This lesson is very indicative of Mister Rogers' outlook[6] and harkens back to the video watched before going to make-believe. Prince Tuesday declines to be in the play, fearing his father's disapproval. When the viewer is taken back to the neighborhood, one of the last things Mister Rogers tells the audience before the episode ends is that everyone loves to be appreciated. So, another tie is made clear between people's actions and the emotions of others. This, too, fits in with the ethic of care elaborated above.

Episode 1664 is the most philosophical of the five. It begins with talk about pretending to shave, followed by a trip to the Neighborhood of Make-Believe. Still concerned because of what happened the day before, and the fact that they appear to behaving warmly with each other, Lady Aberlin sets out to find out what love is. What follows is like one of Plato's dialogues.[7] The first answer is circular: "love is a feeling you have when you love somebody." When Lady Aberlin asks X the Owl to follow up on his answer, he then looks it up in his Benjamin Franklin book, but all that the Franklin book notes is that "love is good" and "love is wonderful." These do not provide any more insight. X concludes that it's "pretty hard to ask important questions, isn't it?" Despite not getting any help on her dilemma, Lady Aberlin still tells X that she loves him before she moves on. She next meets Robert Troll. His first answers, "hugging and kissing" and "getting married," fall into the examples of things you do when you are in love, but do not define the term. As Lady Aberlin points out she loves X the Owl, but does not hug and kiss him and she loves her aunt and uncle, but will not marry them. Robert Troll then offers "love is a feeling" and then, like a true Socratic interlocutor, changes the subject. Lady Elaine says love is what happens when she looks in a mirror. Lady Aberlin thinks that Lady Elaine is not taking the question seriously, but Lady Elaine responds with a key Mister Rogers idea: "you can't love anybody else, if you don't love yourself." This maxim should be added to Mr. McFeely's from Episode 1661. Lady Elaine sends Lady Aberlin off to see her Aunt and Uncle, the Queen and King. Lady Elaine notes that being angry with someone can be a sign of how much you love them. Aunt Sara tells her that you can love even if you don't understand it what it is—it is the most important thing in the world. Loves of music and of family are explored when Mister Rogers meets Peter Ostroushko, a mandolin player, at Joe Negri's music shop. Yo-Yo Ma has noted the importance of music in *Mister Rogers' Neighborhood* for fostering both individuality and community (Zukerman 82). At the end of the episode Mister Rogers tells the audience that love keeps filling up inside: "the more we give away, the more we have to give." This is another maxim to add to Mister Rogers' ethic.

In the last episode of the week, the play is performed in the Neighborhood of Make-Believe. Lady Elaine forgets her lines and everyone tells her they still love her, proving that one can be loved even if one make mistakes. This is echoed by King Friday who wants reassurance that he is still loved, even when he makes mistakes. At this, King Friday seems to be back to his normal self after the end of the play. Interestingly, one never learns what was bothering King Friday. He is loved regardless. A return to the neighborhood shows a visit to the kitchen of Mrs. Schipper, who makes spinach egg rolls for Mister Rogers. She says that "as a way of showing their love and concern for the members of the family, they [her older relatives] teach me how to cook." After singing the "There Are Many Ways to Say I Love You" song again, Mister Rogers articulates one more maxim: "it is tough to love someone who has been mean to you—even if it's yourself."

Revisiting these episodes only reaffirms the way *Mister Rogers' Neighborhood* introduces important themes for children and reinforces ways of treating others. It also shows how Mister Rogers' views as expressed in the show are consistent with the ethic of care discussed above.

Conclusion

William Guy, in his essay "The Theology of *Mister Rogers' Neighborhood*," notes that Mister Rogers' ethic is not one-sided:

> Mister Rogers should be understood as proclaiming an ethic of challenge and responsibility. It is an ethic, however, that understands that care of others is not likely to be tendered by those battered into submission or who doubt their own worth.... So the love-ethic that Mister Rogers propounds relies on the edified psyches of his viewers, whose own worth he is constantly affirming [106].[9]

On this interpretation, Mister Rogers promotes a complete ethic with responsibility and care. Guy further notes that some feel threatened by this notion of care. In a 1985 television review in *National Review*, Aram Bakshian writes that the show is a "daily aerial lobotomy" and that the show is a sugar-coated tranquilizer, while Fred Rogers needs "a generous regimen of hormone injections and a spine transplant" (Bakshian 50). Guy notes that this would seem to align the language of care in Mister Rogers with what was discussed above about Gilligan and the different (feminine) voice (Guy 114–15). In other words, Bakshian equates an ethic of care with being effeminate and thus unworthy.[10]

Thinking about Mister Rogers as an adult academic and as a parent, I am convinced that *Mister Rogers' Neighborhood* is an example of how to learn how to be a good person. I am also convinced that caring is an important part of flourishing as a human being. I wish I could go back in time and tell my younger self to keep watching.

NOTES

1. A similar point is made in Paul Zelevansky's "'The Good Thing': Mister Roger's Neighborhood," *The American Journal of Psychoanalysis* 64.2 (2004): 195–208,

when he compares *Mister Rogers' Neighborhood* to *Sesame Street* and in Thomas Norton-Smith and Linda Norton-Smith's "Two Conceptions of the Value of Individuals in Children's Programming," *The Midwest Quarterly* 34.1 (1992): 112–20 when they *compare Mister Rogers' Neighborhood* to *Captain Kangaroo.* Fred Rogers also extended this from television to computer technology in his "Mister Rogers on Kids and Technology." *TECHNOS* 5 (1996): 33–36.

2. See also Stephen D. Perry and Amanda L. Roesch, "He's in a New Neighborhood Now: Religious Fantasy Themes About *Mister Rogers' Neighborhood*," *Journal of Media and Religion* 4.3 (2004): 199–218, Ronald Bishop, "The World's Nicest Grown-Up: A Fantasy Theme Analysis of News Coverage of Fred Rogers," *Journal of Communication* 53.1 (2003): 16–31, T.L. Warburton, "A Visit with Fred Rogers: A Guided Tour Through a Special Neighborhood," *Journal of Popular Film & Television* 16.1 (1988): 32–40, and also the Laskas and Bianculli essays in the Collins and Kimmel collection.

3. For a reassessment of the differences between Kohlberg and Gilligan, see Cindy J.P. Wood's "Gender Differences in Moral Development and Acquisition: A Review of Kohlberg's and Gilligan's Models of Justice and Care." *Social Behavior and Personality* 24.4 (1996): 375–84. Also, a look at the implications of Gilligan's analysis for legal conceptions of the self can be found in Janice Richardson's "The Law and the Sublime: Rethinking the Self and its Boundaries," *Law Critique* 18 (2007): 229–52.

4. A similar idea about the preservation of the species can be found 100 years later in Darwin's *Descent of Man.*

5. This is reminiscent of Freud's discussion of the futility of "love thy neighbor" in *Civilization and its Discontents*, as any love for your neighbor (who may not deserve it) is love not available for those that do. Noddings and Mister Rogers would probably disagree that love is as limited as care is.

6. This is a lesson many parents struggle with—the "any job worth doing is worth doing well" idea.

7. The *Euthyphro*, in particular.

8. For Gilligan's take on edifying psyches, see her "Recovering Psyche: Reflections of Life-History and History." *The Annual of Psychoanalysis* 32 (2004): 131–147.

9. See Sue Matheson's "Good Neighbors, Moral Philosophy and the Masculine Ideal" in this volume for a discussion of Mister Rogers and masculine moral philosophy.

WORKS CITED

Bakshian, Aram, Jr. "Gone with the Wimp." *National Review* 20 Sept. 1985: 49–50. Print.
Bilsker, Richard. *Four Fundamental Questions: An Introduction to Philosophy.* Dubuque: Kendall Hunt, 2011. Print.
Collins, Mark, and Mary Kimmel, eds. *Mister Rogers' Neighborhood: Children, Television, and Fred Rogers.* Pittsburgh: University of Pittsburgh Press, 1996. Print.
Garfield, Bob. "Foreword: Born Again in Rogers." Collins and Kimmel ix–xv.
Gilligan, Carol. *A Different Voice: Psychological Theory and Women's Development.* Cambridge: Harvard University Press, 1982. Print.
Gilligan, Carol, and Jane Attanucci. "Two Moral Orientations." Gilligan, Ward, and Taylor 73–86.
Gilligan, Carol, Janie V. Ward, and Jill M. Taylor, eds. *Mapping the Moral Domain.* Cambridge: Harvard University Press, 1988. Print.

Guy, William. "The Theology of *Mister Rogers' Neighborhood.*" Collins and Kimmel 101–21.

Hume, David. *A Treatise of Human Nature.* Ed. L.A. Selby-Bigge. Oxford: Oxford University Press, 1888. Print.

Johnston, D. Kay. "Adolescents' Solutions to Dilemmas in Fables: Two Moral Orientations—Two Problem Solving Strategies." Gilligan, Ward, and Taylor 49–71.

Lyons, Nona Plessner. "Two Perspectives: On Self, Relationships, and Morality." Gilligan, Ward, and Taylor 21–48.

"Mister Rogers Talks About Love." *Mister Rogers' Neighborhood.* PBS. MPT, Owings Mills. 22–26 Feb. 1993. Television.

Noddings, Nel. *Caring: A Feminine Approach to Ethics and Moral Education.* Berkeley: University of California Press, 1984. Print.

Rogers, Fred. "A Point of View: Family Communication, Television, and *Mister Rogers' Neighborhood.*" *The Journal of Family Communication* 1.1 (2000): 71–73. Print.

_____. *The World According to Mister Rogers: Important Things to Remember.* New York: Hyperion, 2003. Print.

Rousseau, Jean-Jacques. *Discourse on the Origin of Inequality.* Trans. F. Philip. Oxford: Oxford University Press, 2009.

Schopenhauer, Arthur. *On the Basis of Morality.* Trans. E.F.J. Payne. Indianapolis: Hackett, 1995. Print.

_____. *The World as Will and Representation.* Trans. E.F.J. Payne. Vol. 1. Mineola: Dover, 1966. Print.

Slote, Michael. "Autonomy and Empathy." *Social Philosophy and Policy* 21.1 (2004): 293–309. Print.

Zukerman, Eugenia. "Musical Notes: An Interview with Yo-Yo Ma." Collins and Kimmel 79–87.

Community as Emotional Education: Fred Rogers and Edith Stein

PETER R. COSTELLO

> A human being learns best from another human being.
> That's what it means to be a human being.—Fred Rogers

Mister Rogers' Neighborhood is a show defined by and concerned with an ever-broadening definition of the concept "neighborhood."[1] Although the title and opening music of the show always occur against the background of a slow camera pan across what initially appears to be the same, limited number of buildings, it becomes clear, as Mister Rogers visits neighbors who take care of panda bears at the National Zoo in Washington, D.C., or who take him snorkeling in Florida, that what it means to be a neighbor is not something limited to geographical proximity—not limited simply to Pittsburgh or the show's studio set. To be a neighbor for Fred Rogers, on the contrary, is to be involved in doing something that is often rooted in one place but which transcends that location by being both available and beneficial to others.

Whether the neighbor on the screen is Ella Jenkins, Wynton Marsalis, Eric Carle, or Barbara Bingham, however, it is clear that they are not reduced to their studio, practice room, or particular zoo. Instead, their acts and their creative products allow who they are and what they do to reach toward those who take up their recordings, books, or care as models for their own thoughts, play, and work. This kind of transcendence and communal offering is something that gets extended by the way Rogers approaches his visitors and viewers.

Indeed, as I read his show, Rogers' guests are merely particularly salient examples of the kind of life the children who watch his show can develop by means of their attentiveness, imitation, and reflection. For the self-transcendence modeled in the show's guests / neighbors is really aimed at the self-transcendence of the one watching the show, the one Mister Rogers always calls his "television neighbor." For Rogers, the viewer always already has a role in the neighborhood that is not simply one of consumption or of enjoyment. The television neighbor too is engaged in Rogers' educative project—and encouraged by Rogers to bear witness[2] to the larger function the guests on the show demonstrate themselves to hold. To be a neighbor on Rogers' show, then, whether actor or viewer, is not to be passive, but rather to be engaged (or to be invited to be engaged) within a community of people who search for and create meaningful relations by means of expressing and transcending who they are toward one another by means of the kind of work that they find compelling.

In this essay, I will highlight and comment upon this expanded sense of what constitutes a "neighbor" and on the possibility for self-transcendence that is present in a genuine community, such as the one modeled in Rogers' show. And I will attempt to do my part to bear witness to what I have seen in the show both as a child and as an adult. I will attempt to do these things by reading the show in conjunction with Edith Stein's description of community in *Philosophy of Psychology and the Humanities*.

In my reading of her work, I will pay particular attention to how Stein discusses the roles of the individual member and the leader within the community, the way in which communal emotions can be shared as new occurrences in an individual's life, and the way in which community arises not as a copy of some supposed idea of what a perfect community is but as a striving that is generated through the community's own failure to realize itself fully. These three elements—the articulation of roles, the sharing of new emotions, and the striving toward completion out of real failure—are ones I have selected to emphasize because I also witness these three elements occurring across the episodes of Rogers' show. And so I will also work to locate these three elements and to describe them in what I take to be three representative sets of episodes of *Mister Rogers' Neighborhood*.[3]

Throughout the essay, my goal will be to show how Fred Rogers created and communicated to children a sense of community and of neighborhood that embodies Stein's own description of a legitimate leader and a genuine community. In so doing, I hope to promote a renewed interest in Rogers' show as communicating directly to young children the way in which they are and can be capable of building meaningful, affirming lives of potent interaction.[4]

Re-Viewing Mister Rogers' Neighborhood Episodes

Usually, in each half-hour episode of *Mister Rogers' Neighborhood*, the viewer is able to watch Mister Rogers interacting in the "real world" with a person or group of people who carry out some important function, work, or performance. Then, Mister Rogers sits and presses the button for the trolley, which leads the viewer into another episode of the Neighborhood of Make-Believe. Within that land, ruled at least ostensibly by King Friday and Queen Sara, some similar issues, practices, or conflicts as those discussed in the real world are processed or developed. Following the trolley's re-emergence into the "real world" television set, Mister Rogers then processes that viewing experience and leads the viewer through another more personal discussion (he spends time with just his television neighbor, singing a song to each one while looking directly into the camera, etc.).

This triple movement of introducing the viewer to the community at large, then making a transition to an imaginary community that processes the same sort of issue, and then making a final transition to a direct appeal to the viewer's own situation is a kind of ritual. It has elements of a church service, complete with processional and recessional music ("It's a beautiful day" and "It's such a good feeling" begin and end the time spent together every episode). And it locates the viewer in her or his own relationship between self-experience, communal experience, and empathetic intimacy (the viewer and Rogers as a pair).

What Mister Rogers makes a real point of doing with the viewer who watches his show often is to call explicit attention to the way in which the show is itself fabricated as this triple movement. For example, in Episodes 1530 ("Work") and 1546 ("Making Music") Mister Rogers allows the camera to film the show's set, complete with the edges of the "room" and the set band (including Johnny Costa) who forms the musical background. In Episodes 1530 and 1689, Rogers also shows the viewer that he, Rogers, is the voice and animation of at least four of the puppets in the Neighborhood of Make-Believe. In other episodes, Rogers calls attention to the way in which characters from the Neighborhood of Make-Believe, like Betty Aberlin and Bob Trow, are his real neighbors.

By calling attention to the mechanisms of the show, the way the show transitions from real life to make-believe and back to real again, Rogers makes a point of connecting the motions of the show and the motions within the viewer. And he does this in service to the viewer's own ability to maintain their continuity, his or her own capacity to make the transitions.

Unlike the writers and directors of the show *Sesame Street*, which at the time of Big Bird's first appearance on *Mister Rogers' Neighborhood* would not demonstrate the machinery of its illusions, Mister Rogers did not want his viewers to get lost in their own imaginations and their operations as potentially unconnected to the real world in which those viewers lived. Rather, his goals were decidedly to resist escapism and to promote engagement by encouraging the viewer to process both the show and the viewer's own situation.

Educating the viewer by means of the rational machinery of the television set was (for Rogers) part of the efficacy of the Neighborhood of Make-Believe and its applications to events within a family's life.

Roles Within the Community (Ruling as Education)

Although X the Owl models a love for the work of Benjamin Franklin, and although there is generally within the Neighborhood of Make-Believe an emphasis on democratic participation, self-development, and on the value of individuals within Make-Believe and within the themes that Rogers deals with, the Neighborhood of Make-Believe is nevertheless ruled by a king and queen. In particular the king, King Friday, often tends to act rather imperiously and to assume the leadership role for the community, as if he alone were capable of ruling.

This tendency to imperious rule leads Friday to claim, across a number of episodes, that a comet that will shortly arrive is *his* comet. In Episodes 1562 and 1563, however, the viewer sees how the Neighborhood, particularly in the resistance of Lady Elaine, re-educates the king, who is, after all, educable and not simply imperious. No one can own a comet, or another person, says King Friday, who successfully applies his lesson in limitation even to himself and his relation to his son, Prince Tuesday.

Whatever the given political structure of the Neighborhood of Make-Believe, then, what seems to permeate the entire Neighborhood is the way in which education can reshape politics. And the way in which each person has a role to play in the life of the whole. Roles are not simply based on family ties, or on a competence in a particular technological area (as in the case of Miss Polificate). But the importance of each member is felt within the learning that takes place *as a group*.

The same imperious King Friday, one notices, is the one who graciously helps to plan parties for Ana Platypus and Henrietta Pussycat, the one who is disappointed or upset about not being able to control the size of a party or to have a swimming pool for the children, and who, in Episodes 1486–1488, learns about how he cannot in fact ban playing, even as a response to an injury (of Bob Dog).

Friday is complicated, then, and he is open to others to the extent that he permits himself to be. Indeed, he often seems to permit (even against himself) the others to rule in his place, as evidenced by the fact that it is Lady Aberlin or Lady Elaine or Queen Sara or Handyman Negri who regularly, in the instances mentioned above and countless others, demonstrate their resistance or emotional distance from King Friday's decisions or decrees and who, by distancing themselves, help to shift his position from an initial imperious posture to one much more flexible. It is in their efforts, then, that these other members of the community show King Friday that governance is a shared responsibility, one of re-education and re-shaping, and not one given by a title.

Communal Emotions (Music)

One of the recurring themes throughout Rogers' show is that of feeling, expressing, and working through emotions. Often Rogers will talk about what to do with feelings of anger or sadness or disappointment. But he also talks about how to feel special or valuable. Each person's own private emotional life is important to Rogers, and it is important to help each viewer navigate how to express that life.

In Episodes 1546–1550 ("Making Music"), and in particular in his visit with Yo-Yo Ma in Episode 1547, however, Rogers begins to bridge his discussion of what appears to be private and personal (emotions of happiness or sadness) with the communal.[5] It is music, and particular kinds of expressive musical pieces, that allow us to "dig in" and express anger or happiness.[6] Across the many episodes with music as their theme, the viewer of Rogers' show can see that, for Rogers, music is a kind of codified communal emotional life that allows a place for an individual's emotional life within it.[7]

As Episode 1547 concludes, Yo-Yo Ma plays with Joe Negri and they discuss how they like playing together. The guitar and the cello work together to articulate a very basic song ("Tree, Tree, Tree" by Rogers). The viewer is reminded about how Rogers himself has always seen music as something that bridges people, that allows them to feel together toward something else.

"Feeling together toward"—this is a theme that is developed across the years of the show. And in this light the episodes in which the Neighborhood forms an opera are particularly important. Music for Rogers is communal, not primarily individual, and it is not just the province of professionals but also of amateurs. Anyone can sing. And anyone can be invited to sing. A neighborhood opera is the work of everyone.[8]

More than opera, however, jazz is the soundtrack of the show. And in this light, Episode 1546, where Rogers introduces the viewer to the jazz band of the show in an extended interview, should also be considered very important. The call and response, the variational method of jazz, is part of the way in which music for Rogers involves and enriches community and communication. That no introduction or conclusion to the show is ever played in exactly the same way means something: that the community that is musical is never the same twice, is never the form to which individuals must bend themselves. Rather, the very forms of music that Rogers selects—classical, jazz, opera—imply that the community is at stake in the emotional life of the musician and singer, and they give a kind of freedom to the individual to respond and to shape that community if that individual is also free to hear the others with them.[9]

We feel and play and sing together. And in feeling, playing, and singing together we are given back to ourselves: "Let's just sit and think about what we've heard," Rogers reminds the viewer at the end of Episode 1547. Emotional music, emotion as such, leads to reflection, if it is shared in the codified and co-produced movement of the music that expresses it.[10] And it is precisely this spirit of making music together, this engaging in music as the substance of what it sounds, that founds the episodes concerning the bass violin festival, begun rather imperiously by King Friday, in the Neighborhood of Make-Believe.

Music is that which promotes democracy. Music is that which educates by means of requiring people to follow it and allowing them to create within it.

Community as a Striving

In addition to education and to music, a third way in which community appears within the Neighborhood of Make-Believe is as a striving together towards more equitable, more adequate relationships. To the extent that the episodes of Rogers' show, and of the Neighborhood of Make-Believe within it, can show this striving, it is of course rudimentary and partial. For it is clear that the puppets and the adults who speak to them are attempting to be able to be understood by very young children, who are themselves not quite sure about their own capacities. Nevertheless, the work of being a community, and becoming a better one, is visible across a number of episodes, and it involves children in its content.[11]

In Episode 1508, two of the members, the two friends X the Owl and Henrietta Pussycat, are having a difficult time with each other. They are trying to make a fruit salad with Lady Aberlin for the Royal Picnic. What comes between them is the way in which X becomes bossy through asserting his "expertness" from his OCS cookbook, and the way in which Henrietta's anger overwhelms her. Within Lady Aberlin's mediation, however, the two friends are able to desire to "try again" to be together, to make a salad together out of different fruits. What is embraced by both trying again is not just the possibility of successful community but also the possibility of failure, the possibility of fighting and of feeling emotions that would again tear each other out of intimacy. Nevertheless, and without shutting down the ambiguity involved in trying again, it is precisely this "trying again" that refocuses all three on the salad and the picnic—and on the possibility not just of being friends yesterday and tomorrow but today, now, by means of the friendship being visible within (and important to) the larger community.[12]

Episodes 1528–1530 ("Work") feature the neighborhood trying to work together to build a swimming pool. The shortage of money that King Friday has necessitates that they take turns digging the hole for the pool. A broken pipe then prevents the neighborhood from having the pool, since they have only limited resources and need to decide to replace the pipes instead of putting in a pool—so that they have enough clean water. Episode 1529 shows Queen Sara asking for the entire neighborhood to be consulted, and, because of that, the neighborhood children are asked for their opinion while they are at the school in Someplace Else. The children come up with the idea to fix the pipes with the swimming pool money.

As they finish discussing the way in which the neighborhood could approach the broken pipe, Ana Platypus, dressed as Abraham Lincoln, says in a brief answer to Harriet Cow's question about the Gettysburg address, that Lincoln was thinking about the families who were sad and how he wanted to be with each family, comforting them. It is this heartfelt moment of recognition—the context of a small disappointment occurring within a history of a community striving to respond to each member in the midst of its own failures—that then allows Mister Rogers to make something more important out of a rather ordinary disappointment.

Stein on Community—Roles, Emotion and Striving

The Roles of the Leader and of the Members

For Stein, a community is "the natural, organic union of individuals" (Stein 130). Such a union is not simply "rational or mechanical" as that sort of union would more properly be called an association—something like a trade union. But rather the community, while using reason, functions by each member approaching the other "as a subject": "where the subject accepts the other as a subject and does not confront him but rather lives with him and is determined by the stirrings of his life, they are forming a community with one another" (130). A community, in contrast to an association, then, focuses on each of its members as having a locus of action, of thought, of determination that should be considered. A community shares a common life by allowing the life of each one to be open to the life of every other. Members of a community are "co-determined" by what stirs up the lives of the other members.[13]

What this means is that the emotions, the desires, the decisions of each one's life matter to the others in a community. It is not enough to will a mechanized system of the representation of everyone's interests (as in a republic). It is not enough to live together while permitting each one to develop her or his talents. Rather, a community grows a common life by means of the lives of others mattering. Others are not simply interests or votes. They are lives that stir, that strive, that are not alone.[14]

In Stein's metaphysics of community, each member has a definite role that she or he helps to shape. This role cannot simply be controlled by one person. Stein makes a point of this inability of rulers to shape communities when she contrasts the "demagogue" with "the community man" (131). The community person or leader acts "ingenuously, without calculating the effects of his demeanor, and artlessly receives impressions without initiating surveillance" (131). The community leader "gives herself over" to the members' "inwardness" and artlessly yields to it (131).

The leader of a community, then, does not have a prefabricated idea of what the community is for, or what shapes of life will evolve within it. The leader sees the community as a shared project that externalizes itself out of the members' work at self-expression. The leader of a community, then, sees herself "at the service of the people out of a natural predisposition" and has to "study the people in order to be able to guide them correctly" (132). Community then is about education. One must study, one must learn—and the people must come to express themselves in ever richer ways in order for the one who gives himself or herself over to the community to be able to take on a function, perhaps even one that is less pronounced than the members might like.

To be in community is to be in a process of educating oneself by educating another. To be in a community is to be where a leader does not see herself as given a set of skills but rather a commitment to remain educable and able to guide members to a greater sense of their own stirrings, strivings, and commitments.

Emotions

One of Stein's most important descriptions of community comes in her description of the loss of a leader of a military unit. In the community of the members of that unit, the grief felt is not simply of a personal nature. Rather, there is a grief, perhaps in addition to the personal ones, that is shared, that is "ours": "I feel myself not to be alone with it. Rather, I feel it as *our* grief…. We are affected by the loss, and we grieve over it" (134). To be in community, to be open to the stirrings and life of others, is to be brought within an experience that is of a fundamentally different level or layer than individual experience, it is to feel something different, to feel toward something that we share far more prominently than bread, water, danger, or success. Such a feeling on behalf of the community does not erase one's own capacity for feeling. One is oneself claimed by the feeling—not erased by it. But the feeling nevertheless is not simply one's own either. Stein writes,

> And this "we" embraces not only all those who feel the grief as I do, but all those who are included in the unity of the group: even ones who perhaps do not know

of the event, and even the members of the group who lived earlier or will live later.... I grieve as a member of the unit, and the unit grieves within me [134].

Within a community, then, my role shifts by virtue of my openness. I stand as a member with responsibilities that take me far beyond my own present involvement. My openness means that I no longer end at the boundaries of my emotion. My co-determination means that I feel toward others who share the self-definition of the community.

Stein therefore defines community as shaped by the internal lives of the members who begin to educate themselves by means of their emotions. Community life is education, emotional education, and the emotions people experience as community members move them toward something that they would never have had access to by themselves: "an intention *toward* the communal experience is inherent within the experiences that are directed toward a super-individual object.... We feel the grief as something belonging to the unit, and in the fact that we're doing that, through this grief we're calling for the grief of the unit to be realized" (137, emphasis mine). To be communal is to feel differently, and to ask oneself what it means to feel what one is feeling together with others.

Who is the arbiter of communal feelings? Who can exhaust the meaning of the shared grief, joy, etc.? No one by herself. Neither all together. The life of the community develops on its own by means of concrete, objective feelings that are shared. In shared emotional life, all members are moved toward the whole that is never all at once in front of oneself. The community's members past, present, and future all are at stake in the emotion as it is lived directly here and now. Around the process of emotional education, then, lies the members in their future lives and future relations.

The child is parent to the adult. And that kind of "pre-maturation" occurs in the very sharing of the emotional life of others.[15]

Striving

Perhaps the most poignant example Stein offers of community striving to form itself is in her discussion of "an experience like the suffering of a conquered people" (143). Prescient in its import, this discussion in the middle of her description of community enables the reader to reflect upon how Stein's major insights concerning the metaphysics of community occurs within its breakdown.

To stand as a member of a community within the experience of being conquered, being dominated by suffering or dissolution, is to experience something "so vast that the lone human being stands before it as before something immense and incomprehensible" (143). The dissolution of community, then, is an experience that the community can have. And it places the single human being within an experience of aloneness that does not make sense, that is incomprehensible, given that it is both alone *and shared*.

To be a member of a community in a concentration camp, for example, or to be a child in an abusive home or family, is to become the bearer of communal incomprehensibility. How did we get to this point? Who are we in this suffering? The questions appear in the very faces of those who stand so close together and yet so far apart.

And yet, grieving and lost, these experiences mark out community not as something mechanized, rational, and achieved through steps. Rather, as an indication of the way communities are formed, this collective suffering shows that the "individual experiences that are constitutive for a communal experience ... *target* the communal experience and tend to *try* to encompass it" (144). To experience being conquered, to experience dissolution, is not to undo community but rather to reveal the principle of community's own being—namely the "targeting" and the "trying" of individuals to form together a unity that can withstand difficulty, doubt, and dissolution.

This discussion of striving and its relation to community is even more clearly discussed by Stein when she emphasizes the possibility (or impossibility) of *genuine* community. For Stein, members of a community have "an inclination to reach out beyond themselves toward a complete unification" (285). But the "image" that founds this inclination "can't be achieved by any earthly community—can't in principle and not just accidentally" (285). Where then has this image come from? And what is its status if the members of a community know in advance that the image they are striving toward is impossible?

Stein gives one main hint: the image does not come from on high, but rather as the result of what the community has already been able to achieve. The image of complete unification comes from the success already achieved in addressing the very deep and problematic tension between being a singular person and one who feels on behalf of others: "the possibility of complete community becomes insightfully given on the basis of what *can* be achieved in the midst of the earthly community toward overcoming absolute loneliness" (285). This means, I take it, that the idea of genuine community is ours alone, only ours, and it arises as something that can be further developed, that can further educate us. It arises as a response to our yearning to pursue the knot of individuality and communal life. It arises as the very image of our striving together.

Rogers and Stein Together (A Musical Number)

At first glance, and contrary to what I have been developing here, there might seem to be nothing to Rogers' show that is not, in Stein's words, an "association." Viewers of *Mister Rogers' Neighborhood* could be passive, disconnected, and too young to remember or to process deeply what occurs in thirty minutes on a screen. In fact, as much as Rogers wanted to call his viewer his "neighbor" and "friend," his very attempt at intimacy was surely fraught with empty promises—for there was never just one viewer, and none of the neighbors could claim to be synchronous with Rogers or to have him hear them.

Thus, the project of *Mister Rogers' Neighborhood* might seem to be more aligned with what Stein would call an "association" or a "mass." The viewers were always anonymous and replaceable. If this were true, then Fred Rogers would be a demagogue or merely someone who knew how to manipulate children into feeling good about spending thirty minutes a day in front of a screen and aligning their inner lives with Rogers' own idiosyncratic imagination. Rogers could not be open to and moved by the stirrings of anonymous viewers. The viewers were only "there" virtually.

But that would be to miss what actually occurred for those of us who watched (and still watch) the show. And it would be to misconstrue the role not just of Fred Rogers but also of the music and introductions to persons and practices that the show offered.

Rogers did not mobilize viewers to do anything but reflect on their own emotions, relationships, and self-development. And he did this by means of introducing viewers to art, music, work, and education. So often, by drawing our attention to the works and the workers, Rogers permitted viewers to focus not on him but on a work of art. And in doing so, he allowed the viewer to feel how their "admiration lays a claim that the artwork be given its due" and how their "experience calls for the experience of the community to be engaged and reproduced in itself" (Stein 165). When Rogers would look into the camera and tell the viewer that Barbara Bingham used to go to the zoo when she was a child, when he would ask Yo-Yo Ma what music he played when he was angry—there Rogers was allowing the viewer to become educated as to the experience and the process of emotional life. You can develop your relations as neighbors to one another, and to yourself, Rogers was implying, if you too enjoy what these people do and then take the time to build up a life worthy of sharing with others.

Thus, to the extent that it was possible, Rogers did not simply entertain with his neighborhood. Rather he initiated "a thinking-together" that would be experienced as "*our* common thinking" (Stein 170). To think about one's anger with Rogers would be to remember his song "What Do You Do With The Mad That You Feel?"—it would be to think about how to limit harm while feeling one's anger. And the kind of opening for "one's own contribution" would occur on the basis of what Rogers offered as an educative step.

By turning to the camera in the final parts of the show and addressing each viewer as if their individual lives mattered, as if he were responding directly to each one as a singular person, Rogers modeled what he could not achieve. He modeled the treatment of each person as a subject that a community requires if it is to be genuine, life-affirming, and self-transcending. In this way, he modeled the very notion of striving. Of course a genuine community could not be created through television. Nor should it be. But those of us who watched and still value Rogers' commitments, through acts of writing such as these in this volume, can see that the very image of neighborhood that he created still resounds in our hearing of Costa's musical arrangements. The image that Rogers created is an image borne out of what he really was able to achieve—and in a time before the bewildering multiplicity of cable television and the loss of a sense of common ground.

The image of the neighborhood on Rogers' show was one that was never meant to be self-referential only; it was always one that we were to take out and reshape, reflect on, and rebuild. The image of Rogers' neighborhood, then, to return to Stein's definition, is organic—and it is in danger of being lost by virtue of Rogers' passing. But this fragility is a testament to its genuineness. Any military unit or any family is in danger of being lost when its leaders die. This fragility is even something rooted in Rogers' particular vision and in the particular way in which he made the effort to highlight the works and days that he did. Community is not an address of loss. It *is loss.*

Rogers' vision is not really compromised by the passing away of the leader of the group of us who assigned our emotional lives to its classroom. It is attempting to confirm itself. But there is a very real danger—and the real danger lies in the possibility that no one else steps forward, that the members do not sense the imminence of the demand. The danger is in the very growing of the associational mechanisms of our life now within a society that is further away from shared values and from education as the very definition of community.

Certainly Fred Rogers lived by what Stein asserts as the mechanism of community within a structure of given leadership: "even when I'm sweeping the other guy along toward an action he wouldn't be capable of on his own, he's still got to commit himself to my influence" (193). We were given an opportunity to commit to Rogers, and remain committed to Rogers' influence not because of his power but because of his invitation to see his show as a springboard to self-development. It is *because* he saw himself as one who could disappear from view in order for the neighborhood to become what was real—it is because we knew this, I suspect, that those of us who took up what he sang and said did what we did.

To this day, those of us who began our lives with regular viewings of his show, and who defined ourselves by means of its music and values, see Rogers and each other within a shared set of values and commitments. We are a generation of viewers who have a "zone of reciprocal understanding" (Stein 206) that makes community possible. This was of course visible at his acceptance speech for his lifetime television award, and it was represented for us by the man (to us also the child) in his wheelchair who said to Rogers what Rogers had said all along to us "It's You I Like."

For Rogers, community, being a neighbor, was always "founded essentially in individuals" (Stein 238). His movement into mass media was done by breaking with the very mechanisms of that media. What Rogers achieved with us was a process of education that was enjoyable, that spoke and sang in ways that functioned as the touchstones of memory. And in this process of education, the "genuine being of the community" shone through (Stein 263).

Community for Rogers and for us was rooted in the "further evolution of the common mind" (Stein 263), a mind that was musical, literary, focused on work and relationships. Community for Rogers was the very notion that education was what each person required in order to feel toward others, in order to move toward others. Community was the tension between being alone, between him not being able to see or hear us, and becoming together by means of playing alongside each other, on behalf of each other in the future, when we would meet on the basis of our striving to make real what most mattered—how to live well.

We could not know it then, but those of us who viewed him were an opera: One that was both work and music. We were becoming the kinds of persons who could treat each other as subjects, who could live together by means of shared projects, who could maintain individuality while being together even in the midst of great pain. It's such a good feeling to know that we can try again. It's such a good feeling to remember that Rogers always opened with a question, an appeal: to be asked, to be invited—not just to come and play but to *be* a neighbor.

NOTES

1. For a philosophical development of the notion of neighbor see Karol Wojtyla's *The Acting Person.* See also "Pope John Paul II's Participation in the Neighborhood of Phenomenology" by Costello in Billias, Curry, and McLean (2008).

2. See John Russon's *Bearing Witness to Epiphany* for an excellent philosophical discussion of how consciousness develops itself by means of its ability to bear witness to its own creative powers of synthesis and relation. Of particular importance is Russon's focus on desire and erotic commitment.

3. These episodes are currently available on Amazon prime videos or through the website of Family Communications. I have included episode numbers for easy reference.

4. This essay thus takes up the argument of my two articles on children's literature: the one on Arnold Lobel's *Frog and Toad Are Friends* and the other on Russell Hoban's *The Mouse and His Child.* In both of these, I work to show how children in

these stories are addressed by means of the relationships described—in both what I take to be operative is a combination of Maurice Merleau-Ponty's arguments in "The Child's Relations With Others" and of D. W. Winnicott's discussion of play in *Playing and Reality.*

5. See the work of Kym Maclaren for an excellent development of emotions as intercorporeal and intersubjective. In particular see "Life is Inherently Expressive."

6. Fred Rogers: "Music is the one art we all have inside. We may not be able to play an instrument, but we can sing along or clap or tap our feet" (2003, 18).

7. I am indebted for my thinking about music to Licia Carlson. See her excellent article on the children's book *Are You My Mother?* in *Philosophy in Children's Literature,* 2011.

8. Fred Rogers: "as you play together in a symphony orchestra, you can appreciate that each musician has something fine to offer. Each one is different, though, and you each have a different 'song to sing.' When you sing together, you make one voice. That's true of all endeavors, not just musical ones" (*The World According to Mister Rogers,* 154).

9. See John Russon's *Human Experience,* chapter one, and *Bearing Witness,* "The Music of Everyday Life," for an important discussion of music as indicative and exemplary of the human ability to synthesize, to make sense. See also my book *Layers in Husserl's Phenomenology* for an extended treatment of jazz as the music of intersubjectivity.

10. Fred Rogers: "It's important to know when we need to stop, reflect, and receive" (*The World According to Mister Rogers,* 129).

11. The work of Thomas Wartenberg in *Big Ideas for Little Kids* as well as that of Gareth Matthews and Matthew Lippman across their careers demonstrates the principles of Rogers' work as it relates to philosophy. Children are already "partners in inquiry" as Matthews argues, and they should be treated as having critically important responses to literature or philosophical issues.

12. Fred Rogers on events after September 11, 2001: "I'm so grateful to you for helping the children in your life to know that you'll do everything you can to keep them safe and to help them express their feelings in ways that will bring healing in many different neighborhoods" (*The World According to Mister Rogers,* 173).

13. For more background on the issue of community in Stein, and on Stein's work in general, I suggest reading the work of Marianne Sawicki and Antonio Calcagno. Both are substantial Stein scholars; Sawicki, in particular, is responsible for Stein's prominence in philosophy circles in North America. I have included relevant pieces of theirs in the works cited.

14. See Nick Longo's *Why Community Matters* for an excellent discussion of the role of neighborhood community, especially in the chapter entitled "The Neighborhood Learning Community."

15. For a discussion of how children are pre-mature, please see a beautiful article by Maurice Merleau-Ponty entitled "The Child's Relations with Others." It pairs well with Rogers' own work on the "archaeology of emotions" in his *World According to Mister Rogers.*

Works Cited

Baseheart, Mary Catherine. "Edith Stein's Philosophy of Community." *Personalist Forum* 8 (1992): 163–173.

Borden, Sarah. *Outstanding Christian Thinkers: Edith Stein.* London: Continuum Press, 2003.

Calcagno, Antonio. "Thinking Community and the State from Within." *American Catholic Philosophical Quarterly* 82:31–45.

Carlson, Licia. "Are You My Mother? Finding the Self in (M)others." *Philosophy in Children's Literature*. Ed. Peter Costello. Lanham: Lexington Books, 2011. 63–82.

Costello, Peter. *Layers in Husserl's Phenomenology: On Meaning and Intersubjectivity*. Toronto: University of Toronto Press, 2012.

_____. *Philosophy in Children's Literature*. Lanham: Lexington Books, 2011.

_____. "Pope John Paul II's 'Participation' in the 'Neighborhood' of Phenomenology." *Karol Wojtyla's Philosophical Legacy*. Ed. Nancy Mardas Billias, Agnes B. Curry, and George F. McLean. Washington, D.C.: Council for Research in Values and Philosophy, 2008. 45–60.

Jacobson, Kirsten. "Heidegger, Winnicott and *The Velveteen Rabbit*: Anxiety, Toys, and the Drama of Metaphysics." *Philosophy and Children's Literature*. Ed. Peter Costello. Lanham: Lexington Books, 2011. 1–20.

Longo, Nicholas. *Why Community Matters: Connecting Education with Civic Life*. Albany: SUNY Press, 2007.

Maclaren, Kym. "Life Is Inherently Expressive: A Merleau-Pontian Response to Darwin's *The Expression of Emotions*." *Chiasmi International* 7(2005): 241–61.

Merleau-Ponty, Maurice. "The Child's Relations with Others." In *Primacy of Perception*. Chicago: Northwestern University Press, 1964.

Nancy, Jean-Luc. *The Inoperative Community*. Minneapolis: University of Minnesota Press, 1991.

Rogers, Fred. *The World According to Mister Rogers: Important Things to Remember*. New York: Hyperion, 2003.

Russon, John. *Bearing Witness to Epiphany: Persons, Things, and the Nature of Erotic Life*. Albany: SUNY Press, 2009.

_____. *Human Experience: Philosophy, Neurosis, and the Elements of Everyday Life*. Albany: SUNY Press, 2003.

Sawicki, Marianne. *Body, Text, and Science: The Literacy of Investigative Practices and the Phenomenology of Edith Stein*. Dordrecht: Kluwer Academic Publishers, 1997.

Stein, Edith. *Philosophy of Psychology and the Humanities*. Washington, D.C.: ICS Publications, 2000.

Wartenberg, Thomas. *Big Ideas for Little Kids: Teaching Philosophy Through Children's Literature*. Lanham: Rowman & Littlefield, 2009.

_____. *A Sneetch Is a Sneetch: Finding Wisdom in Children's Literature*. London: Wiley-Blackwell, 2013.

Winnicott, D. W. *Playing and Reality*. London, Routledge, 2005.

Structure and Story
in the Operas

MAURA GRADY

Mister Rogers' Neighborhood had many things in common with its television predecessors and contemporaries in the 1960s—local and regional variety shows like *Captain Kangaroo, Bozo the Clown, Romper Room, The Shari Lewis Show, The Howdy Doody Show, Princess Pat's Storybook Castle,* and the show's predecessor, *The Children's Corner* (Rowe 105, Hollis 35, 17). Most of these shows featured a congenial host, regular visiting guests, puppets and direct engagement with the television audience. Many scholars and critics have detailed the ways in which Fred Rogers very consciously set out to create a unique program based on the latest and most trusted work by child psychologists, such as D.W. Winnicott (Nancy Curry Oral History),[1] that would not only entertain children, but also comfort and educate them. Rogers' use of transitions, make-believe, and practical, down-to-earth lessons have also been documented (Curry, Townley, Linn, Friedrich Cofer), as has Rogers' use of his own compositions, performed by the cast of players and puppets and accompanied by the show's music director, jazz pianist John Costa (Laskas, Zukerman, Murray Zoba).

But one of the most remarkable innovations unique to Rogers' show is his use of opera to tell stories that teach his familiar lessons of empathy, cooperation, and growth, but that also could introduce children to a classical art form only rarely produced for television. Rogers composed thirteen episode-length original operas ("Mr. Speedy Delivery Talks")[2] for the series.[3] The first of these, "Babysitter Opera," was produced in 1968 and featured baritone John Reardon, who would star in all but one of the subsequent operas. This opera featured Mister Rogers dressed in a top hat and cape, demonstrating the use of opera glasses and depicted people attending a staged opera performance by the puppets (Neighborhood Archive Ep. 0045).[4] Several of the songs performed would become part of the regular repertoire of the series, such as "I'm Taking Care of You" and "Tree Tree Tree," while others ("It's Hard to Say Goodbye" and "I'm Missing Someone Badly") were performed only in this instance and one other time, respectively (Neighborhood Archive Ep. 0045). Throughout the series, Mister Rogers continued to innovate and exercise his talent for music and whimsy with the operas, which departed from the simplicity of "Babysitter Opera" to feature unique sets, costumes, and characters as well as a fully integrated musical play with original music unique to the episode.

While a number of these operas are now available for streaming via Amazon.com and PBS.org, only two operas are available with their full week of lead-in episodes, 1980's "Windstorm in Bubbleland" and 1984's "A Granddad for Daniel."

Viewed within the context of Rogers' experience in music, television, and televised opera in its early years, the series "Windstorm in Bubbleland" is a shining example of the fusion of Mister Rogers' talents to convey the lessons of cooperation, empathy, and personal growth, as well as introduce children to a classical art form in a unique-for-television format.

One of Rogers' first television work experiences was in the earliest televised opera productions. After graduating from Rollins in 1951 with a bachelor of music degree, Rogers had planned to go to seminary right away, but in his senior year he went home for a vacation and saw television for the first time. Rogers says he then applied for "any position" at NBC and he was accepted to "work on the music programs" starting in October 1951 (Fred Rogers Interview).

In a 1999 interview, Rogers explained one of his first television jobs was as a floor manager for *NBC Opera Theatre*, noting that composer Giancarlo Menotti was

> [i]nvited to write an opera for the NBC Theatre.... They wanted a Christmas opera and so Menotti actually wrote it for the *NBC Opera Theatre*. After the dress rehearsal Toscanini said to Menotti in Italian, "this is the best you've ever done." And of course, *Amahl and the Night Visitors* continues on stage ... even puppet theatres have done it and done it well [Fred Rogers Interview].

Rogers left commercial television for public broadcasting and in 1971 founded Family Communications to produce his show ("About Us"), largely because he didn't want to abuse power to influence viewers, noting,

> Radio began as a vehicle to broadcast classical music. Television in the early days was doing the same thing. Until television became such a tool for selling, it was a fabulous medium for education. That's what I had always hoped it would be [Fred Rogers Interview].

In this interview, he describes the duties of a floor manager: "I timed programs ... we had to get off the air at just the right second or else we'd be cut off the air … we had seven or eight sets" in the studio (Fred Rogers Interview). This sense of timing followed him in his work in public television, where he was known for his insistence on precise repetition of the rehearsed material. Like his colleague, jazz pianist John Costa, Rogers was a skilled improviser (as has been noted in his work on *The Children's Hour*) but chose to be precise in the filming of his shows. One way in which he brought careful preparation to the show was via his use of music, the importance of which he frequently discussed on air, especially noting how music can be used to express emotions like anger and sadness (Episode 1740 is one of many examples).

In interviews, Fred Rogers frequently discussed the importance of music in his work, and in the above interview he relayed that his very first instruments were a pump organ and later a Hammond organ, the sounds of which feature heavily in his operas, as well as in the usual music for his show. While many children's television shows feature musical acts and interludes, Rogers' experience in early television opera was no doubt an influence on him, as he saw what might be possible working within a tightly scripted and precisely timed studio opera event. Unlike the earliest opera for television, Rogers had the advantage of an ensemble cast familiar with his methods, as well as tape and editing options not available in the early days of televised opera when programs were broadcast live from the studio.

In one of the few extended studies of the genre of "television opera," *Television Opera: The Fall of Opera Commissioned for Television*, Jennifer Barnes notes that the first opera commissioned for television was Menotti's *Amahl and the Night Visitors* in 1951 on the *NBC Opera Theatre*, where Rogers worked. Olin Downes, music critic for the *New York Times*, in writing about *Amahl* first used the term "television opera" to describe an opera commissioned for television, and not one that was a live relay from the opera house or live broadcast of a previously performed opera on television, whether live or recorded (Barnes 2). Rogers' operas followed the trend in early operas to emphasize, if not realistic stories and settings, realistic style in terms of the camera work and effects (Barnes 8).

Barnes discusses the question of categorization and the quality judgments attached to what has variously been called "television opera" and / or "opera for television." Barnes notes that "by 1971, the Television Opera was perceived by many as an opera dominated by television techniques and, in ways never fully specified, compromised by its television origins" (Barnes 2). While some, such as Jack Bornoff, argued that television opera only qualified for the title if it *could not* be adapted for the stage, others have disputed this categorization and indeed some of the most famous operas commissioned for television would not fit this definition.

An early example of the challenges presented by translating theatrical, live opera to the television format as it existed before home recording and home video is that of Benjamin Britten's *Billy Budd* in 1952. *Billy Budd*'s nearly three-hour onstage running time was a challenge for the expectations of television audiences. Nevertheless, a successful version was eventually staged effectively as "Scenes from *Billy Budd*." Britten's willingness to experiment, even if he wasn't always satisfied with the results, led to other composers being willing to consider television. According to the *New York Times* "opera index," Britten "often worked outside opera's conventional boundaries, *writing operas for children*, for the church, *and even for television*" (emphasis mine, "The 20th Century"[5]). The dismissive judgment signaled in "even for television" illustrates the general assumption that opera is not naturally an art form that lends itself to children's television entertainment. *Mister Rogers' Neighborhood* was self-consciously innovative in a number of thematic and formal ways, and Rogers' use of opera was consistent with that innovation. Like early practitioners (Barnes 79), Rogers eschewed lip-synching to playback in favor of live performance for the cameras. Indeed, director John Lloyd Davis commented that for a television opera to succeed, the creator would need to be a "composer, librettist, director, designer, lighting designer, and conductor all rolled into one" (Barnes 100). Rogers' near-total artistic control over his show suggests a reason for the success of the opera format on *Mister Rogers' Neighborhood.*

Peter Herman Adler, under whose direction of *NBC Opera Theatre* Fred Rogers worked (Fred Rogers Interview),[6] speculated in *Opera for Television* about a future of operas developed specifically for television, favoring operas broadcast from the studio over those performed live, such was the promise of the early years of television and its power to expand and revolutionize older art forms such as music, theatre and opera. While Barnes argues that television opera "neither formed an artistic identity nor established distinguishing characteristics" (97), Rogers' operas succeed because they make use of television techniques, but keep the effects simple. "Windstorm in Bubbleland" uses television monitors on the stage, first to imitate a TV newsroom, and later to connect Hildegarde Hummingbird via television monitor with the Bubblewitness News team who plead (through the television) for her to return to them. In "Spoon Mountain," television's shooting and editing capabilities allow the use of an elaborate mountain set, as well as the "magic" of entering a door standing alone on the mountain and finding a huge room inside (a sleight of hand trick employed on contemporary shows such as *Doctor Who* and *I Dream of Genie*). "Star for Kitty" uses perhaps fewer TV tricks, but the format of television allows for multiple locations to be used in quick succession without the need to break the action for a scene change.

While any of Rogers' operas *might* be adapted for the stage for new performers, and could make a fun afternoon of entertainment for children in new venues, any contemporary production of one of the Neighborhood operas would lack the guiding hand (and voice) of Mister Rogers. In all operas save "Spoon Mountain," Mister Rogers' voice is featured via the puppets (especially Lady Elaine and Daniel Striped Tiger). "Spoon Mountain" is notably the only one of the thirteen operas in which the puppets do not appear. Moreover, unlike other well-known composers that have translated operas from their stage format to the TV studio, Rogers envisioned the episode-length performances specifically for his show's format and for the cast of actors and singers with whom he worked regularly. The young audience's familiarity with them was key to maintaining the simplicity of each opera's message. The low-tech effects, costumes, and make-up may of course have been employed for budgetary reasons, but it is far more likely that Rogers chose them to ease the transition from "standard episode" to "opera" so that the children watching would not be confused or disoriented. The transition to an entirely new story with unknown characters, plot, and setting is greatly eased through the use of familiar cast members, puppets, instruments, as well as through Mister Rogers' bookending introduction and concluding remarks framing the opera's story and its characters.

Though usually referred to as "Windstorm in Bubbleland," Episode 1475 aired on Friday, May 23, 1980, with the title card "Mister Rogers Makes an Opera" and was preceded by four episodes (Monday-Thursday), which featured themes culminating in the Friday show, as was typical for the show's weekly format, but with a longer rehearsal period ("Chuck Aber Oral History").[7] Chuck Aber, who sang in "Spoon Mountain," "A Star for Kitty," "Granddad for Daniel" and "Josephine the Short-Necked Giraffe," notes the cast would rehearse two or three days for each opera, as opposed to a quick run-through of songs featured in a regular episode ("Chuck Aber Oral History").

While the opera episodes differ from the "usual" *Mister Rogers* episode structure, they still adhere to some basic guidelines for successful children's programming, including use of a simple, linear storyline that conveys a clear message to the audience. Screenwriter Brooks Wachtel boasts over 100 screenwriting credits, with a number of those for PBS series *Liberty Kids* and *Clifford the Big Red Dog* and other childrens' programming. He argues screenwriting for children must keep to a simple, B follows A storyline, meaning that the "B story is the emotional story that is affected by the plot of the A story" (Wachtel), should use age appropriate language and should "avoid subtext [because] kids say what they mean and what they feel in direct and straightforward ways" (Wachtel).

In the first of the "Windstorm in Bubbleland" episodes, the audience is told that Reardon is working on an opera. In conversation with Handyman Negri, Lady Elaine says she wants to participate and play a Hummingbird named Hildegarde who will "pop bubbles"—this is Lady Elaine's symbolic role, as she "bursts the bubble" of Bubble Land and its vision of unchanging perfection. Negri tries to come up with a role to play himself. Francois Clemmons wants to be a Porpoise. Miss Paulificate wants to be a blower of bubbles. Mister Rogers sums up the episode saying, "Bubbles don't last very long but they're beautiful while they're here."

In this pre-opera four-episode arc, Rogers encourages the audience members to imagine roles for themselves if they were writing an opera. After asking each person to think about what he or she might like to pretend to be, he connects imaginative play where each person can pretend to be something different with love and being loved by stating, "we all need to be loved." Before segueing into one of his standard tunes ("It's You I Like"), he develops this sentiment with this explanation:

> Every person that you see in this world needs to be loved. And the marvelous thing about being human is that while we're very much alike, each one of us is very different. Isn't it great that we can care about each other the way we do?

The second episode of the arc, "Makes an Opera" #2 or "How People Make Sweaters," starts with Mister Rogers showing a photo of his mother who made by hand all the sweaters he wears on television. He then visits Bob Trow, who has a sweater machine at his workshop, where he also has a bubble machine. The Neighborhood of Make-Believe segment features Reardon receiving a new sweater from Lady Aberlin. King Friday says he likes his operas on Fridays, leading the audience to understand how long they will have to wait. Rogers frequently reminded children that although waiting is hard to do, they can learn to do it without being frustrated, often singing "Let's Think of Something to Do While We're Waiting."

In the episode "Makes an Opera" #3 or The Story of 'Bubble Trouble'" (Episode 1471), Mister Rogers introduces a synthesizer that he has in his front room and shows the variation in sounds that imitate various instruments, encouraging the audience to identify the different instrument sounds just by listening. Rogers sings "Look Carefully, Listen Carefully" explaining that grown-ups like to play too. As in #2, #3 offers the cast members an opportunity to show that they are talented in their usual milieu, but also capable and willing to participate in the Neighborhood ensemble. For example, in this episode Francois Clemmons (who was frequently featured as "Officer Clemmons," a police officer in the Neighborhood of Make-Believe and as the owner of a music and dance studio in *Mister Rogers' Neighborhood*) sings "There's a Boat That's Leaving Soon for New York" from Gershwin's American opera *Porgy and Bess* with accompaniment from John Costa. This choice demonstrates Clemmons' training and experience as a performer on Broadway and at the Metropolitan Opera Studio and foregrounds his position as an African-American performer of classical American music. Throughout his long career, Clemmons performed the role of "Sportin' Life" in *Porgy and Bess* over 100 times, his 1973 recording of the role on London Records with the Cleveland Orchestra winning a Grammy Award ("Francois Clemmons Sings"), and he founded the Harlem Spiritual Ensemble, a group dedicated to performing, preserving, and commissioning American Negro spirituals. In his professional career outside of *Mister Rogers' Neighborhood*, he was inspired to reach out to all types of people and to unite them in a love of music.

According to a story about his retirement on Middlebury College's website, Clemmons "wanted the music to unite and invigorate the singers in a glorious shared experience. Clemmons unwittingly made himself an impromptu ambassador of campus diversity" ("Francois Clemmons Sings"). In a 2012 interview with Guy Hutchison on the *Adventure Club Extra* Podcast, Clemmons notes that he was touring with Fred Rogers doing children's concerts and that because the children's concerts were over by the evening, he was able to attend many theater, orchestral, and operatic performances in the cities they visited. He says, "After a few years of doing this, I said to Fred [Rogers], why in the world aren't there any Black choral organizations specializing in Negro Spirituals?" (Interview with Dr. Francois Clemmons). Clemmons notes that he formed just such a group, the Harlem Spiritual Ensemble, in the 1980s and worked with Mister Rogers' management to coordinate the touring schedule of his group with his appearances on and performances associated with *Mister Rogers' Neighborhood*. Then, in 1991, Mister Rogers visited a rehearsal of the HSE on an episode of the show (Harlem Spiritual Ensemble).

To help create his opera character, Chef Brockett makes recipes with bananas, including Banana Boat Sundae. This choice ties in with both Clemmons' "There's a Boat That's Leaving Soon" performance as well as Brockett's role in the opera as Banana Boat Captain. A visit to the Neighborhood of Make-Believe finds Lady Aberlin and Reardon describing costumes and the plot for the opera to King Friday, who congratulates them on having "a lot figured out already." Lady Aberlin agrees but then urges the others in a leading suggestion: "We need a way to put all [the elements] together." This show uses its entertaining segments to encourage the audience to think creatively. In the *Mister Rogers' Playbook,* a guide for parents on encouraging imaginative play, the foreword by Rogers states, "Each time a child learns how something works or what it can do, he or she is gaining a little more understanding and mastery … more tools to *create* with" (Rogers MRP 8, ellipses in original text). By encouraging the on-screen puppet children and by extension, the viewing audience to learn what operas are as well as to learn how they are created, Rogers encourages the viewers to see how they too can make up stories, plays, songs, and even operas to entertain themselves and flex their imagination muscles.

Reardon goes to the familiar school in the Neighborhood of Make-Believe to sing some opera to the schoolchildren and explains about how he loved to sing as a little boy. He then sings a little medley recapping many operas performed in the Neighborhood, and in an unusual production move, the audience is shown tape from the following past operas though they are not named on-screen: "The Key to Otherland" (1975), "A Monkey's Uncle: The Organ Grinder Opera" (1971), and "Potato Bugs and Cows" (1973). Describing and revisiting these operas in this episode reminds viewers that operas are not something unfamiliar, but rather that they have a history on the show and can be built upon when writing the next opera, as when Reardon lets the children brainstorm ideas for the new opera. Francois Clemmons then "improvises" a song for his character, the "Friendly Porpoise with a Purpose," to Queen Sara, which is the main theme for the Opera: "There's never any trouble here in Bubbleland."

This structure and sequence designed for children not only show how someone might compose an opera, but also how to make up a story, create roles, and imagine costumes, all encouraging the viewers to engage in imaginative play on their own. At the end of the episode, Mister Rogers asks the viewers to imagine what might make trouble for bubbles and hints it has something to do with the air (i.e. the wind), setting up the creation of the opera's villain, W.I. Norton Donovan (W.I.N.D.). The last episode before the opera ("Makes an Opera" #4) is about the wind. Mister Rogers visits a weather station, is shown the radar equipment and a weather balloon by the meteorologists, and on Day 5 the opera is presented as a self-contained work, without reference to the preceding "creating" episodes. In an abbreviated version of the standard opening of the show, Mister Rogers, already in his sweater and sneakers, walks up to and sits on his front porch singing, "It's a beautiful day in the neighborhood, a beautiful day for an opera, should we make one? Sure, we'll make one." Rogers explains the roles each of the neighborhood regulars will be playing and what the first song will be about, an example of what Curry describes as interpreting and narrating a sequence of encounters, which help "the child move back and forth between highly idiosyncratic thinking called primary process thinking and secondary process thinking, which reflects the child's increasing experiences with and understanding of reality" (Curry 58).

Rogers gives a brief introduction to the plot and then the viewer hears a drumroll on the timpani to transition to an establishing shot of the Bubblewitness News television studio. Reardon (as Robert Redgate) is center frame and sings the main theme: "There's never any trouble here in Bubbleland."

The transition to this new set is eased through the familiar musical sounds and visual punctuations. The glockenspiel, the usual instrument used to play the show's theme, is heard along with harp for opening music prior to the Mister Rogers greeting. When Robert Redgate is shown, he has four TV monitors behind him emphasizing what's important (himself, Bubbles, spray sweaters). The song is accompanied by jazz piano, and high hat drum kit. It's jazzy and breezy (the familiar touch of Johnny Costa), thus making a nice transition for the kids watching. Because this is the same support structure the audience members are used to for Mister Rogers' music, the addition of Reardon's operatic vocal over the top of it increases the comfort level with the operatic, bel canto vocal style, which may be new to them. When a potential complication is introduced throughout the sequence, the music signals the shift—for example, a synthesizer introduces the National Bubble Chemical Company's theme, indicating there is something artificial about the company and its products.

The familiar Betty Aberlin (appearing here as owner of Betty's Better Sweaters) sounds a warning, interrupting Redgate's breezy tune and cheerful pitch for the National Bubble Chemical Company's Spray Sweater in a Can. She does so by singing "It's a fraud!" in a minor key. The shift in tone is so abrupt that the children would understand that she is telling them to doubt what Redgate has just told them about the spray sweater, even though they likely cannot identify or name the musical shift to minor.

When weather forecaster Hildegarde Hummingbird (the puppet Lady Elaine Fairchilde in a hummingbird costume) lends her voice to the warning by saying she has word of a coming windstorm, her entrance is greeted by diminished chords. Here, Hildegarde might represent the child who is trying to point out the obvious, or who has good reason to worry about something but is told by adults there is nothing to worry about. "Why won't you believe me?" she asks the members of the news team, who respond, "because we don't want to!" The team does explain why: "a windstorm would blow all our bubbles away, our business would suffer such pain. A windstorm would give us a terrible day, so don't mention a windstorm again. Not again!" This response, sung in three-part harmony by Aberlin, Reardon, and Clemmons (as Porpoise), is also in a minor key, signaling trouble.

Like most of the *Neighborhood* operas, "Windstorm in Bubbleland" adheres to the three-act structure, familiar to audiences of American film and television, and this is not surprising. According to Motti Aviram and Louise Gikow (both writers and showrunners), writing for *Script* magazine,

> Scriptwriting for kids, just like for any other audience, is based on the classic three-act plot structure. And just like any other script, a children's film or TV episode requires a good turning point to move the plot forward and steer it to fascinating places [Why Write for Kids?"].

In "Windstorm in Bubbleland," the turning point (the danger the wind will pose to the bubbles) is punctuated by musical shifts and character movements. When Hildegarde Hummingbird realizes she is being asked not to "speak the truth," she determines to leave, saying "someday you will wish I was here," a familiar sentiment among the audience of young children who often feel misunderstood or ignored when they try to express something important. Hildegarde's departure (at ten minutes into the episode) marks the end of the first act. The minor key warning sounded by Hildegarde and Betty is echoed in the following scene, at the dock by a banana boat, and is sung by Chef Brockett as the Banana Boat Captain, who sings, "It's funny ... the water in the sea looks slightly strange to me.... I think I even saw a wave or two!" Hildegarde floats by (the puppet is on a wire) who tells him she is leaving. He is then joined by Theresa, a bubble seller played by Miss Paulificate (a neighborhood regular) who notes that her bubble business is down. She dismisses his concerns about the air by singing a breezy little 3/4 time waltz, "All I Ever Blow Is Bubbles." A tip of the boat signals danger, and the Porpoise appears with a warning and tells them that Robert Redgate and Betty have gone to the National Bubble Chemical Company to investigate. Aviram and Gikow also note,

> A scriptwriter who wants to write for children must be familiar with the wants and needs of the target audience, their cognitive abilities, principles of humor for the very young, basics of writing for puppets and animation and more. It helps to be capable of conceiving exciting plots that speak to the hearts of children and to love the characters that children love: characters like princes and princesses, monsters, witches, fairies, talking animals and superheroes ["Why Write for Kids?"].

While this story does not feature every one of these elements, it does present a number of them along with a problem to solve and it lets the children in the audience to use their sensitivity to musical motives and visual cues to determine what's wrong in Bubbleland.

The set for the National Bubble Chemical Company is modern and angular in tones of silver, black, and gray, and the sounds that accompany this visual are that of a synthesizer. The synth music is ominous and mischievous and contrasts with the more chromatic modulations from earlier music. Betty confronts Redgate, stating, "all that's in these cans is just plain air. No needles, no yarn, no skill of any kind. No heart. No, no spray-can can make a sweater." When Betty sings here about the truth, the music is a complex classical moment, with more complicated chromatic modulations than have been heard. The profundity of speaking the truth is underscored by this musical choice.

Betty's bravery speaks to Aviram and Gikow's assertion that "most of all, the writer needs to be able to create characters with pluck, wit, and passion ... characters who want to move forward and reach goals, characters with real needs they must fulfill" ("Why Write for Kids?").

The best representative of this lesson in "Windstorm" is no doubt Hildegarde Hummingbird. Robert Redgate, though the symbol for authority due to his status as a news anchor, responds to W.I.N.D.'s gleeful admission of guilt in starting the windstorm with a vapid, pseudo-patriotic theme, stating "Bubblewitness News is always the first" to report anything of import. For the journey to the newsroom to report to the public on the problem is the familiar traveling theme used to transition Mister Rogers from place to place in his Neighborhood.

When Betty Aberlin reminds everyone of Hildegarde's bravery, her song is sung in major arpeggios:

> It was Hildegarde Hummingbird, smallest of all
> Who told us this morning in this very hall
> That a windstorm was coming and we should beware
> And how did we treat her? [Redgate]: We sent her elsewhere.

With all characters now pleading to the camera for Hildegarde to hear them if she is listening, Betty, Reardon and the Porpoise sing a little trio pleading for "Hildegarde Brave" to forgive them "and come back and save your Bubbleland neighbors." This trio, which transitions visually from the newsroom set to a TV set that Hildegarde is watching, is in a 6/8 lilting meter which keeps it distinct from the triumphant theme of the news station, which is also in arpeggios but more like a march with its 4/4 time signature. The scene continues with Hildegarde in the foreground and the trio on the television screen behind her.

Responding that she is "not all that interested in saving your bubbles," Hildegarde then expresses the central compassionate lesson of the opera with a little melodic aria:

> A hummingbird cares about people and creatures with fur and with wings.
> A hummingbird cares about feelings but doesn't care much about things.

When the trio responds that they are "scared and need" her, Hildegarde turns to the screen and announces she is coming and they should "start building a wall." The music of intention increases, with the trio deciding the "wind will be down by the ocean—that's where the wall ought to go. Let's bank on our strongest emotion to help us beyond all our woe. Let's go!" with "Let's go!" on a new chord indicating resolve and strength. This scene, which ends the second act, shows the characters ready to work together to defeat the Wind, and though they still are thinking first about saving their bubbles, they have begun to realize that their greatest strength comes from uniting together.

The start of the third act is back at the dock, showing the Banana Boat Captain and Theresa in a state of despair, singing sadly: "Oh what sadness, oh what fear. There hasn't been a windstorm here in at least 2,000 years." The sorrow is countered by the energetic collaboration of all the characters, who cooperate to build a wall with banana crates and a sweater, knit by Betty, to cover it all. Video of ocean waves is overlaid with an image of the W.I.N.D. in a flowing robe and long, silvery whiskers. The accompaniment for the W.I.N.D. is jazz piano in minor with diminished arpeggios as well as an irregular meter that speeds up as he sings louder: "I'm the wind, I'm the wind, I'm offshore picking up speed. There's no one to stop me save one Hildegarde but she's gone."

When Hildegarde returns, the cast sings, "Blow, Wind, blow if you must but try not to bust our bubbles." To this Hildegarde reminds them of what is important: "You and you and you and you and you can blow more bubbles. But you can't blow more you." Hildegarde engages each character directly as she sings "you," just as Mister Rogers does when he speaks directly to his viewers, thus illustrating the importance of each individual.

The W.I.N.D. is then flown in on a wire, cackling and singing, "You're scared of me," with a melody alternating between duple rhythms and little triplets, indicating instability, and a more topsy-turvy feeling than the more stable trio and quintet of the previous segment. The W.I.N.D. unleashes his strongest power but Hildegarde counters that she is "as strong as the wind." Rushing wind sounds accompany their battle, as well as sounds of a synthesized Theremin's wobble standing in for hummingbird wings. The W.I.N.D. is atonal at his defeat, singing exhaustedly: "I think I'll have to retreat soon. This bird will cause my defeat soon." As Hildegarde also loses her strength, she urges the others to "try flapping your own wings. If you all try together, you too can be strong as the wind" with the Theremin-as-hummingbird sounds underscoring it. The wind sounds fade, and the cast joins together in a triumphant major trio: "The wind is gone, the sea is calm and who do we have to thank? But Hildegarde, Our Hildegarde!" This theme ends with a big major chord on "Brave Hildegard" but transitions to chromatic diminished chord, when Hildegarde appears to be lifeless, shown in a rapid close-up to the puppet on the ground among fallen bananas. The mood changes with a very romantic use of a chromatic, melodic line with Robert Redgate singing a sad lament: "Hildegarde, dear Hildegarde. Our regard for you is the highest. You will always be through all our history Brave Hilde, Hildegarde." The others join in on a reprise to celebrate her memory. When Hildegarde wakes up, she asks them to repeat the song, and they cheer for her.

At this time, Hildegarde does what Mister Rogers frequently does at the end of his episodes—summarize the day's lessons—by asking, "Well, did you learn anything from it all?" They respond in succession:

[ABERLIN]: Hummingbirds are really strong.
[REDGATE]: Sweaters are better than bottled-up air
[PORPOISE]: When friends tell you something caringly, you should listen carefully.

[THERESA]: Bubbles are nice. Also, people are different from bubbles.
[CAPTAIN]: People are far more important than bubbles.

Redgate then jumps in with "one more thing" and reprises the "There's Never Any Trouble" theme but with an important difference this time: "There's never any trouble here in Bubbleland, that we good friends together cannot end."

With the complexity in the art form of Opera, Rogers is juggling a lot of artistic, musical, and thematic concerns. But his talents and those of his collaborators provide the opportunity for the program to present and work through an extended series of metaphors and lessons. According to Wachtel, children's television should feature emotional lessons that are "easy-to-understand, 'kid-relatable' issues" (Wachtel), and the operas each oblige, clarifying the messages through repetition. This opera summarizes its lessons clearly at the end, yet also weaves in a critique of commercialism (the sponsorship of a news program and the town's concerns for its bottom line negatively affect the integrity of the news broadcast), a reminder that all things worth doing are not come by easily ("it takes time to make a sweater"), and that friends need to care about each other more than they do about their own fame, businesses, or property.

Wachtel identifies trends in children's screenwriting that *Mister Rogers' Neighborhood* pre-dated, such as avoiding any disturbing storylines involving death or threats of bodily harm. Given these current guidelines, Hildegarde's seeming death might not be permitted today when, according to Wachtel, scripts with even "an element of sadness" are rejected.

"Windstorm in Bubbleland" illustrates one of Fred Rogers' favorite themes, articulated here in a book of collected quotations:

> Human relationships are primary in all of living. When the gusty winds blow and shake our lives, if we know that people care about us, we may bend with the wind ... but we won't break [*The World According to Mister Rogers* 94].

Rogers makes those metaphorical winds literal and embodied, giving the friends something to unite against and push back (though not defeat violently—instead they counter the wind's power with their own strength. The hummingbird's small size is emphasized repeatedly to communicate to children that they do not need to be big to be brave or strong. As Rogers relates, "When I was a boy I used to think that strong meant having big muscles, great physical power; but the longer I live, the more I realize that real strength has much more to do with what is *not* seen. Real strength has to do with helping others" (Rogers, *The World* 41). The selflessness of Hildegarde and the success she has in uniting the others to defeat the wind illustrate this strength clearly to children.

The episode closes with Mister Rogers reiterating the lessons learned by the characters and how the value they found in each other can also be found in each child, but also reminding children about the power of music and how they can always carry it with them before John Costa's trio plays over the closing credits with jazzy variations on the Bubbleland theme:

> So, they all found out that friends are far more important than things. When a bubble's gone you don't see it anymore with your eyes. And when an opera's over, you don't hear it anymore with your ears, but you can remember. You can remember what bubbles look like and what operas sound like and what friends feel like. And you'll always have them with you in your memory. You always make each day a special day, by just your being yourself. And people can like you just the way you are.

Mister Rogers' themes of friendship, empathy, and child development were expressed to audiences for over thirty years, and although they represent a small percentage of the overall output of *Mister Rogers' Neighborhood*, the operas can continue to make an impact on children and their caregivers, especially as they illustrate the breadth of talent and creativity possessed by Rogers and his collaborators. In a 2009 interview with William V. Madison, Betty Aberlin said,

> The operas were Fred at his whimsical best. The operas still focused on the beautiful themes that were pertinent to children, but Fred was allowed to be more expressive. For some reason or another, he said that PBS was not so fond of them, but I thought they were it. I loved them [Betty Aberlin Interview].

Although Rogers' last opera was broadcast over twenty years ago, and the last episode of *Mister Rogers' Neighborhood* was produced in 2001, audiences continue to have access to the archive of the show online through PBS.org, Fred Rogers.org, Amazon.com Prime and other outlets.

Whether children will still discover and choose *Mister Rogers' Neighborhood* when the last of the nostalgic parents, who themselves watched the episodes on broadcast television, are gone is another question. What is not in question is the lasting value of a show that transitions slowly and calmly in real time. As Roderick Townley describes in "Fred's Shoes: The Meaning of Transitions in *Mister Rogers' Neighborhood*," studies of preschoolers who had watched *Mister Rogers' Neighborhood* were "better able to concentrate and stick with an activity than were children who had been shown high-action cartoons" (69). The opera episodes especially require the child's concentration and attention, and they are unique in the annals of television and television opera.

Notes

1. http://www.fredrogerscenter.org/media/curriculum_toolkit/Curry1-Formatted. pdf. One example of Winnicott's work showing up in a Neighborhood opera is "Spoon Mountain." In this opera, unique in that it did not feature Rogers' puppets, the characters (expressing empathy for anyone in trouble) work together to rescue Purple Twirling Kitty from his imprisonment by the villain Wicked Knife and Fork. But in

the end, the villain gains sympathy from the others when he reveals he has been a victim of taunting which mischaracterizes him, singing: "All I ever wanted was a spoon ... but all they ever gave me was a knife and fork. They even called me Wicked Knife and Fork," illustrating child development specialist D.W. Winnicott's concept of the "True Self" and the "False Self."

2. http://archives.cnn.com/2001/SHOWBIZ/TV/08/31/mcfeely.chat.cnna.

3. "Babysitter Opera" (1968), "Campsite Opera" (1968), "Teddy Bear / Whaling Ship Opera" (1969), "Pineapples and Tomatoes" (1970), "Monkey's Uncle" (1971), "Snow People and Warm Pussycat" (1972), "Potato Bugs and Cows" (1973), "All in the Laundry" (1974), "Key to Otherland" (1975), "Windstorm in Bubbleland" (1980), "Spoon Mountain" (1982), "A Granddad for Daniel" (1984), "A Star for Kitty" (1986). A three-episode musical play, "Josephine the Short-Necked Giraffe" (1989), was aired as a tribute to John Reardon, who died of complications from AIDS in 1988 (*New York Times* obituary, http://www.nytimes.com/1988/04/19/obituaries/john-reardon-58-noted-baritone-and-champion-of-modern-opera.html).

4. http://www.neighborhoodarchive.com/mrn/episodes/0045/index.html.

5. http://topics.nytimes.com/top/reference/timestopics/subjects/o/opera/index.html.

6. During a 1983 interview with Joan Rivers on *The Tonight Show*, Rogers says he began by working as a floor manager for, among other things, the *NBC Opera Theatre* right after college (*Hit Parade, Kate Smith Hour*) (YouTube).

7. http://exhibit.fredrogerscenter.org/early-life-education/videos/view/950/.

Works Cited

Aberlin, Betty. Interview with William V. Madison. *Billevesées*. Billmadison.blogspot.com, 2009. 6 Aug. 2013. Web.

"About Us." Fred Rogers Company. Fredrogers.org http://fredrogers.org/FRC/about-us.html. Web.

Barnes, Jennifer. *Television Opera: The Fall of Opera Commissioned for Television*. Woodbridge, Suffolk, UK: Boydell & Brewer, 2003. Print.

The Billboard Illustrated Encyclopedia of Opera. General Editor Stanley Sadie. Fullham, London: Flame Tree Publishing, 2003. Print.

"Chuck Aber Oral History." Fred Rogers Center. Feb. 27, 2007. Web.

Cofer, Lynette Friedrich. "Make-Believe, Truth, and Freedom: Television in the Public Interest." Collins and Kimmel, 145–161. Print.

Collins, Mark, and Margaret Mary Kimmel, eds. *Mister Rogers' Neighborhood: Children, Television, and Fred Rogers*. Pittsburgh: University of Pittsburgh Press, 1996. Print.

Curry, Nancy E. "The Reality of Make-Believe." *Mister Rogers' Neighborhood: Children, Television, and Fred Rogers*. Ed. Mark Collins and Margaret Mary Kimmel. Pittsburgh: University of Pittsburgh Press, 1996. 51–64. Print.

"Francois Clemmons Sings a Joyous Farewell." Middlebury Arts. 26 Apr. 2013. http://www.middlebury.edu/arts/news/node/450328. 13 Aug. 2013.

Fred Rogers Interview with Karen Herman. 22 July 1999. Emmytvlegends.org. Web. 6 Aug. 2013.

Harlem Spiritual Ensemble. MRN Program Number: 1635. Fred Rogers Center. http://exhibit.fredrogerscenter.org/early-life-education/videos/view/942/. Web.

Hollis, Tim. *Hi, There, Boys and Girls! America's Local Children's TV Programs*. Jackson: University of Mississippi Press, 2001. Print.

Interview with Dr. Francois Clemmons. Guy Hutchinson. *Adventure Club Podcast*. 3

Sept. 2012. http://www.adventureclubpodcast.com/2012/09/interview-with-dr-francois-clemmons.html. 13 Aug. 2013. Web.

Laskas, Jeanne Marie. "What Is Essential Is Invisible to the Eye." *Mister Rogers' Neighborhood: Children, Television, and Fred Rogers.* Ed. Mark Collins and Margaret Mary Kimmel. Pittsburgh: University of Pittsburgh Press, 1996. 15–34. Print.

Linn, Susan. "With an Open Hand: Puppetry on *Mister Rogers' Neighborhood.*" *Mister Rogers' Neighborhood: Children, Television, and Fred Rogers.* Ed. Mark Collins and Margaret Mary Kimmel. Pittsburgh: University of Pittsburgh Press, 1996. 89–99. Print.

"Mr. Speedy Delivery Talks." David Newell Interview by Carol Lin. Cnn.com. http://archives.cnn.com/2001/SHOWBIZ/TV/08/31/mcfeely.chat.cnna/.

Murray Zoba, Wendy. "Won't You Be My Neighbor?" *Christianity Today,* 6 Mar. 2000. pp. 38–46. Print.

Rogers, Fred. *The World According to Mister Rogers: Important Things to Remember.* New York: Hyperion & Family Communications, 2003. Print.

Rogers, Fred, and Barry Head. *Mister Rogers' Playbook: Insights and Activities for Parents and Children.* New York: Berkley Books, 1986. Print.

Rowe, Claudia. "Some Things Never Change, and Thank Heavens Mister Rogers Is One of Them." *Biography.* Mar. 2000. 102–105, 116. Print.

Townley, Roderick. "Fred's Shoes: The Meaning of Transitions in *Mister Rogers' Neighborhood.*" *Mister Rogers' Neighborhood: Children, Television, and Fred Rogers.* Ed. Mark Collins and Margaret Mary Kimmel. Pittsburgh: University of Pittsburgh Press, 1996. 67–76. Print.

The 20th Century. *New York Times* Opera Navigator. http://topics.nytimes.com/top/reference/timestopics/subjects/o/opera/index.html. 6 Aug. 2013. Web.

Wachtel, Brooks. "Author Q & A: Animation Writer Brooks Wachtel." Writeonline.com. http://writeononline.com/2009/07/24/author-qa-animation-writer-brooks-wachtel/. 13 Aug. 2013. Web.

"Why Write for Kids?" Motti Aviram and Louise Gikow. Feb. 26, 2013. http://www.scriptmag.com/features/why-write-for-kids. A division of *The Writers' Store.* 13 Aug. 2013. Web.

Winnicott, D.W. "Ego Distortion in Terms of True and False Self." *The Maturational Process and the Facilitating Environment: Studies in the Theory of Emotional Development.* New York: International University Press, 1965. 140–52. Web.

Zukerman, Eugenia. "Musical Notes: An Interview with Yo-Yo Ma." *Mister Rogers' Neighborhood: Children, Television, and Fred Rogers.* Ed. Mark Collins and Margaret Mary Kimmel. Pittsburgh: University of Pittsburgh Press, 1996. 79–87. Print.

Fred Rogers and the Early Use of Puppetry on American Children's Television

Mark I. West

Almost ten years before Fred Rogers assumed the on-air television persona of Mister Rogers, he performed as a puppeteer on a local children's television program. In 1954 WQED, an educational television station in Pittsburgh, hired Rogers to work on *The Children's Corner*. This live unscripted program featured Josie Carey as the show's host. She interacted with a series of puppet characters created and controlled by Rogers. Although Rogers did not appear in person on this program, he provided the voices for the puppet characters. Through his work on *The Children's Corner*, Rogers played a significant role in the early use of puppetry on American children's television. As a puppeteer, he drew inspiration from other puppeteers who performed on television a few years before he made his debut, but he also influenced the work of puppeteers who entered the medium of television after he achieved success on *The Children's Corner*. When viewed from a historical perspective, the launching of Rogers' television career is inextricably tied to the larger story of how the American television industry embraced puppetry during the late 1940s and early 1950s.

Puppetry and the Origins of American Children's Television

Before the 1940s, the American public showed little interest in puppetry. While puppeteers had toured the United States since the 1700s, their shows were generally regarded as novelty acts. In contrast, European puppeteers enjoyed a long history of public appreciation. Puppet characters figure in the popular culture of most European countries. Great Britain has Punch and Judy, France has Guignol, Sicily has Orlando, just to name a few (Baird 93–129). In America, however, no puppet characters captured the imagination of the general public until the 1940s and 1950s when suddenly Kukla, Ollie, Howdy Doody, King Friday XIII, and a number of other puppet characters became famous. This rise in the popularity of puppetry can be directly attributed to the emergence of television.

The history of television goes back to the 1930s, but it was not until after the Second World War that television stations began broadcasting on a regular basis. During the first few years after the war, the broadcasting networks provided minimal programming, which meant that individual stations had to develop their own programs if they wished to be on the air for more than a few hours per day (Wilk 2). However, due to financial and technical limitations, television stations found it difficult to produce programs that made full use of television's visual capabilities. In their efforts to improve the quality of their programming, television producers began experimenting with various types of programs, and they soon discovered that puppeteers could work around the constraints of this new medium. In an article titled "Puppets on Television," Joe Owens, a puppeteer who regularly performed on WRGB in Schenectady, New York, during the late 1940s, explained why the television producers of that period were drawn to puppetry:

> The reasons why puppets are already a success on television are many. They are liked by the studio staff. Being small and therefore requiring a small stage they are more easily and effectively lighted than are live actors.... The camera men like puppets because they can roll their cameras right up to the stage for a close-up, elevate them for low angles, or get an effective shot looking down on top of the set [22–23].

Another reason television producers liked puppet programs is that these shows usually required less rehearsal time than most other programs in part because puppeteers did not need to memorize their lines. In some cases, they would simply ad lib the dialogue. In other cases, they would read the script. Since the puppeteers were out of camera range, the television audience could not tell that the script was being read. In fact, it was a puppeteer who invented the prototype of today's teleprompter (Baird 234–35). An off-camera floor mike was used to pick up the puppeteers' voices instead of the boom mike that was usually used with live talent. For this reason, the sound quality on puppet programs was exceptionally good for this early period in television programming (Owens 23).

During the late 1940s, numerous television stations produced their own puppet programs. WWJ in Detroit aired a puppet program called *Let's See Willie Dooit. Musical Marionettes,* a show on KSTP in Minneapolis, featured dancing marionettes that were dressed in various national costumes. WPIX in New York aired *Pixie Playmate,* a show that featured a dragon, a witch, and several other puppets. In Milwaukee, WTMJ aired a program titled *Hi, Kids* in which area children would present their own puppet shows (McFadden 73). Perhaps the most important of these locally produced puppet programs was Burr Tillstrom's *Kukla, Fran and Ollie,* which first aired on WBKB in Chicago in 1946 (Gehman 30).

As the 1940s were coming to an end, programming on the television networks was beginning to blossom. The number of stations on the air grew at a rapid rate, and the expansion of the coaxial cable made it possible for a large percentage of these stations to carry network programs. The network executives realized that television could become an important mass medium if more people could be persuaded to buy televisions sets. This realization led to the expansion of network programming for children. The network executives reasoned that parents would be inclined to purchase television sets if they felt that their children would benefit from watching television (Melody 35–36). From 1948 through 1951 the networks continually expanded the number of hours they devoted to children's programs (Shelby 248). An outgrowth of this trend was the emergence of several network programs that featured puppets.

The first puppet program to be broadcast over a network was *Howdy Doody.* In 1947, Warren Wade, the executive in charge of NBC's television programming, approached Bob Smith with the idea of developing a puppet-based program for children. Smith already produced a children's radio program for NBC, and Wade and Smith decided the new television program would star a marionette version of a character from Smith's radio show. The program got its name from the greeting that his character always used. Frank Paris made and operated the puppet, and Smith provided its voice. The first telecast of the program occurred on December 27, 1947. At first, *Howdy Doody* was a weekly program, but within a month it was on the air three days a week. By the fall of 1948, *Howdy Doody* aired each weekday from 5:30 to 6:00 p.m. (Wilk 208).

A number of puppet characters regularly appeared on *Howdy Doody* in addition to the program's namesake. A puppet named Mr. Bluster served as the show's villain. Other puppets included Dilly Dally, Inspector, and Fluba-dub. The program also featured two human characters. Bob Smith appeared on the show as Buffalo Bob, and Bob Keeshan, who later became Captain Kangaroo, played the role of Clarabell, a mute clown (McPharlin 573–74).

By 1949 the coaxial cable had reached Chicago, making it possible for network programs to originate out of the Midwest. Since Tillstrom's *Kukla, Fran and Ollie* had been doing well in Chicago, the program executives at NBC decided to broadcast the show over the network. Beginning in the spring of 1949, Tillstrom's puppet show aired on NBC from 7:00–7:30 p.m., and it quickly built a large and loyal audience of children and a surprising number of adults ("Tillstrom Kids" 47–48). Except for Fran, all of the characters on *Kukla, Fran and Ollie* were hand puppets. During the shows, Fran stood in front of the stage and interacted with the puppets. Before each show, Tillstrom and Fran, whose full name was Fran Allison, would plan the day's performance. Tillstrom had mastered the art of improvisational puppetry at an early age, and he never used a script when he was performing (Turner 8–9).

Following the success of *Kukla, Fran and Ollie,* the networks added several other puppet programs to their schedules. CBS, for example, aired a puppet program called *Lucky Pup.* The chief puppets on this program were Lucky Pup, who played the role of a millionaire dog, and Foodini, an evil but ineffectual magician. Two other network programs that featured puppets were *The Small Fry Club* and *The Singing Lady* ("Stars on Strings" 70).

The number of hours the networks devoted to children's programming reached a peak in 1951 when the networks aired a weekly total of twenty-seven hours of children's shows. The following year, the total dropped to a little over seventeen hours (Shelby 268). The main reason for this decline is that advertisers were shifting their support to adult programs, for they felt that advertising dollars were better spent on shows that were directed at adult viewers. Numerous children's programs were cancelled, and others were moved out of prime time (Melody 38). This development adversely affected the position of puppetry on network television.

Although *Howdy Doody* survived this round of cuts, *Kukla, Fran and Ollie* was not so fortunate. In the fall of 1951, NBC decided to cut the daily program from half an hour to fifteen minutes. This decision came about after Proctor and Gamble and *Life,* two of the show's sponsors, withdrew their support. NBC arranged for *Bob and Ray,* a satirical show aimed at adults, to be aired during the time slot they took away from *Kukla, Fran and Ollie.* The move angered many viewers. NBC received over 2,000 unsolicited letters of protest the day after the decision was announced ("Shrinking Oasis" 50). Other network programs that featured puppets, such as *Lucky Pup,* were simply cancelled.

The mid 1950s witnessed several significant changes in the networks' approach to children's programming. The networks began scheduling children's programs on Saturday mornings and weekday afternoons rather than on prime time. Also, the nature of children's programs was changing. Live shows were being phased out in favor of filmed programs, such as *The Mickey Mouse Club* (Shelby 248). Another important development in the area of children's programming was the emergence of made-for-television animated series pioneered by William Hanna and Joseph Barbera (Melody 45–46). As a result of all of these factors, the position of puppetry on network television was considerably weakened.

Fred Rogers' Career as a Television Puppeteer

Fred Rogers' debut as a television puppeteer occurred at the same time as the commercial television networks were moving away from airing programs featuring puppets. In April 1954, Rogers began performing with hand puppets on a program titled *The Children's Corner*, which aired on Pittsburgh's WQED (Hollis 246). As the nation's first community-owned television station, WQED emerged as an early leader in the area of educational television. After having received a grant from the Emerson Radio and Phonograph Company to develop a high-quality television program for children, WQED turned to Rogers to make this program a reality (Levine and Hines 265).

Rogers' career in television had begun a few years earlier when he accepted a position at NBC in New York City. Shortly after graduating with a music degree from Rollins College in Florida, he signed on with the NBC Television Opera Theatre. He worked at NBC from 1951 through 1953 during which time he learned a great deal about the technical side of producing television programs. As an employee of NBC, he was familiar with NBC's *Kukla, Fran and Ollie* and this program provided him with a model when he moved to Pittsburgh to work for WQED (Laskas 180).

From its very inception, *The Children's Corner* shared many characteristics with *Kukla, Fran and Ollie*. Both shows featured hand puppets interacting with a young woman who would sit in front of the puppet stage at more-or-less eye level with the puppets. In both shows, the puppeteers remained off camera, but they provided the voices for the puppets. Both shows relied on improvisation, and both featured a small cast of puppet characters who reappeared in episode after episode.

In the case of *The Children's Corner*, Rogers created a cast of four puppets: Daniel Striped Tiger, "X" the Owl, Lady Elaine Fairchilde, and King Friday XIII. These four puppets not only appeared on *The Children's Corner*, but they also went on to become regulars on *Mister Rogers' Neighborhood*. As fellow puppeteer Susan Linn notes, Rogers' gift as a puppeteer was in his ability to endow his puppet characters with complex and believable personalities:

> The physical puppets themselves are simple, primitive creatures…. Their mouths do not move. Their eyes do not tack. They have no feet…. We do not watch the Neighborhood of Make-Believe to marvel at flawless manipulation. Nor do we sit in awe of the puppets' design. We watch because we have come to care about the essence of these characters. We, and our children, watch because we know them. We recognize ourselves in their complexity [Linn 89–90].

With the debut of *The Children's Corner* in 1954, Rogers emerged as a pioneer in the development of educational television programing for children. Very soon after the show began airing, it began attracting national attention.

In 1955, the show won the "Sylvania Award for best locally produced children's television program in the United States" (Levine and Hines 265). Also in 1955, NBC briefly picked up the show, but it continued to produced and aired on WQED (Hollis 246).

The Children's Corner remained on the air until 1961, but the end of the show did not result in the demise of the puppet characters featured on the program. In 1963, Rogers moved to Toronto, where he developed and starred in an educational television program for the Canadian Broadcasting Corporation. Titled *Misterogers*, this program combined puppetry with on-camera appearances by Rogers himself. After a one-year stay in Canada, Rogers moved back to Pittsburgh and to his previous employer, WQED. With the support of a grant from the Sears Roebuck Foundation, Rogers and the producers at WQED created *Mister Rogers' Neighborhood* in 1966. This program was soon distributed nationally through the newly formed Public Broadcasting Service (Laskas 20). Through all of these transitions, Rogers continued to perform with the same puppets that he used in *The Children's Corner* in the 1950s (Linn 90–91).

Puppetry on Public Television

Mister Rogers' Neighborhood quickly became a mainstay of public television. Rogers' success in the area of educational television programming for children encouraged others to develop such programming for the then fledgling Public Broadcasting Service. About a year after the debut of *Mister Rogers' Neighborhood,* the Children's Television Workshop, under the leadership of Joan Ganz Cooney, set to work on producing *Sesame Street.* Like *Mister Rogers' Neighborhood,* this new program featured puppets. Jim Henson created the puppet characters that appeared on *Sesame Street,* and he and his team brought the puppets, called Muppets, to life on the program (Dircks 216–17).

The enduring popularity of both *Mister Rogers' Neighborhood* and *Sesame Street* resulted in puppetry finding a secure niche on the Public Broadcasting Service. Rogers played a key role in this development in the history of puppetry on American television. Rogers' roots as a television puppeteer reach back to *Kukla, Fran and Ollie* and the other early puppet shows that aired on the commercial television networks during the late 1940s and early 1950s. However, even after the commercial networks lost interest in producing puppet programs, Rogers, as a result of his longstanding association with WQED and his early support for the Public Broadcasting Service, helped keep puppets in front of American audiences through programming aired on public television.

WORKS CITED

Baird, Bil. *The Art of the Puppet*. New York: Macmillan, 1965.

Dircks, Phyllis T., ed. *American Puppetry: Collections, History and Performance*. Jefferson, NC: McFarland, 2004.

Gehman, Richard B. "Mr. Oliver J. Dragon and Friends." *Theatre Arts* Oct. 1950: 26–30.

Hollis, Tim. *Hi There, Boys and Girls: America's Local Children's TV Programs*. Jackson: University of Mississippi Press, 2001.

Laskas, Jeanne Marie. "What Is Essential Is Invisible to the Eye." *Mister Rogers' Neighborhood: Children, Television, and Fred Rogers*. Ed. Mark Collins and Margaret Mary Kimmel. Pittsburgh: University of Pittsburgh Press, 1969.

Levin, Robert A., and Laurie Moses Hines. "Educational Television, Fred Rogers, and the History of Education." *History of Education Quarterly* 43.2 (2003): 262–75.

Linn, Susan. "With an Open Hand: Puppetry on *Mister Rogers Neighborhood*." *Mister Rogers' Neighborhood: Children, Television, and Fred Rogers*. Ed. Mark Collins and Margaret Mary Kimmel. Pittsburgh: University of Pittsburgh Press, 1969.

McFadden, Dorothy L. "Television Comes to Our Children." *Parents' Magazine* Jan. 1949: 23+.

McPharlin, Paul. *The Puppet Theatre in America: A History*. Boston: Plays, 1969.

Melody, William. *Children's Television: The Economics of Exploitation*. New Haven: Yale University Press, 1973.

Owens, Joe. "Puppets on Television." *Puppetry 1946–1947*. Ed. Paul McPharlin. New York: Hastings House, 1947.

Shelby, Maurice E. "Children's Programming Trends on Network Television." *Journal of Broadcasting* 8.3 (1964): 247–256.

"Stars on Strings." *Time* 17 Jan. 1949: 68–70.

"Shrinking Oasis." *Time* 10 Dec. 1951: 50–52.

"The Tillstrom Kids." *Newsweek* 22 Aug. 1949: 47–48.

Turner, Gerry A. "Kukla, Fran and Ollie: T.V.'s Wonderful Puppets Are Flesh and Blood to Millions." *Design* Jan. 1951: 7–9.

Wilk, Max. *The Golden Age of Television: Notes from the Survivors*. New York: Dell, 1976.

Chronology

March 20, 1928	Fred McFeely Rogers is born in Latrobe, Pennaylvania, near Pittsburgh.
1951	Rogers graduates from Rollins College in Winter Park, Florida, where he receives a degree in music, and begins working in the fledgling medium of television at NBC in New York City. He is the assistant producer on *The Voice of Firestone*.
1952	Rogers marries Joanne Byrd.
1953	Rogers returns to Pittsburgh and joins WQED, which becomes the nation's first public television station. He develops a new series, *The Children's Corner*, with Rogers as puppeteer and Josie Carey as host. It is a live, unscripted TV show, introducing puppet characters King Friday XIII, Lady Elaine Fairchilde, Daniel Striped Tiger, and X the Owl, that proves to be the genesis of *Mister Rogers' Neighborhood*. Rogers begins wearing sneakers on the set so as to move about more quietly.
1954	WQED goes on the air.
1955	*The Children's Corner* wins the Sylvania Award as the nation's best locally produced children's show and earns national recognition. NBC runs it briefly on Saturday mornings.
1959	Joanne Rogers gives birth to the couple's first child, James.
1961	Joanne Rogers gives birth to the couple's second child, John.
1963	Rogers moves to Ontario, Canada, and works on a new series based on *The Children's Hour*. Titled *Misterogers*, the fifteen-minute show introduces story elements such as the trolley and the castle and, more importantly, features Rogers as himself on camera for the first time. The series runs on CBC for three years.
1963	Rogers is ordained as a Presbyterian minister.
1964	Rogers returns to Pittsburgh.

1966	Rogers obtains the rights for his show from CBC and rejoins WQED in Pittsburgh, where he had worked with Carey on *The Children's Corner*. His new show, which is renamed *Misterogers' Neighborhood* and incorporates the Neighborhood of Make-Believe, is bookended by live-action segments featuring Rogers. It airs on educational stations throughout the Northeast, including the major markets of New York City, Boston, and Washington, D.C.
1967	After one hundred episodes, the series is cancelled due to a lack of funding. The Sears Roebuck Foundation responds with support, enabling the show to reach a nationwide audience. Taping begins in October.
1967	Rogers writes what becomes his signature song, "Won't You Be My Neighbor?"
February 19, 1968	Bearing a slightly changed title, *Mister Rogers' Neighborhood* begins airing nationally on PBS and wins its first Emmy Award.
1968	Rogers is appointed chairman of the Forum on Mass Media and Child Development of the White House Conference on Youth.
1969	Rogers wins the first of two Peabody Awards for excellence in television.
March 23, 1970	*Mister Rogers' Neighborhood* airs an episode in which Rogers addresses the death of his pet goldfish. The episode is well-received and encourages Rogers to tackle more serious subjects.
1971	Rogers forms his own production company Family Communications, Inc.
1973	Rogers adopts his song "It's a Good Feeling" as the closing theme of each show.
1975	Rogers stops production on *Mister Rogers' Neighborhood*.
February 20, 1976	Original episodes of *Mister Rogers' Neighborhood* end, although PBS still carries the show in reruns.
1978	Rogers creates a new series for PBS, *Old Friends, New Friends*, about older people.
August 27, 1979	*Mister Rogers' Neighborhood* series resumes production, integrating fresh new episodes with older ones. Rogers begins grouping episodes of *Mister Rogers' Neighborhood* into week-long series exploring special topics such as death, war, anger, and competition.
1981	Eddie Murphy satirizes *Mister Rogers' Neighborhood* in a *Saturday Night Live* spoof titled "Mister Robinson's Neighborhood." It is the first of many spoofs of the show that was a familiar part of American childhood.

1984	The Smithsonian Institution's National Museum of American History places one of Rogers' trademark zippered sweaters, hand-knitted by his mother, on permanent display.
1984	Rogers demands that Burger King withdraw ads featuring a character with his likeness.
1987	In a gesture of peace, Rogers and a children's TV host from the Soviet Union appear on one another's shows.
1990	Rogers sues the Ku Klux Klan after the organization sends racist telephone recordings featuring imitations of Rogers' voice, phrases, and theme song. The offensive messages are stopped.
1989	Idlewild Park, an amusement park in Ligonier, PA, near Pittsburgh, opens a new attraction, Mister Rogers' Neighborhood of Make-Believe.
1991	At the onset of the Gulf War, Rogers tapes segments to allay fears and reassure children of their safety and well-being.
1996	Johnny Costa, who provided the jazzy music for the *Mister Rogers' Neighborhood*, dies and is replaced by Michael Moricz.
1996	*TV Guide* names Rogers one of the fifty greatest TV stars of all time.
1996	Rogers appears in an episode of one of his favorite TV dramas, *Dr. Quinn, Medicine Woman*, in a cameo role as a preacher. It is the only time he plays a character other than himself on TV.
1997	Rogers receives a lifetime achievement award from the National Academy of Television Arts and Sciences and the Television Critics Association and is recognized in his hometown as Pittsburgher of the Year by *Pittsburgh* magazine.
1998	Rogers gets a star on the Hollywood Walk of Fame.
1998	The Pittsburgh Children's Museum opens a Mister Rogers exhibit featuring his original puppets.
February 27, 1999	Rogers is inducted into the Broadcasting Hall of Fame and says, "We can either choose to use the powerful tool of television to demean human life, or we can use it to enrich it."
2000	Carnegie Science Center launches a planetarium show that includes characters from *Mister Rogers' Neighborhood*.
2000	The Religious Communicators Council presents Rogers with the Wilbur Award for support of religious values in the media.
2000	*Mister Rogers' Neighborhood* stops production of new episodes. In his thirty-three years of national production, Rogers tapes over a thousand shows.
August 31, 2001	PBS removes *Mister Rogers' Neighborhood* from its daily syndi-

	cated schedule, but many stations chose to continue airing it in reruns.
February 21, 2002	Along with First Lady Barbara Bush, Rogers is given an Elsie Award for community service at Pittsburgh's Carnegie Hall in Oakland. The awards were begun by Elsie and Henry Hillman in 1996.
July 2002	President George W. Bush presents Rogers with the Presidential Medal of Freedom.
August 2002	Rogers' prerecorded public service announcements for PBS encouraging parents to read to their children and advising them how to handle the first anniversary of the 9/11 terrorist attack are aired.
December 2002	Rogers is diagnosed with stomach cancer.
January 1, 2003	On New Year's Day, Rogers serves with Bill Cosby and Art Linkletter as grand marshal of the Tournament of Roses Parade in Pasadena, California, where people shout, "Welcome to the neighborhood, Mister Rogers."
January 2003	Rogers undergoes surgery for a terminal condition and chooses to die at home.
January 19, 2003	The Dallas Symphony Orchestra premieres a children's concert titled *The Neighborhood Symphony*, arranged by Richard Kaufman and Lee Holdridge and featuring some of Rogers' tunes, including "You Are Special," "Look and Listen," and "It's Such a Good Feeling." Rogers is slated to attend the performance but cancels, presumably due to illness.
February 27, 2003	At age seventy-four, Rogers dies at his home in Pittsburgh's Squirrel Hills with his wife of fifty years at his side. At the time of his death, *Mister Rogers' Neighborhood* is still airing in reruns in ninety-four percent of America. The website provides helpful information for parents and caregivers on how to respond to children who ask about Rogers' death.
September 2003	The Pittsburgh Children's Museum opens an expanded 2,500-square-foot exhibit of Mister Rogers' Neighborhood.
September 3, 2007	Various PBS affiliates begin replacing *Mister Rogers' Neighborhood* with new programs, including *Super Why!*, *WordGirl*, and *WordWord*.
August 28, 2008	PBS discontinues *Mister Rogers' Neighborhood* from its daily syndicated schedule, along with *Reading Rainbow*, *Boohbah*, and *Teletubbies*.
September 3, 2012	*Daniel Tiger's Neighborhood*, an animated spin-off of *Mister Rogers' Neighborhood* featuring familiar characters from the Neighborhood of Make-Believe, debuts on many PBS stations.

A Selective Bibliography of Works by and About Fred Rogers

CAMILLE MCCUTCHEON

Books Written/Co-Authored by Fred Rogers

Rogers, Fred. *Adoption.* New York: Putnam, 1994.

_____. *Dear Mister Rogers: Does It Ever Rain in Your Neighborhood? Letters to Mister Rogers.* New York: Penguin, 1996.

_____. *Divorce.* New York: G.P. Putnam's, 1996.

_____. *Extraordinary Friends.* New York: Putnam, 2000.

_____. *The Giving Box: Create a Tradition of Giving with Your Children.* Philadelphia: Running Press, 2000.

_____. *Going on an Airplane.* New York: Putnam, 1989.

_____. *Going to Day Care.* New York: Putnam, 1985.

_____. *Going to the Dentist.* New York: Putnam, 1989.

_____. *Going to the Doctor.* New York: Putnam, 1986.

_____. *Going to the Hospital.* New York: Putnam's Sons, 1988.

_____. *Going to the Potty.* New York: Putnam, 1986.

_____. *If We Were All the Same.* New York: Random House, 1987.

_____. *Life's Journeys According to Mister Rogers: Things to Remember Along the Way.* New York: Hyperion, 2005.

_____. *Making Friends.* New York: Putnam, 1987.

_____. *Many Ways to Say I Love You: Wisdom for Parents and Children from Mister Rogers.* New York: Hyperion, 2006.

_____. *The Mister Rogers Parenting Resource Book.* Philadelphia: Courage Books, 2005.

_____. *Moving.* New York: Putnam, 1987.

_____. *The New Baby.* New York: Putnam, 1985.

_____. *No One Can Ever Take Your Place.* New York: Random House, 1988.

_____. *Stepfamilies.* New York: G.P. Putnam's Sons, 1997.

_____. *When a Pet Dies.* New York: Putnam, 1988.

_____. *When Monsters Seem Real.* New York: Random House, 1988.

_____. *Wishes Don't Make Things Come True.* New York: Random House, 1987.

_____. *The World According to Mister Rogers: Important Things to Remember.* New York: Hyperion, 2003.

_____. *You Are Special: Words of Wisdom from America's Most Beloved Neighbor.* New York: Viking, 1994.

Rogers, Fred, and Barry Head. *Mister Rogers' How Families Grow.* New York: Berkley Books, 1988.

_____. *Mister Rogers' Playbook: Insights and Activities for Parents and Children.* New York: Berkley Books, 1986.

_____. *Mister Rogers Talks with Parents.* New York: Berkley Books, 1983.

Rogers, Fred, and Clare O'Brien. *Mister Rogers Talks with Families about Divorce.* New York: Berkley Books, 1987.

Books about Fred Rogers and Mister Rogers' Neighborhood

Collins, Mark, and Margaret Mary Kimmel, eds. *Mister Rogers' Neighborhood: Children, Television, and Fred Rogers.* Pittsburgh: University of Pittsburgh Press, 1996.

Comstock, George A., and Erica Scharrer. *Media and the American Child.* Rev. ed. Boston: Elsevier, 2007.

DiFranco, JoAnn, and Anthony DiFranco. *Mister Rogers: Good Neighbor to America's Children.* Minneapolis: Dillon Press, 1983.

Hollingsworth, Amy. *The Simple Faith of Mister Rogers: Spiritual Insights from the World's Most Beloved Neighbor.* Nashville: Integrity Publishers, 2005.

Long, Michael G. *Peaceful Neighbor: Discovering the Countercultural Mister Rogers.* Louisville: Westminster John Knox Press, 2015.

Stanley, George Edward. *Mr. Rogers.* New York: Aladdin Paperbacks, 2004.

Stewart, David C. *The PBS Companion: A History of Public Television.* New York: TV Books, 1999.

Newspaper and Periodical Articles about Fred Rogers and Mister Rogers' Neighborhood

Alpert, Hollis. "A Nice Neighborhood for Kids." *Woman's Day* Apr. 1968.

Bakshian, Aram, Jr. "Gone with the Wimp." *National Review* 20 Sept. 1985: 49–50.

Banas, Casey. "Mr. Rogers of TV Works to Ease Fear in Children." *Chicago Tribune* 24 Nov. 1976.

Bandler, Michael J. "Mister Rogers: Everybody's Neighbor." *Parents Magazine* Mar. 1989: 118.

Belcher-Hamilton, Lisa. "The Gospel According to Fred: A Visit with Mr. Rogers." *Christian Century* 13 Apr. 1994: 382–384.

Bender, Bob. "Mr. Rogers Never Left the Child Behind." *USA Today* 15 Apr. 1984.

Berkvist, Robert. "Misterogers Is a Caring Man." *New York Times* 16 Nov. 1969: D21+.

Bianco, Robert. "Children Lose a Quiet, Honest Friend." *USA Today* 28 Feb. 2003: E5.

_____. "The Quiet Success of Fred Rogers." *Pittsburgh Press Sunday Magazine* 26 Mar. 1989.

Bishop, Ronald. "The World's Nicest Grown-Up: A Fantasy Theme Analysis of News Media Coverage of Fred Rogers." *Journal of Communication* 53.1 (2003): 16–31.

Blau, Eleanor. "Rogers Has New TV Series on School." *New York Times* 20 Aug. 1979: C16.

Boyum, Joy Gould. "The Tube as Childhood Friend." *Wall Street Journal* 7 Apr. 1972: 8.

Briggs, Kenneth A. "Mr. Rogers Decides It's Time to Head for New Neighborhoods." *New York Times* 8 May 1975: 45.

Buck, Jerry. "Misterogers Caters to Tots' Development." *Hartford Courant* 15 June 1969: 60.

Bunce, Alan. "Mr. Rogers Explores the Rhythms of Childhood—and Life." *Christian Science Monitor* 9 Mar 1987: 33+.

_____. "Mister Rogers: TV's Best Neighborhood." *Christian Science Monitor* 2 Feb. 1993: 13.

Campbell, Chari A. "An Overview of Mr. Rogers and His Work with Children." *Elementary School Guidance & Counseling* 28.1 (1993): 4+.

Carvajal, Doreen. "Still around the Neighborhood." *New York Times* 10 Apr. 2001: E1+.

Cernkovic, Rudy. "'Misterogers' Show Is from Children." *Washington Post, Times Herald* 18 Dec. 1967: C8.

Christy, Marian. "How Mr. Rogers Keeps His Neighborhood Ticking." *Boston Globe* 17 Feb. 1985.

Coates, Brian, and H. Ellison Pusser. "Positive Reinforcement and Punishment in 'Sesame Street' and 'Mister Rogers.'" *Journal of Broadcasting* 19.2 (1975): 143–151.

Coates, Brian, H., Ellison Pusser, and Irene Goodman. "The Influence of 'Sesame Street' and 'Mister Rogers' Neighborhood' on Children's Social Behavior in the Preschool." *Child Development* 47.1 (1976): 138–144.

Cobb, Nathan. "Can You Say Mr. Rogers?" *Boston Globe* 16 Mar. 1988.

Collins, Glenn. "TV's Mr. Rogers—A Busy Surrogate Dad." *New York Times* 19 June 1983: H1+.

Cross, Robert. "No Kid Stuff for Mr. Rogers When It Comes to Business." *Chicago Tribune* 17 Mar. 1983.

Curtis, Carrie L. "Meet Mister Rogers, Everybody's Neighbor." *Pennsylvania Heritage* 23.3 (1997): 22–31.

Daley, Eliot A. "Is TV Brutalizing Your Child?" *Look* 2 Dec. 1969.

Davis, Flora. "Mr. Rogers Talks to Mothers." *Redbook* Jan. 1975.

Delatiner, Barbara. "On Television: The Charm of 'Misterogers.'" *Newsday* 20 Jan. 1968, Nassau ed.: W351.

Dohrmann, Rita. "A Gender Profile of Children's Educational TV." *Journal of Communication* 25.4 (1975): 56–65.

Dundon, Susan. "Pretend, Just Pretend, That Mr. Rogers Is an Adult's Friend." *Philadelphia Inquirer* 14 Apr. 1981.

Estrada, Louie. "Children's TV Icon Fred Rogers Dies at 74; 'Neighbor' Offered a Reassuring Presence." *Washington Post* 28 Feb. 2003: A1.

Evans, Phyllis. "Meet Mr. Rogers." *American Baby* Aug. 1981.

Farhi, Paul. "TV's Gentle Giant; Mister Rogers, We Liked You Just the Way You Were." *Washington Post* 28 Feb. 2003: C1.

"Fred Rogers." *Variety* 3 Mar. 2003: 77.

Gaines, Donna. "The Father of Us All." *Village Voice* 9 Feb. 1993: 47+.

Geist, Eugene A., and Marty Gibson. "The Effect of Network and Public Television Programs on Four and Five Year Olds Ability to Attend to Educational Tasks." *Journal of Instructional Psychology* 27.4 (2000): 250–261.

Graves, Susan B. "Mr. Rogers: The Little Peoples' Spokesman." *Good Housekeeping* Feb. 1970.

Gregory, Jane. "Mr. Rogers: A Special Friend Takes on a Special Problem." *Chicago Sun-Times* 2 Feb. 1980.

"Growing Up with Mister Rogers." *Boston Globe*: 9 May 1971: D14+.

Hallett, Vicky. "There Goes the Neighborhood." *U.S. News & World Report* 10 Mar. 2003: 4.

Hamill, Sean D. "Pittsburgh Journal: It's Still a Beautiful Day in His Neighborhood." *New York Times* 18 Mar. 2010: A19.

Harrington, Richard. "Mister Rogers' Gift: A Sweater for the Smithsonian." *Washington Post* 21 Nov. 1984: D1+.

Harvey, Doug. "Zen and the Art of Make-Believe: A Date with Mr. Rogers." *Art Issues* 52 (1998): 19–23.

Henderson, Keith. "Mr. Rogers' Neighborhood Keeps on Growing." *Christian Science Monitor* 13 Jan. 1986: 29.

Hendrick, Kimmis. "'Misterogers'—He Talks with Children Where They Are." *Christian Science Monitor* 22 Mar. 1969: 19.

Hendrickson, Paul. "Behind that Soothing and Sincere Facade, A Soothing and Sincere Man." *Washington Post* 18 Nov. 1982: C1+.

Henry, William, A., III. "Mister Rogers in Person Is Mister Nice Guy." *Boston Globe* 12 June 1978: 17+.

"Interview with Mister Rogers." *Instructor* Mar. 1979: 26–27.

"It's You We Like, Mister Rogers." *Christian Science Monitor* 31 Aug. 2001: 10.

Judson, Bay. "Art Museum in Mister Rogers Neighborhood." *School Arts* 81 (1982): 27–29.

Junod, Tom. "Can You Say. .. 'Hero?'" *Esquire* Nov. 1998:132.

Kastelic, Robert L. "Mr. Rogers and the Neighborhood as a Model for Understanding Human Behavior." *SKOLE: The Journal of Alternative Education* 15.1 (1998): 92–96.

Kimmel, Margaret Mary. "A Rose for Fred." *Children & Libraries: The Journal of the Association for Library Service to Children* 1.2 (2003): 32–35.

King, Janet Spencer. "Christmas with Mr. Rogers." *Ladies' Home Journal* Dec. 1988.

Krasnow, Iris. "Celebrity Profile: Fred Rogers Content in 'Neighborhood.'" *Hartford Courant* 23 June 1985: AH45.

Lapinski, Susan. "Mr. Rogers: A Friend of the Family." *American Baby* Aug. 1987.

Laskas, Jeanne Marie. "The Good Life—and Works—of Mister Rogers." *Life* Nov. 1992: 72+.

Laurent, Lawrence. "'MisteRogers': TV Idol for the Tots." *Washington Post, Times Herald* 7 July 1969: D1+.

Leo, Peter. "Kids Like Fred Rogers Just the Way He Is." *Pittsburgh Post-Gazette* 17 Apr. 1979.

Levin, Doron P. "Loved by Kids for His TV 'Neighborhood,' Mr. Rogers is a Hit in Boardrooms, Too." *Wall Street Journal* 22 Apr. 1981: 31.

Levin, Robert A., and Laurie Moses Hines. "Educational Television, Fred Rogers, and the History of Education." *History of Education Quarterly* 43.2 (2003): 262–275.

Lewis, Daniel. "Mister Rogers, TV's Friend for Children, Is Dead at 74." *New York Times* 28 Feb. 2003: A1+.

Lowry, Cynthia. "'Misterogers' Makes It in Kiddie Field." *Hartford Courant* 10 Mar. 1968: H4.

Marazon, Renee Alda. "Mister Rogers' Neighborhood"—As Affective Staff Development for Teachers of Young Children: A Story of Conflict, Conversion, Conviction, and Celebration." *Young Children* 49.5 (1994): 34–37.

Margulies, Lee. "Mr. Rogers Is What He Is." *Los Angeles Times* 19 Dec. 1982: U2.

Maynard, Fredelle. "Mr. Rogers' Neighborhood: Where Small Children Feel at Home." *Image* Mar. 1974.

McGinn, Daniel. "Everybody's Next-Door Neighbor." *Newsweek* 10 Mar. 2003: 61.

Millman, Joyce. "What Mr. Rogers Could Have Taught Michael Jackson." *New York Times* 9 Mar. 2003: AR10.

Moore, Scott. "PBS's Good Neighbor Policy." *Washington Post* 15 Feb. 1998: CH6+.

Neuhaus, Cable. "Fred Rogers Moves into a New Neighborhood—and So Does His Rebellious Son." *People* 15 May 1978.

Norton-Smith, Thomas M., and Linda L. Norton-Smith. "Two Conceptions of the Value of Individuals in Children's Programming." *Midwest Quarterly* 34.1 (1992): 112–120.

Oberlin, Loriann Hoff. "Mister Rogers' Neighborhood." *Saturday Evening Post* Jan./Feb. 1993: 78–81.

O'Connor, John, J. "Mr. Rogers, a Gentle Neighbor." *New York Times* 15 Feb. 1976: D33.

_____. "An Observer Who Bridges the Generation Gap." *New York Times* 23 Apr. 1978: D33.

Pae, Peter. "This Neighborhood Hasn't Changed a Bit over the Decades." *Wall Street Journal* 2 Mar. 1990: A1+.

Pannone, Olga R. "Mister Rogers' Neighborhood Ideal Children's Entertainment." *Hartford Courant* 23 June 1974: 4+.

Perry, Stephen D., and Amanda L. Roesch. "He's in a New Neighborhood Now: Religious Fantasy Themes about Mister Rogers' Neighborhood." *Journal of Media & Religion* 3.4 (2004): 199–218.

Poniewozik, James. "He Was Not Afraid of the Dark." *Time* 10 Mar. 2003: 72.

"WQED-TV Sets New Show." *New Pittsburgh Courier* 26 Nov. 1966, city ed.: A6.

Raab, Scott. "Mister Nice Guy." *Entertainment Weekly* 14 Mar. 2003: 14.

"'Rainbow Power' Keynotes Children's TV show." *New York Amsterdam News* 15 Dec. 1973: 17.

Reed, Jennifer. "America's Most Beloved Neighbor: TV's Fred Rogers Provided Gentle Guidance for Three Generations of Children." *Success* Nov. 2010: 74+.

Rice, Mabel, and Patti L. Haight. "'Motherese' of Mr. Rogers: A Description of the Dialogue of Educational Television Programs." *Journal of Speech & Hearing Disorders* 51.3 (1986): 282–287.

Rogers, Fred. "Communicating with Children through Television." *Clinical Pediatrics* 10.8 (1971): 456–458.

_____. "Divorce as a Growth Experience." *Boston Globe* 25 Nov. 1981: 25+.

_____. "How Do We Make Goodness Attractive?" *Federal Communications Law Journal* 55.3 (2003): 569+.

_____. "Part of Our Neighborhood." *Exceptional Parent* 26.6 (1996): 78+.

_____. "Mr. Rogers Tells How to Get Through to Children." *Family Circle* July 1973.

_____. "No Wasted Time." *Media & Methods* Sept. 1981: 8.

_____. "Nurturing Creative Energy." *New York Times* 21 Aug. 1983: SM64+.

_____. "The Past and the Present Is Now." *Young Children* 39.3 (1984): 13–18.

_____. "A Point of View: Family Communication, Television, and Mister Rogers' Neighborhood." *Journal of Family Communication* 1.1 (2001): 71–73.

_____. "That Which Is Essential Is Invisible to the Eye" *Young Children* 49.5 (1994): 33.

_____. "Understanding Differences: Listening and Learning with Mister Rogers." *Exceptional Parent* 10.4 (1980): 14–16.

_____. "What Comes First in Learning." *Educational Forum* 56 (1992): 331–333.

_____. "What Do You Bring To TV?" *Saturday Evening Post* 1 Sept. 1978: 50+.

Rogers, Fred, and Hedda B. Sharapan. "How Children Use `Play.'" *Education Digest* 59.8 (1994): 13+.

Rowe, Claudia. "Some Things Never Change, and Thank Heavens Mister Rogers Is One of Them." *Biography* Mar. 2000: 102+.

Santoli, Al. "I Like You Just the Way You Are." *Washington Post* 28 Mar. 1993: L4+.

Schaer, Sidney C. "Mr. Rogers, Neighbor of America's Children." *Newsday* 27 Dec. 1981, Nassau ed.: A1+.

Sedgwick, John. "Welcome to 'Mister Rogers' Neighborhood.'" *Reader's Digest* Feb. 1991: 127–131.

Seiler, Michael. "Listening to What Mr. Rogers Says." *Los Angeles Times* 18 June 1975: F1+.

Shain, Percy. "$150,000 Sears Grant Saves 'Misterogers.'" *Boston Globe* 12 July 1967: 4.

_____. "Misterogers: Pied Piper of Educational TV Is a Presbyterian Minister." *Boston Globe* 14 May 1967: C2+.

Sharapan, Hedda. "How Early Childhood Educators Can Apply Fred Rogers' Approach." *YC: Young Children* 67.1 (2012): 36–40.

_____. "'Mister Rogers' Neighborhood': Dealing With Death on a Children's Television Series." *Death Education* 1.1 (1977): 131–136.

Shepard, Richard F. "TV: On Superheroes." *New York Times* 4 Feb. 1980: C19.

Shipp, Randy. "A Neighborly Visit with Mister Rogers." *Christian Science Monitor* 21 Aug. 1979: B8+.

Singer, Jerome L., and Dorothy G. Singer. "Can TV Stimulate Imaginative Play?" *Journal of Communication* 26.3 (1976): 74–80.

_____. "Come Back, Mr. Rogers, Come Back." *Psychology Today* Mar. 1979: 56.

"A Special Goodbye: Mister Rogers Was a Good TV Neighbor." *Washington Post* 28 Feb. 2003: C12.

Spiegelman, Barbara M., and Susan M. Melnick. "Access to the Neighborhood of Mister Rogers: Creating a Source for Research." *School Library Journal* 32 (1985): 136–141.

Spitz, Ellen Handler. "The Magical Neighborhood of Mr. Rogers." *Chronicle of Higher Education* 28 Mar. 2003: B16.

Stevens, Melanie Chadwick. "Mister Rogers' Neighborhood." *Parents* May 1982: 76–80.

Sucher, Cynthia. "Mr. Rogers: An Insightful Talk with an Extraordinary Man." *Access* Feb. 1981.

Wagner, Judith. "When Children Ask about Handicaps." *American Education* 11 (1975): 28–31.

Warburton, T.L. "A Visit with Fred Rogers: A Guided Tour through a Special Neighborhood." *Journal of Popular Film & Television* 16.1 (1988): 32–40.

Wardlow, Jean. "Tiny Voices Vote for 'Mr. Rogers.'" *Miami Herald* 29 Nov. 1969.

Wecker, David. "Mr. Rogers Is the Real Thing." *Cincinnati Post* 9 May 1985.

Weingrad, Jeff. "Rogers Moves His Neighborhood." *New York Post* 7 Dec. 1977.

Weiskind, Ron. "Fred Rogers Lays Himself Out for TV Critics." *Pittsburgh Post-Gazette* 16 Jan. 1986.

White, Betty. "Christmas in Mr. Rogers' Neighborhood." *Saturday Evening Post* Dec. 1977: 24–26.

Zaleski, Carol. "Mister Rogers." *Christian Century* 19 Apr. 2003: 35.

Zelevansky, Paul. "The Good Thing": Mister Roger's Neighborhood." *American Journal of Psychoanalysis* 64.2 (2004): 195–208.

Zoba, Wendy Murray. "Won't You Be My Neighbor?" *Christianity Today* 6 Mar. 2000: 38–46.

Fred Rogers Archive

Located in Latrobe, Pennsylvania, where Rogers grew up, Saint Vincent College established the Fred Rogers Center for Early Learning and Children's Media in September 2003 to preserve Fred Rogers' legacy. The Fred Rogers Center houses the Fred Rogers Archive and the multimedia Fred Rogers Exhibit.

The Fred Rogers Center website (http://www.fredrogerscenter.org/) states that the Archive "preserves and organizes in a single location all the materials related to Fred Rogers personally and to the public person that became the iconic Mister Rogers. Archival materials are an essential resource for the work of the Fred Rogers Center for Early Learning and Children's Media, but they are also intended to be a source for other scholarly and applied research into children's television, early childhood development, and Fred Rogers's unique role in bridging both fields."

According to Emily Uhrin, the Fred Rogers Center Archivist, "the Archive holds a wide-range of materials, including many original, handwritten texts by Rogers. These items include letters to personal friends and professional colleagues; ideas and outlines of programs ranging from his earliest children's television program (*The Children's Corner* with Josie Carey) to public service announcements for both children and adults, and speeches. The Archive also houses many of Rogers' awards and citations; programs from a wide variety of events such as commencements, funerals, and memorial services; and photographs from several different sources." The website notes that there is also "a collection of oral history interviews of people who knew and worked with Rogers throughout his life" and that there are "more than 1,100 videos of *Mister Rogers' Neighborhood*, *The Children's Corner* and other programs [that] are part of the digital Archive."

About the Contributors

Richard L. **Bilsker** is a professor of philosophy and social sciences at the College of Southern Maryland. He has broad teaching and research interests in philosophy, political science, sociology, psychology and the humanities. He is the author of two books and has published in a variety of journals.

Chris **Buczinsky** is the director of the English program and chair of the Liberal Arts Department at Calumet College of St. Joseph. He is the creator of A Child's Voice, a children's poetry performance company in Arlington Heights, Illinois, and co-author and illustrator of *Pied Poetry*, a collection of poems and pictures for children.

Peter R. **Costello** is a professor of philosophy at Providence College. His research in phenomenology focuses on the works of Edmund Husserl, Maurice Merleau-Ponty and Edith Stein. He is the editor of *Philosophy in Children's Literature* (Rowman and Littlefield, 2011) and the author of *Layers in Husserl's Phenomenology: On Meaning and Intersubjectivity* (University of Toronto, 2012).

Steven M. **Emmanuel** is a professor of philosophy at Virginia Wesleyan College. His research interests lie in the history of philosophy (East and West), with a special emphasis on moral and religious thought. His major publications include *Kierkegaard and the Logic of Revelation* (SUNY, 1996), *The Guide to the Modern Philosophers: From Descartes to Nietzsche* (Blackwell, 2001), *A Companion to Buddhist Philosophy* (Blackwell, 2013), and *Kierkegaard's Concepts*, 6 volumes (Ashgate, 2013–15).

Maura **Grady** is an assistant professor of English at Ashland University, where she writes on film, television, literature and fan culture. She has published on the television programs *Mad Men* and *Doctor Who*, films such as *Kill Bill* and *The Shawshank Redemption*, and on *Beowulf*-inspired fiction. Her research interests include the intersection between fans and film tourism.

Kathy Merlock **Jackson** is a professor of communication at Virginia Wesleyan College, where she specializes in media studies, animation and children's culture. She has published numerous articles and chapters and seven books, including *Disneyland and Culture: Essays on the Theme Parks and Their Influence* and *Walt Disney, from Reader to Storyteller: Essays on the Literary Inspirations* (both co-edited with Mark I. West, and from McFarland).

165

Susan **Larkin** is a Batten Associate Professor of English at Virginia Wesleyan College, where she teaches courses in children's and adolescent literature, women's literature and women's studies. Her research interests are diverse and include issues of identity and illusion in adolescent literature, collaborative pedagogies and Laura Ingalls Wilder.

Tim **Libretti** is a professor of English, women's and gender studies, and Latina/o and Latin American studies at Northeastern Illinois University. He has published numerous book chapters and articles in such journals as *Melus, Modern Fiction Studies, Women's Studies Quarterly, Radical Teacher, College English, Amerasia Journal, Against the Current*, and *Race, Gender, and Class*, among others. He regularly writes political commentary for PoliticusUsa.com and People's World.

Sue **Matheson** is an associate professor of English at the University College of the North in Manitoba, Canada. She specializes in American popular culture and film, frontier literature and children's literature. She has edited three collections of essays, and her articles have appeared in numerous periodicals.

Camille **McCutcheon** holds the rank of librarian and serves as the coordinator of Collection Management at the University of South Carolina Upstate Library. As liaison to the School of Education, she is in charge of collection development for the library's juvenile collection. Her research interests include children's and adolescent literature, film history and film star biographies.

Valerie H. **Pennanen** is an assistant professor of history and coordinator of the History Support Area at Calumet College of St. Joseph. Her research interests include sacred and spiritual themes as reflected in literature, art and popular culture through the ages, and the use of first-person accounts (autobiography and memoir) to illuminate the past and make it exciting for today's readers.

Mark I. **West** is a professor of English at the University of North Carolina at Charlotte, where he teaches courses on children's and young adult literature and serves as chair of the department. He has written or edited fifteen books, including *Disneyland and Culture: Essays on the Parks and Their Influence* and *Walt Disney, from Reader to Storyteller: Essays on the Literary Inspirations* (both co-edited with Kathy Merlock Jackson, and from McFarland).

Index